The Manager's Guide to Systems Practice

The Manager's Guide to Systems Practice

Making Sense of Complex Problems

By Frank Stowell
and
Christine Welch

WILEY

A John Wiley & Sons, Ltd., Publication

This edition first published in 2012
Copyright © 2012 John Wiley & Sons Ltd

Registered office
John Wiley & Sons Ltd, The Atrium, Southern Gate, Chichester, West Sussex, PO19 8SQ,
United Kingdom

For details of our global editorial offices, for customer services and for information about how
to apply for permission to reuse the copyright material in this book please see our website at
www.wiley.com

Wiley publishes in a variety of print and electronic formats and by print-on-demand. Some
material included with standard print versions of this book may not be included in e-books or
in print-on-demand. If this book refers to media such as a CD or DVD that is not included in
the version you purchased, you may download this material at http://booksupport.wiley.com.
For more information about Wiley products, visit www.wiley.com.

Designations used by companies to distinguish their products are often claimed as
trademarks. All brand names and product names used in this book are trade names, service
marks, trademarks or registered trademarks of their respective owners. The publisher is not
associated with any product or vendor mentioned in this book. This publication is designed to
provide accurate and authoritative information in regard to the subject matter covered. It is
sold on the understanding that the publisher is not engaged in rendering professional services.
If professional advice or other expert assistance is required, the services of a competent
professional should be sought.

Library of Congress Cataloging-in-Publication Data

Stowell, Frank A.
  The manager's guide to systems practice : making sense of complex problems / by
Frank Stowell and Christine Welch.
       p. cm.
  Includes bibliographical references and index.
  ISBN 978-1-118-34563-4
1. Problem solving.   2. Systems analysis.   3. System theory.   4. Decision
making.   5. Management.   I. Welch, Christine Elizabeth.   II. Title.
  HD30.29.S76 2012
  658.4'032–dc23
                               2012012668

ISBN: 978-1-118-34563-4 (hbk)   ISBN: 978-1-118-34562-7 (ebk)
ISBN: 978-1-118-34561-0 (ebk)   ISBN: 978-1-118-34727-0 (ebk)

A catalogue record for this book is available from the British Library.

Typeset in 10/14 pt Kuenstler480BT-Roman by Toppan Best-set Premedia Limited
Printed and bound by CPI Group (UK) Ltd, Croydon, CR0 4YY

To
June, Samantha, Alison and
the memory of Mum and Dad
FAS

To
Geof and Freda Ford
CEW

Table of Contents

Acknowledgements

This book has been written to support three areas of learning. The first is to provide support for workshops, which we have found to be increasingly popular amongst busy managers looking for ideas that may be useful to them in dealing with their ever present, day-to-day problems. Second, for the student or practitioner who is studying methods of organizational enquiry and finally, for the more advanced learner who wants to know more about the ideas themselves. Some early parts of the text appear tantalizingly easy but as the reader progresses through the chapters, s/he will begin to discover that there is more to these ideas than at first appeared.

We have attempted to describe many, but not all, methods and ideas of Systems practice that we have found to be useful. In this respect the book is ambitious because it attempts to describe several approaches rather than being dedicated to a single method. We have written it in this way because we have spoken with managers, involved in 'real world' situations, and realize that they may require different methods to help make sense of changing situations. The style of text is suited to students too as it is right that they are made aware of the different ways of making sense of complex issues.

In order to achieve our ambition to produce a text that is of practical value but also provides some intellectual support for the ideas within we discussed the many facets of Systems practice with respected colleagues in the Systems community. They provided insight and critical feedback to our idea which has helped structure the text. We would like to acknowledge the contributions of colleagues who have helped us and encouraged us to write this text.

The idea for *The Manager's Guide to Systems Practice: Making Sense of Complex Problems* sprang from the success of the Systems practice for managing complexity network (SPMC). This network begun in 2001 with a three-year EPSRC research grant which had been awarded to Ray Ison (OU) and Frank Stowell (DMU now UoP). (Note:

The spmc web page is currently hosted by the University of Northumbria -spmc- http://www.northumbria.ac.uk/spmc.) The network continues to offer one-day workshops for managers and practitioners at various locations throughout the UK and has become self-sustaining.

The network would not have flourished were it not for its contributors. To this end we wish to acknowledge some of the many contributors and participants who have been a part of the network over the past ten years: in particular, Petia Sice at the University of Northumbria, Monica Shelly and Jacqueline Eisenstadt at the Open University. These colleagues have organized a number of management and practitioner workshops over the years dealing with topics as varied as regional police reorganization, tourism, the NHS computer project and some workshops on urban regeneration. The early chapters in the text have been written by taking into account the response and feedback we have received from these workshops.

In addition to the feedback which shaped the early chapters we also invited comment about some of the early drafts of the later chapters from undergraduate and postgraduate students: their feedback has been reinvested where appropriate in these chapters. Thanks are due to undergraduate and postgraduate students at the Universities of Portsmouth and Northumbria, for feedback received.

We also acknowledge the Stowell and West text *Client Led Design* (1994) from which some ideas have been included albeit refined and developed. Some ideas contained within the text have been the result of various research projects with which we have been involved. These include the work of Donna Champion, who has made contributions to both Client Led Information Systems Creation (CLICS) and to the thinking about Organisational Intervention. Shavindrie Cooray, who took the ideas embedded in CLICS and developed them a step further by exploring and using the ideas of Sir Geoffrey Vickers. The work of Ying Laing and Junkang Feng's research into technical definition has also contributed to the thinking about ways of bridging the gap between client needs and their technical fulfilment.

Susan Smith's research and the management workshops have added to the lessons about using AIM as a means of gaining understanding of the many strands involved in complex decision making. Peter Bednar's work, focusing on socio-technical analysis and contextual dependencies, has also contributed to thinking about user-driven design by providing a framework to explore unique individual perspectives on systems of interest.

The pioneering work and ideas of Sir Geoffrey Vickers, Peter Checkland, Stafford Beer, C. West Churchman and Russ Ackoff have provided inspiration for much of the thinking behind *The Manager's Guide to Systems Practice: Making Sense of Complex Problems*.

This text has also had the benefit of feedback and criticism from a number of respected colleagues including Stephen Probert, John Martin and Peter Bednar. Members of the Joint Systems Department at DSTL Portsdown West have helped us by using and evaluating earlier versions of Parts 1 and 2 of the text. We have also benefited from ideas generated through the Community of Practice of business improvement professionals led by Tammi Sinha of Portsmouth Business School and Nigel Ward of the National School of Government.

Finally we would like to thank the enthusiasm of Neil McBride who suggested the need for a text which would cater for new Systems practitioners and for those practitioners and students who wished to learn more about Systems. Thanks are also given to the UK Systems Society Board of Directors, namely Laurence Brookes, Stephen Probert, Pam Hearne, Ian Roderick and Jennifer Wilby for their enthusiastic support for Systems thinking and practice at a time when the use of these ideas has never been more important.

Preface

The idea for this book grew out of many years' experience in using, and teaching others to use, Systems concepts, methods and techniques to address complex problems. The usefulness of Systems ideas has been proven over many decades but anyone wishing to inform him/herself about them is obliged to search through many different sources, each dealing with a different aspect of Systems theory or practice, some of which are no longer in print. When leading workshops for managers, or teaching Systems concepts on undergraduate or postgraduate courses, we have often been asked the question 'What should I read in order to gain an overview of the principles and techniques of Systems?' This has been a difficult question to answer since the available literature has mainly been comprised of books and articles dedicated to particular perspectives or methodologies.

This book is therefore intended to meet the needs of three groups. First, managers who attend professional development workshops to explore useful Systems techniques require a primer with which to consolidate the skills and knowledge they acquire for practical purposes. Secondly, members of academic communities (staff and students) need a text that provides both a practical and a theoretical guide to Systems ideas. The third group are people already well versed in Systems as a framework for thinking about complex issues, who wish for a reference work with which to add to their knowledge. These might be members of the UK Systems Society, the Systems Practice for Managing Complexity Network, the International Society for Systems Science or one of the many Systems Societies from around the world. The text is therefore divided into four sections which are intended to satisfy the beginner, who may be attending a one-day workshop (Chapters 1–3), the learner who wishes to understand how the various ideas from Systems can be brought together as problem-solving methods (Chapters 4 and 5); and the advanced learner who wishes to understand the theory behind the practice and the origins of modern Systems thinking and practice (Chapters 6 and 7). A fourth section (Chapters 8 and 9) provides case studies that can be used in a classroom situation.

This book is therefore an ideal resource for busy managers whose time is scarce. It provides a rapid introduction to straightforward yet powerful techniques that enable users to address real world problems. When time presses, we need methods that can take us rapidly to the heart of a messy situation, without losing sight of the bigger picture. Systems theory and practice is predominantly a framework for thinking about the world, in which holistic views are maintained. In this it contrasts with some familiar techniques of management science, in which problem situations are broken down into their constituent parts with resultant loss of coherence. However, we do not see Systems thinking as a rival to the techniques of management science but rather as complementary tools within the manager's armoury.

'Systems' as an academic discipline has evolved over decades with contributions from many respected writers and researchers. Works by these influential men and women have been discussed throughout the text, and in particular in Chapters 4 and 5. There are many institutions of learning in which Systems is taught both inside and outside the UK, and thousands of individuals hold degrees and higher qualifications in this field. However, as this text makes clear, the strength of this discipline lies in its foundation for practice. Studying Systems is never simply an opportunity for intellectual stimulus but the foundation for addressing 'wicked' problems which have otherwise eluded efforts to find a workable solution. Systems is essentially about interconnectedness. When managers adopt such a framework for thinking, it becomes possible to seek resolution to problems without causing adverse 'knock-on' effects elsewhere in an organizational setting.

In designing this text, we have endeavoured to give our readers an overview of the whole 'family' of Systems approaches. The basic building blocks of Systems thinking (emergence, hierarchy, communication and control) are common to a range of different ways of conceiving situations and problems. We can, for instance, distinguish between 'hard' and 'soft' approaches. The former accepts an assumption that the problem domain can be clearly defined, and therefore that solutions can be found by applying suitable tools of analysis. The latter, on the other hand, is useful in messy and/or fluid situations in which it is difficult or impossible to give a definitive description of the problem to be addressed from the outset. Soft approaches empower analysts to explore situations using tried and tested techniques in order to clarify, describe and define the particular issues to be addressed.

Systems ideas have developed over time, incorporating influences from a number of different fields. Some of the founding Systems thinkers worked in biology, for instance, recognizing the interconnectedness of nature. Many key Systems ideas owe their origins to observation of living organisms, and a number of writers on Systems have used analogy with the structures and processes inherent in living things within their approaches to modelling. Other influences underpinning Systems ideas arose from studies in mathematics, physics or engineering. It is one of the strengths of our field that we draw upon concepts from diverse sources, including fundamental areas of knowledge that have been studied for decades. Systems is a meta-discipline, reflecting and benefiting from the complementary nature of human knowing. We begin to explore these influences in Chapters 4 and 5 of the text and in later chapters, especially Chapter 6, we go on to examine philosophical principles underpinning Systems ideas in greater depth.

Not only does Systems theory and practice derive from many sources, it has also generated a range of opinions about the nature of human problems and the ways in which they need to be addressed. Nowadays we can choose from different groups of tools, techniques and methodologies that share a basis in key systemic concepts but differ in the types of tools they offer. These are explored and illustrated in the second part of the book. A further dimension to the field of Systems thinking is the way in which it has influenced other disciplines. While there are many people who regard themselves as Systems practitioners, using the tools and ideas set out in this book to address real world problems, there are many others who make use of Systems ideas in other ways. Systems as a school of thought can be found embedded in a range of subject disciplines including geography, archaeology, sociology and economics. A detailed discussion of all the applications of Systems concepts is beyond the scope of any one text. However, we have endeavoured to provide pointers within the text and links to further reading that we hope will encourage interested readers to journey further into related fields.

Systems ideas have proved their worth to countless decision makers and managers in public and private sector organizations, and the holistic perspective they provide has never been more important than it is today. Successive governments in the UK and elsewhere have recognized the need for 'joined-up thinking' to address the key issues of State – the economy, health and social welfare, international relations and defence. Businesses need Systems ideas in order to design integrated and optimal internal processes and to deal with the interconnected forces in the business environment, including the power of customers, suppliers, competitors and regulators. We have written this text in the shadow of one of the deepest economic and financial crises of the post-War years, and during a period in which wars are ongoing in many different regions of the world. Problems of hunger and endemic disease confront much of the world's population every day. Our scientists are engaged with causes and consequences of global warming. Our politicians and economists struggle to bring stability to financial markets and to the banking system. In our everyday lives, we endeavour to balance our incomes and expenditure and cater for the needs and desires of the different members of our families. All of these we face in the 21st century and they require us to think holistically, to consider how the various aspects of life interconnect, and to seek for optimal solutions.

In business we try to balance the books, protect our jobs and improve our performance. We can all point to examples of business failure that can be attributed to short sightedness. Many small businesses have failed, despite a popular product, a full order book and an efficient work system, because of cash flow problems. Perhaps the proprietor failed to consider how flows of money into and out of the business were related and balanced. Systems thinking can help us to structure problems, investigate failings and model solutions holistically. Experience has shown us that Systems ideas can be beneficial to modern managers whose prime task is to maintain their company's relationship to its changing and challenging environment.

Structure of the Text

Part I: Key Systems Ideas

In **Chapter 1**, the reader is introduced to some of the most fundamental concepts involved in working with systems. We unravel some of the confusion surrounding the use of the term 'system' in everyday speech. We discuss how a system is defined from the perspective of an observer, who chooses to draw a boundary reflecting that interest and give the system a name. We go on to introduce the reader to some of the diagrams used in Systems modelling including 'Black Box' diagrams, influence diagrams, Rich Pictures and systems maps.

In **Chapter 2**, we build on what we have learnt about modelling, distinguishing between different types of systemic models and showing how they can be used as templates to structure approaches to problem situations. In this chapter, readers learn how to select and use the right modelling methods to address particular management problems. In this chapter we introduce aspects of Systems theory relating to control such as Ashby's Law of Requisite Variety.

Chapter 3 further develops the modelling concepts addressed in the first two chapters, and introduces the reader to the use of methods and methodologies for systemic analysis. In doing so, we discuss work of influential researchers in the Systems field, such as Sir Geoffrey Vickers, Stafford Beer and Peter Checkland. This chapter illustrates how these ideas have been developed and used in significant and complex areas faced by those tasked with managing.

Part II: Systems Thinking

Chapter 4 places emphasis on Systems as a framework for thinking about the world, not just a set of useful tools. Here we talk about the key defining concepts of emergence, hierarchy, communication and control which distinguish systemic approaches from other aspects of management science. Some more of the ideas in Systems theory are introduced at this point, as we begin to look at the impact of Systems approaches in dealing with real world problems. These include socio-technical principles by which work systems may be designed; and paradigms used to reflect upon perceptions of risk and/or failure in problem situations.

In **Chapter 5**, we explore some of the main approaches to problem structuring which use Systems ideas as their foundation. We introduce the reader to some of the modelling techniques of System Dynamics, which deals with the responses of systems to changes in inputs from the environment and the impact upon their outputs. We use Vickers' concept of Appreciative settings to discuss his view of organizations as relationship-maintaining rather than goal-seeking systems. Churchman's discussion of the problem of reductionism is the next step in the discussion. Here it is important for the reader to grasp the role of Systems ideas in promoting learning about problem situations, in contrast to some techniques that may support a premature and uninformed rush towards a 'solution'. The chapter goes on to introduce readers to the Soft Systems Methodology and the Viable Systems Model and builds on ideas touched on in earlier chapters such as Ashby's Law of Requisite Variety as examples of approaches promoting systemic learning and understanding.

Part III: The Contributions of Philosophy and the Social Sciences

Chapter 6 takes the interested reader deeper into ideas underpinning Systems theory and practice. This chapter explores the origins of some Systems ideas and their relationship to other areas of scholarship such as science, social science and hermeneutic philosophy. The discussion contained in this chapter, though quite demanding, will give valuable insights to those who desire a deeper understanding of the foundations of systemic perspectives.

Chapter 7 deals with the nature of Systems inquiry as Action Research, i.e. research in which inquirers are themselves part of the field of investigation. This chapter we believe will be valuable for any reader wishing to expand their thinking about the nature of problems and problem solving and the role of research in expanding human knowing. Action Research is focused on the creation of a productive learning circle (or spiral) relating to a focused area of inquiry. Checkland's FMA model is discussed as a useful mnemonic to guide inquiry and to illustrate how this cyclical process unfolds in practice.

Part IV: Case Studies

In **Chapter 8**, we set out two case studies in which we elaborate and illustrate the application of some specific systemic approaches in practice. Ideas used in the case studies include Soft Systems Methodology, CLICs, Dynamic Modelling and the Viable Systems Model.

Chapter 9 contains further case studies which can be used as self-learning tools or material for discussion in formal classroom settings. Two full-length and four short cases are provided, all of which relate to common management problem situations from contemporary settings.

How to Use this Book

It is our intention that those who have worked through this text should be able to:

1. Gain an understanding of the practice of Systems thinking.
2. Define and distinguish between so-called hard and soft Systems thinking and associated methods.
3. Discuss the importance of boundary setting in defining fields of inquiry and relevant systems, including the impact of differing worldviews (*Weltanschauungen*) among stakeholders.
4. Use appropriate tools for systemic inquiry into business organizations and their environments, e.g. Rich Pictures, influence diagrams, concept maps.
5. Model Systems behaviour using systemic concepts such as: *boundary, owner, actors, transformation, control, communication, resources.*
6. Synthesize practical recommendations from the analysis of organizational situations in terms of planning and control, innovation and creating value.
7. Appraise inquiry into complex systems and an holistic appraisal of strategic decision making, the challenges of strategic management and the management of change.
8. Through the application of various Systems tools appraise prior knowledge, critically analyse and synthesize strategic issues facing organizations; evaluate alternatives, and make appropriate recommendations for change and its implementation.
9. Appraise the challenges of strategic management and the management of change.

10. Integrate and critically evaluate the concepts, main framework and theories of Systems thinking, including the paradoxes in their applications in different contexts.
11. Gain insight into the basis of organizational models and differentiate between reductionist and holistic models and the underpinning concepts behind them.
12. Appraise prior knowledge, critically analyse and synthesize strategic issues facing organizations and make appropriate recommendations for change and its implementation.
13. Demonstrate awareness of the interconnected nature of business structures and relationships, using suitable models and examples.

Although the text has been created as a coherent whole, each of the four parts has a distinct purpose. Those who are new to Systems ideas may wish to read quickly through the first part, in order to gain a general overview of the power and purpose of the concepts and tools set out in Chapters 1–3. Having done so, those who wish to make use of these ideas may benefit from a second, more reflective reading of the chapters.

Many readers will then feel equipped to try out Systems tools and techniques within their own areas of management. In doing so, they will find that they have become Action Researchers in their own right – creating productive learning spirals about the problem situations they seek to address. When reflecting upon the outcomes of these endeavours, some people will begin to desire a deepened understanding of this framework for inquiry. Part II of the book is intended for them, but is also useful as a text for those in formal study settings who are preparing both for assessments and for later professional practice using Systems methodologies. The case studies contained in Part IV will also provide useful material for discussion and reflection among managers and students falling into these categories.

The material in Part III is clearly intended for those readers whose appetite for Systems ideas has been whetted by considering and applying the concepts they have learned from Parts I and II. This material will require careful study and it may be beneficial to scan it quickly before going over these chapters again more thoroughly. Experienced managers and practitioners, and postgraduate students in Systems or Management, will clearly find these latter chapters interesting and rewarding.

Frank Stowell
Christine Welch
December 2011

PART I

KEY SYSTEMS IDEAS

Chapters 1, 2 and 3

The following three chapters are designed to introduce the learner to some simple yet powerful ideas. Following a short introduction to the ideas plus some exercises the ideas can be soon learnt and put into practice. Each chapter in this section contains self-assessment exercises and exercises that will help consolidate what has been learnt. It is worth pointing out that there are one-day workshops available, for example, those offered by the systems practice for managing complexity network (spmc) where opportunities are available to practise the ideas under the guidance of an experienced tutor. For more detail see http://www.northumbria.ac.uk/sd/academic/ceis/enterprise/spmc/

1

Understanding Things: The Manager's Guide to Systems Practice

Introducing some basic (but powerful) ideas

Begin at the Beginning – What is a System?

We encounter the word 'system' often in our daily lives. It crops up in many different contexts – some technical, some social and some philosophical. This text is for people who are intrigued by the concept of 'Systems' and want to clarify and develop understanding of its usefulness. In this text, we will explore use of the word 'System' and related terms such as 'Systems Thinking' and attempt to resolve some of the confusion surrounding these terms. As the chapters progress, we will introduce further aspects of Systems practice, and elaborate upon its usefulness in dealing with the challenges of life in the 21st century.

We will deal with the origin of the word system and its meaning later in the text as we do not need that now, but what we do need is to understand what it means in a practical sense. In everyday conversation we use the term loosely which helps to confuse understanding. In everyday speech we often refer to a 'system' when we mean a computer system. Many people, when told that one is involved in systems, assume that we mean that we are computer engineers. In other instances, people may use the term generally and speak of a system when referring to a government department. Such generalization is often the case when we complain about the unfairness of something: we blame the system. In recent times we hear newscasters and government spokes-persons reporting a failure as being systemic, which seems to mean that no individual is to blame as the failure was a failure of the whole enterprise.

The way that we use the term system in everyday speech is imprecise and relies upon the listener interpreting what the speaker means. If there is plenty of agreement between the speaker and listener it suggests that the conversation is going well and that the speaker and listener inhabit the same area of interest (at least they assume that they do) but there is no guarantee that the system to which the speaker refers is the same one that the listener had in mind. The imprecise way that we use the word can be misleading, often resulting in the participants ending up with completely dif-ferent understandings of the situation and worse, if we think of such a situation in terms of practitioner and client, what appears to be the right answer but is actually inappropriate to their particular problem.

A useful starting point in the practice of Systems thinking is to consider carefully what we mean when we refer to a system and define what system it is we are talking about. For example, if we were to discuss a transport system we need to decide what transport system it is we are considering. Is it freight? Is it a public transport system or is it a personal transport system that we mean (i.e. motor cars)? Do we include bicycles and other types of personal vehicle, and so on? Even when it seems we are referring to a computer system, do we mean just the hardware and software or are we including the people who are using it too? So let us agree some rules:

i. Always give the system a name.
ii. Agree that the name of the system to which the client is referring means the same thing to you!

Like many ideas in Systems, implementing such a simple idea is easier said than done but we have other ideas that can help us and the client to clarify what system it is we are interested in.

Some Simple Tools

Boundary and Environment

Most would agree that in any given circumstances it is wise to take into account as much of the situation as is possible before taking action. We need to see the situation in its entirety – that is to say to take in the whole, what we call adopting a holistic perspective. Many of us assume that we do this instinctively but often our horizons are limited by lack of experience of a new situation or awareness that things are changing from the familiar to something more challenging. When confronted with a new or a complex situation it is difficult to know where to start. The complexity of the situation itself can be overwhelming and it is not unusual at this stage that we can retreat to the safety of familiar techniques or rely on an individual within the situation to tell us what they think the problem is.

It is self evident that in any situation of interest we need to make decisions about what to include and what to leave out. Clearly a situation must have a beginning and an end point, and there must be some form of boundary around the system. If we do not do this then the alternative is that we will have to take the whole planet into account, which of course we cannot do; or conversely we slice up the problem into small pieces, but with this comes the danger that we might ignore important areas. One useful Systems idea is a simple yet powerful practical tool to help with this difficulty. The idea behind the 'tool' is the notion of boundary and environment.

What are these ideas and why are they useful? Many may be tempted to ask if they are just a fancy way of packaging up common sense. Well there is nothing common about common sense and the ideas which at first seem simple often have hidden depths which are realized as a user becomes more adept at using them. Despite the fact that, when confronted with a problem, most of us will consider the 'system' and make a mental note about what it seems to comprise, most do not represent it explicitly. We do not provide a clear enough description for the listener to understand and provide critical appraisal of what is being said. Using the idea of boundary we can begin, with those involved, to enrich understanding about the system – the situation of interest. But how do we set about deciding what is part of the system of interest and what is not? The first thing to remember is to beware a quick assessment. A hasty judgement can inhibit thinking, so take care. When you first draw your boundary remember that as you begin to understand what it contains, so will the boundary alter to reflect your richer understanding of the system of interest.

Let us consider an example. Imagine 'A Manufacturing System' is our area of interest. Where should we draw the boundary? We can start by thinking of things to exclude, including service industries and local government and obvious things like the entertainment industry and libraries. But what should we include? Well are we thinking of all aspects of manufacturing or specific areas such as those using metal? Do we wish to include all manufacturing or just those institutions within a given country? We need to decide what constitutes manufacturing. But, I hear you say, we would know the industry we were called upon to examine. This might be true but equally the practitioner might be asked to look into a changing manufacturing environment in which the company concerned needs to react.

Initially, our boundary and environment might look like Figure 1.1 below:

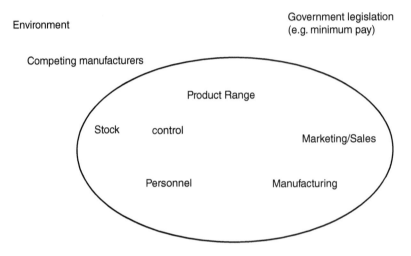

Figure 1.1: Drawing a boundary

This diagram enables us to begin discussions with the members of the enterprise. As more is learned about the situation the boundary might add more sub-systems such as Production Control, Research and Development, Drawing Office and in its environment 'Parent Company' (which may control the policy that determines the market within which the enterprise can trade), Suppliers, Skills Availability and Sources of Capital. We may find as we begin to gain greater insight that one or more systems in our environment might be better placed within the boundary of the system itself or vice versa. For example, the parent company might have a Board member on the Board of the subsidiary, in which case a sub-system relating to that role should be within the boundary. It might be that the R&D department is part of the parent company and should be in the environment (it might be a separate cost centre that is contracted by various parts of the holding company's portfolio).

Following discussions with all concerned, the final diagram might now look like Figure 1.2:

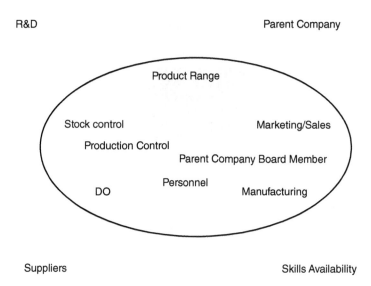

R&D   Parent Company

Product Range

Stock control   Marketing/Sales

Production Control

Parent Company Board Member

Personnel

DO   Manufacturing

Suppliers   Skills Availability

Figure 1.2:   Boundary and environment

Using what appears to be a simple diagram we can begin to gain an appreciation of the system itself and what is in its environment. The process of developing the diagram will play its part in enriching the understanding of those involved. The simple idea of drawing a boundary around the system of interest demands clarification about what the system is (it requires a name) and what component elements make it up. Once an agreement about the system has been reached the next stage is to decide what is in its environment and what is not. In this way we are beginning to be more precise in our description of the system of interest and its surroundings. The development of the diagram is a part of a process of learning for all those involved, the outcome of which is an agreed representation of the situation of interest and the context in which it exists.

We now move on to another apparently simple idea, that of a 'black box'.

Black Box Diagrams

Another simple analytical tool that helps us make sense of complex issues is called a Black Box diagram. This thinking tool is borrowed from engineering where it is used to represent situations where the inner working of the product is less important than is the relationship between each of the sub-systems that make it up (see Figure 1.3).

Black Box diagrams provide a useful means of representing a complex situation using the notion of 'input → process → output' which is common to many systems diagrams (see Figure 1.4):

BLACK BOX MODELLING

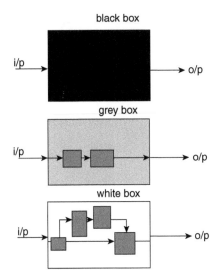

Figure 1.3: Black Box modelling

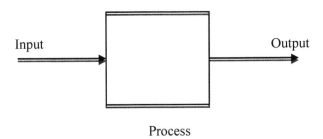

Figure 1.4: Input–Process–Output diagram

The strength of a Black Box diagram is that there is no need to understand all the detailed processing that is undertaken inside the system as a whole, it is enough to recognize that 'something' happens and that this 'something' has particular inputs and outputs which can be identified. A further advantage of a Black Box diagram is that by obeying a few simple 'rules' the process can lead to a comprehensive learning exercise.

The first stage is to represent the whole system (i.e. the situation under investigation), as a single 'input → process → output' diagram. The system is named and the inputs to this system are listed and drawn and shown to be feeding into the system – let's call it stock control. The outputs of this system are then identified and shown flowing out of the system as illustrated in Figure 1.5 below:

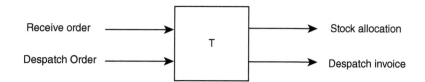

Figure 1.5: Simple first level Black Box diagram

The given system is then 'broken down' into smaller wholes, or sub-systems, and the process of identifying the different inputs and outputs for each sub-system is undertaken until a list of all relevant sub-systems has been developed. The completed diagram may look as shown in Figure 1.6:

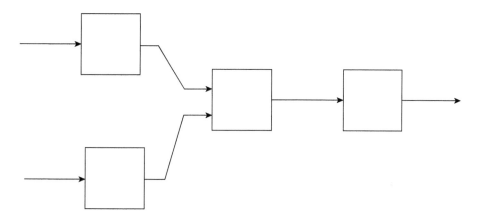

Figure 1.6: Outline of developed Black Box system

As is the case with most systems diagramming the idea is quickly learned but there are pitfalls as it is possible to get it wrong if the conventions of deductive logic are not followed. This and an example of a more complex Black Box diagram, are given in the next chapter. Why not try to represent a system of interest to you – say your central heating system. If you do you will learn that you can produce quite a complex diagram without the need to become a heating engineer.

Another diagramming method we have found to be useful is the influence diagram. These diagrams allow us to represent a situation in terms of the relationships and outcome of various interactions.

Influence Diagrams

Our experience of life shows us that the way we react or the way that things interact with each other will produce some kind of effect. So we can represent our system of interest as a series of relationships or influences. For example, we can say that, by and large, the number of calories we consume will influence our weight. This is not true for everyone but generally speaking it is true. Using this simple idea we can build up quite complex models of any given situation. Let us take a simple representation showing the relationship between consuming chocolate and weight gain, shown in Figure 1.7:

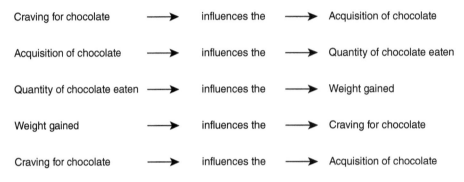

Figure 1.7:   Example of possible influences of chocolate upon weight

The diagram is an oversimplification of course as it is not true that everyone who consumes chocolate gains weight. The value of influence diagrams lies in their simplicity and in their power to represent the relationships between complex issues. These diagrams can be extended and translated into a computer program using building blocks as part of what is called System Dynamics (SD). System dynamic programs allow us to represent a situation using the notion of feedback to discover what might happen if we alter inputs, what effect certain influences might have upon the system. SD is a useful aid for assisting us to make decisions. We will return to feedback and influence diagrams in the next chapter and deal with System Dynamics in Chapter 3. Meanwhile why not try to represent a situation familiar to you as a set of influences?

Feedback – Positive and Negative

It is obvious that the way we influence things can be in a positive or a negative way. Influence is not a neutral thing. In Systems we do have a way of representing these kinds of influences but at first they seem counterintuitive. Positive feedback can be a bad thing and negative a good thing. Too much positive feedback or lack of negative feedback will cause the system to collapse. Think about what happens when an electrical device gets near a microphone: there is an unpleasant howl isn't there? The characteristics of a system, which has only positive feedback, will be that it is driven in

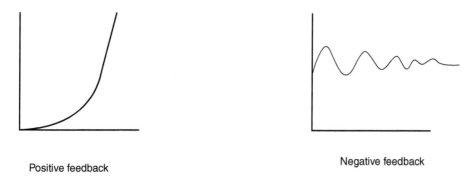

Positive feedback

Negative feedback

Figure 1.8:   Positive and negative feedback

the same direction until it collapses. The characteristic of a fire provides a good example of positive feedback. We light a fire and it burns until all the fuel has been consumed. We can delay it going out by replenishing the fuel, but it will eventually run out of fuel and go out. Negative feedback on the other hand seeks equilibrium and stability. The control it exerts seeks to find equilibrium and stability. For systems to survive there must be a sufficient amount of negative feedback to maintain stability (see Figure 1.8).

Systems Maps

You will have seen this style of diagram elsewhere and called them by another name but we use them in a slightly different way to that which you may have experienced. For example, you would be correct in thinking that they resemble a Venn diagram but because we use them in a particular way and for a particular purpose we call them systems maps.

So what is particular about the way we create and use these diagrams? Well we use them in two ways. First and most importantly, we use them as a means of helping us to think about a situation of interest (which we will call our notional system). When thinking about what makes up our system of interest, we need to consider boundary and environment (see page 4). Once we have decided what it is we go on to consider what components (call them sub-systems for now) make up our notional system. The second reason we use the maps is as a simple means of communicating our ideas to other interested individuals. Do not underestimate the educational value that the process of creating a systems map provides. Remember that the map is the means for you to present your thoughts to others. You should take time to develop the map and consider it as complete only when you have exhausted every aspect of the area of interest. Remember that there is no right or wrong answer to your map because it is your view of the situation (we sometimes call this our *Weltanschauung* but we will come back to that later in the text).

What is the difference between a systems map and the notion of boundary and environment that we discussed earlier? Well the notion of boundary and environment is a means of deciding what is relevant to your area of interest, what is outside in the environment and what is of no interest at all. The systems map on the other hand is a diagram of all the elements that make up your notional system. Let us take one of the components from the boundary example above: marketing. For this example of a map we will be considering 'what is marketing?' (the proposition). Remember that this activity is part of an exercise in learning so you are not expected to be an expert in marketing but the map provides you with an opportunity to explore your thinking before you discuss your ideas with colleagues. The systems map might look like Figure 1.9:

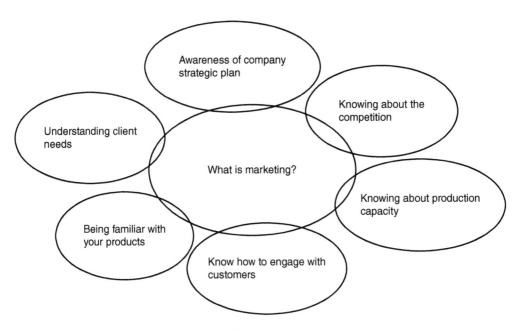

Figure 1.9:   Example of a systems map

This of course is by no means THE map of marketing but it is (in this case) my map. All of the sub-systems overlap the central element, which we now call the proposition, because, in the opinion of the drawer, these make up Marketing. Needless to say you would require clarification and confirmation of each of the sub-systems but more of this in later chapters. For the moment just practise producing a systems map of your own which represents something you are interested in, such as a hobby or a holiday.

Rich Pictures

If you happen to be familiar with Soft Systems Methodology (SSM) you will recognize this as one of the early stages in SSM mode 1 (SSM is discussed in detail in the next section). The idea of a Rich Picture is to represent a situation of interest in the form of a cartoon-like diagram. We all know how a good cartoonist can capture a whole event or series of events in one picture. This is a general idea behind RPs. Like all systems of interest you and your clients will have to decide where your boundary lies but as you have learnt already the boundary gradually unfolds as you learn more about the situation. The key to a successful picture is not so much your skills as a cartoonist but your ability to capture a rich representation of the situation but without putting a rigid structure around the elements contained within your picture. The RP should be an unstructured account of the situation of interest. What do we mean by unstructured? Well we do not mean a random set of images but a representation which is the result of the interaction between the structure and the processes within the situation and the issues that arise from them. What we do not want is a pictorial representation of a list – that is to say we do not want a formal account of each part of the situation as one might create a list. For example, in the case of a manufacturing enterprise we do not want to see all of the production activities in one corner, marketing in another, stores in another and so on. What we are looking for is the emergence of issues and resultant activities which, together, portray the situation as a whole. You can try this by drawing a picture from a short piece reported in a newspaper. You can ask a friend to look at your picture and see if it tallies with what was written down. There are few examples of Rich Pictures publicly available but most are contained within the numerous studies undertaken by postgraduate and Open University students over the last 30 years. The picture in Figure 1.10 is taken from an SPMC workshop in 2009 and depicts the summer heatwave of 2003 which had a profound impact upon the United Kingdom with complex effects being experienced both immediately and into the future. The most widely reported result was the large number of excess deaths directly attributable to the weather, but the effects upon businesses, individuals, the emergency services, hospitals, the justice system, insurance services, utility companies, tourism and transport services to name but a few, whilst not as widely or comprehensively reported, were wide ranging.

Although the Rich Picture in Figure 1.10 provides the observer with a full account of the situation it is possible to produce a picture (see Figure 1.11) which is as rich but perhaps not as 'pretty':

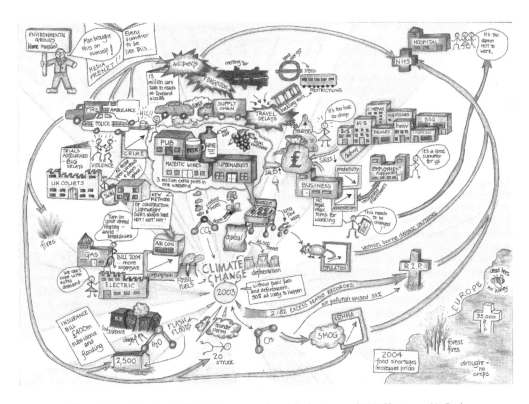

Figure 1.10:   Example of a Rich Picture: perception of the heatwave of 2003 (Courtesy of L. Day)

Activity or Conceptual Models

For those familiar with Soft Systems Methodology mode 1 you will be familiar with the Conceptual Modelling stage. Here we refer to it as an 'activity model'. An activity model is a model of a series of activities which show how a given system functions. It is a diagram where activities of a named system are identified and expressed using the verbs of the English language as their main component. The form of the diagram is built around the logical dependencies of the activities involved with arrows linking them. The activities themselves are placed within cloud-shaped boundaries as a means of emphasizing that they represent the working of a given notion system (an example of an activity model can be seen in Figure 1.12). The activities that have been named are not necessarily real-world activities – they are the activities that need to take place if the notional system is to function. In SSM, the conceptual model has traditionally been described as being purely a description of an ideal type that is developed from a detailed and carefully composed description (a Root Definition) of some notional system. However, practice has shown that we do not need to adhere strictly to the Root Definition-Conceptual Model conversion, but instead may produce an activity model

Figure 1.11: Rich Picture of the same situation but less artistic!

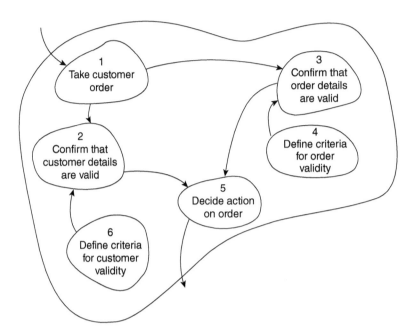

Figure 1.12:   Example of an activity model of an Order Validation System (see Stowell and West, 1994, p. 87)

directly from some appreciation of the activities of any named system (for example, one identified in a Black Box diagram or a systems map).

The activities themselves describe purposeful activity, each activity is doing something and as such each description of an activity begins with a verb. The relationship between each activity is a logical one rather than an incremental one. If the activities are numbered then it should be taken as an address rather than a representation of the order of execution of a set of actions. Care should be taken to ensure that the activities in the model are all at the same level of resolution; as a rule of thumb an activity model should not have more than 7 ± 2 activities. If not, it may be necessary to conduct further modelling in order to decompose activities. An example of an activity model is given in the next chapter.

In order to develop an activity model the system of interest must be carefully named (e.g. expressed in terms of the transformation to be effected together with its associated perspective). Then the next step is to begin to assemble verbs which relate to the activities that must be undertaken in order to achieve the stated transformation. Once these activities have been identified they are arranged by identifying their logical dependencies using arrows to link the activities. A system boundary needs to be added and it is worthwhile to try to identify the input and output of the system (and sub-systems). Finally, since we are interested in viewing the named activities as a collected whole, or system, we need to be concerned with the continuity of the system which can be brought about by monitoring and controlling it. For this reason it is usual to include the monitor and control activities within the overall system boundary. But we will return to activity models in more detail in the next chapter.

Summary

The above examples show different ways of both representing and gaining understanding of a situation of interest. We need to remind ourselves that a diagram is a representation of the way that we, or if used correctly, those involved, see the situation. It is not the situation itself but an interpretation of it. These diagrams are useful thinking tools in their own right but, as you will learn later in this text, in Chapters 2 and 6, when used as part of a method or methodology they take on a greater significance. When they are considered within a particular intellectual framework the way in which they are used becomes more demanding.

Each of the Systems methods and methodologies described later in this text all share the same aim and that is to produce a model of some kind as a way of learning and of gaining an appreciation about the situation of interest. But it is important to remember that these are models and as such a representation of a thing or situation at a given moment in time and which is the view of those who create the model.

CHAPTER 2

Models and Modelling

Introduction

The preceding chapter has provided examples of some practical diagramming tools which have been found useful in modelling complex situations. As we have seen, modelling is a useful way to reflect on the situation of interest without losing a holistic view and avoid the need to take hasty or uninformed actions. Diagrams are a way of describing a situation of interest but whenever we describe or express some activity, either through words or diagrams, we are creating an abstraction of our perception of 'reality'. We select the modelling medium to highlight and emphasize what *we* take to be important aspects of the activity which we wish to model. You should remember that it is our perception of 'reality' and is also a simplification of the situation: an intellectual construct. Wilson reminds us that '. . . the measure of success in modelling is not that you can produce a model that is bigger and more sophisticated than anyone else's but that it adequately answers the original question for which it was developed' (Wilson 1984, p. 7). A situation might be modelled in different ways, each of which might show it in a different light. Stowell and West (1990, p. 55) point out that to a great extent the success of the modelling exercise rests upon the skill of the modeller in terms of their ability to:

i. Understand the activity, or situation, to be modelled,
ii. Understand the nature of different models, together with their implications and
    significances, and
iii. Select and use these models in a meaningful and useful fashion.

But there are many kinds of models so is it any wonder we stick to the ones that we
were taught? Well, some decades ago Ackoff (1962) produced a general description of
what he argued were three types of model to which most models can be assigned. He
defined these as Iconic, Analogic and Analytic, which can be described as follows:

> An iconic model is a model of reality, the properties of which equate to those of
> the real article such that (albeit on a different scale), so that the model can be
> expected to behave in the same way as the real thing (e.g. a bridge or building
> tested for the effects of stress).

> An analogic model is an attempt to simulate the behaviour of the original
> although its physical appearance is quite different to that of the article being
> modelled (e.g. WiFi game).

> An analytic model is created from mathematical or logical relationships that are
> believed to lead to the behaviour of some situation of interest (e.g. a spreadsheet).
> This model may provide the data for an analogic model.

To these Wilson (1984) added a further type of model which he called 'Conceptual'.
Conceptual because this type of model may include pictures or symbolic models which
are often used before any other type of modelling takes place. These models are used
to represent the subjective and qualitative aspects of a situation.

We can say that something used to represent a situation can be classified as a model
if the users find the method to be useful although we would be hard pressed to find a
model which does not fall into one of the above categories. Ackoff et al. (1972) reflected
on the process of producing models in the following way:

> What an individual perceives, is conscious of, and remembers in a choice situa-
> tion and what he feels about it constitute the raw material from which his model
> of the situation is constructed. Therefore his model influences what he takes
> from the situation, and what he takes from it influences his model (Ackoff et al.,
> 1972, reported in Ackoff, et al., 2006 p. 78)

In order to choose the 'right' kind of model that we feel will represent the situation of
interest we must be clear about its purpose and use. Remember we are using our model

as a kind of surrogate representation of some situation. It is the very process of forming, reforming and structuring our model that assists us in learning about the situation of interest and of its similarities and differences to the situation itself. This process may make us decide to reinvestigate areas as we discover where our understanding is deficient. Modelling provides us with a useful way to learn more. The model encourages us to compare the 'real' situation with what is effectively an 'ideal' type representation of the situation.

So the act of building a model provides us with a way of trying out something to see what effect an action might have on the 'real' situation, enables it to be tested bearing in mind that the model is an abstraction of the 'real' thing but is capable of providing results for a specific set of circumstances. In this sense the model may allow us to 'simulate' a particular series of events and assess the results without having to risk doing this in the 'real' situation (e.g. using System Dynamics). A model can also provide us with the means of communicating to others our ideas about a situation and what reactions we might experience in certain circumstances.

Wilson reminds us of the dangers inherent in modelling; he says '. . . because modelling is so fascinating there is a danger that it can become an end in itself' (1984, p. 7). It is important to remember that whatever our use of a model it is, with varying degrees of accuracy, an abstraction of *our* perception of 'reality'. A model is not the real situation and is sometimes merely a vague representation of reality. We should remember that this warning applies equally to models of 'soft' human activity which are shaped by our personal views and experience and 'hard' models of situations which are represented by quantifiable facts. It is always possible to find some deviation from 'reality' in our model whether it is because of the assumptions that we used to build the model or because we were unable to provide absolute measures of 'reality'. As Stowell and West point out '. . . A model of a situation, regardless of size or complexity, is the result of an individual's understanding of a situation and the aspects we choose to model will be the result of what Vickers calls our "readinesses" (or lack of them) to take note of or recognise aspects of reality as being relevant to our model' (Stowell and West 1994, p. 56). It is easy to forget that a model is a *simplification* of the situation it is trying to represent.

Modelling, whether it is through diagrams or in a verbal form, plays an important part during our 'Appreciation' of a situation of interest. But it is important that we do not let the modelling tools we use get in the way of gaining understanding. In Systems we use a variety of tools to help us 'Appreciate'. These include diagrams and modelling which can help in this process of learning. An advantage of the tools discussed in Chapter 1 of this text is that each of them provides the means of representing a situation in its entirety rather than a segment of it, which is characteristic of the more familiar 'reductionist' models commonly used.

In the following section, we will add to the knowledge gained from Chapter 1 and suggest how you may add to the practical experience you should now have gained from using the tools we described earlier. The models described here are not intended as an exhaustive account of models and modelling but some models found useful in the practice of Systems thinking. We begin with feedback.

Feedback

The idea of feedback control is not new since its origins can be traced back to the third century BC (Mayr, 1970). It was the recognition that the principles of feedback control systems, which can be seen in engineering mechanisms (e.g. thermostats), could be applied to other systemic activity that led to the exploitation of these ideas in other areas of human endeavour (e.g. Production Control; Quality Control; Management).

Open Loop Control

This is an arrangement where the output is not connected to the input for measurement and correction. For example most traffic lights are open loop where they run in a cycle irrespective of the number of vehicles on either side. A simple electric light system is another example as the lights remain on until switched off (in this case one could suggest such systems are closed loop when a human being has decided that it is light enough without the artificial light and switched it off, but left to itself it is open loop with no control system). This is a useful example of the importance of boundary drawing (see Chapter 1) – do we choose to include a human being as part of the system or outside it? In the case of open loop control we have an input, a process and an output. The system is controlled in the design phase when an objective is achieved without thought of modification in the light of changing circumstances.

Closed Loop Control

A system can be characterized as exhibiting feedback control by its closed loop structure. It can be defined as one 'which tends to maintain a prescribed relationship of one system variable to another by comparing functions of these variables and using the difference as a means of control' (Schoderbek, et al., 1990, p. 439). By exercising feedback control we are attempting to reduce the effect of change to a system caused by

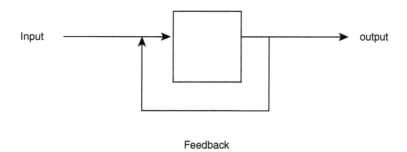

Feedback

Figure 2.1: Simplified diagram of feedback control

changes in desired output, environmental disturbances and inconsistent inputs and system processing behaviour. We do this by compensating for the difference between the actual and the required output of the system. We call this type of control 'closed loop control' since we are closing the loop between output and input. As can be seen in Figure 2.1, samples of the actual output may be taken and compared to the desired output so that suitable decisions can be made about a strategy for future action that helps to compensate for the deviation detected.

It is not always easy to exercise control since it may take time for the effects of the changes to the input (the results of the 'correction' strategy) to reach the output. The time delay between the moment of operating the control and the effect appearing in the output is called *lag.* Lag is a common term used in engineering and can be either counteracted or used to benefit when considering the design of, for instance, information systems. It may be necessary to ensure that the lag in a closed loop control system does not result in the controller over-controlling the system because earlier control actions have not had time to filter through and be picked up at the output sample point. If we consider an example of a stock control system, messages travelling through the system that are subject to lag can result in the system served running out of stock completely because replenishment is not timely. Alternatively, over-controlling action could lead to unwanted stock building up which ties up business capital unnecessarily. In other cases lag may be a useful way of slowing down and making the control of a system more manageable and, hence, more stable (e.g. the Stock Exchange).

Positive and Negative Feedback

The type of feedback used in a closed loop control system can be of two kinds: positive and negative.

Positive feedback: As the output of a system moves in any direction (increases or decreases), the feedback message acts on the input in such a way as to cause the output

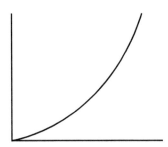

Figure 2.2: The 'shape' of positive feedback

to move in the same direction even further (see Figure 2.2). For example, think about the effect of a computer-based information system in a Stock Market (e.g. London or New York). If, as happened in the recent economic difficulties, computer programs are designed to detect patterns in the sale of shares this can trigger off a share-selling program. The traders' reaction to what they see triggered more selling and soon developed into a selling frenzy. The cycle repeats until it self-destructs. Positive feedback, unless interrupted, will finally destroy the system through perpetual growth or perpetual decay. This is not to say that positive feedback should be avoided at all costs: it may be used to great effect if there is some need to promote growth (e.g. to start a business enterprise) or to encourage decay (e.g. reducing waste).

Negative feedback: As the output of a system moves away from the desired output, then control action is induced and the output is pulled back towards the desired output. The lag in the control system means that the output is likely to continue past the desired state. But here the comparison of the actual output with the desired output invokes control action and pulls the output back to the desired state. The overall behaviour of this is to oscillate towards the desired state until equilibrium is achieved resulting in stability.

Because of the characteristics of negative feedback it is used to control systems because it acts to reduce errors and enable the 'goal' of the system to be achieved (see Figure 2.3). A good example of the practical effect of negative feedback in a business enterprise

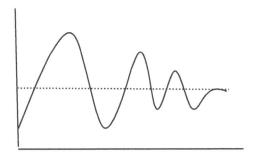

Figure 2.3: The 'shape' of negative feedback

is the use of a management information system (MIS) which enables control to be exercised over the business as a whole. The MIS provides up-to-date details enabling management to take action to ensure that the company is maintaining its relationships to its environment (more of this later).

As discussed in the first chapter, consider a phenomenon which most of us have experienced: the howling effect that we sometimes get on a public address system. At a particular frequency a 'howl' is audible indicating that the public address system is unstable at this frequency and, hence, could be said to exhibit positive feedback. This frequency is related to the delay of the sound from the loudspeaker back to the microphone. At other frequencies there is the same amplification but because of the delay in the feedback path the signal that is fed back does not augment the input signal so there is negative feedback at others, despite the fact that the feedback path has not been altered. To ignore the effects of feedback can have serious consequences: we only have to reflect upon some of the environmental difficulties that we, the human race, currently face. At the time of writing this book we are still trying to overcome the economic difficulties of the first part of the 21st century. The loss of confidence in the financial markets has introduced a catastrophic series of events which at first sight seem unrelated, e.g. it is claimed there has been an 89% jump in the number of men seeking treatment for hair loss in the UK since the start of the recession. So says a report commissioned by LA Science, (http://newslite.tv/2010/08/09), who specialize in hair treatment. Bias, perhaps, but one form of hair loss is caused by stress.

Activity Models

In Chapter 1 and at the start of this chapter we said that something can be considered to be a model if it is used as a means of communicating to a third party. Whilst this is true in a general sense the importance of the assertion lies in the transitive verb, communicating. In order for a model to be a vehicle for communicating the receiver must be aware of the conventions of the particular model. For this reason when we represent a situation of interest we should take care that the symbols that we use are easily understood and as unambiguous as possible. As we have seen, Ackoff referred to three kinds of model. Whilst an activity model could be considered to be a form of analogical model, perhaps it is Wilson's notion of a conceptual model in which he incorporates pictorial/symbolic models that is more representative.

Activity models are representations of the relationship between actions that are considered necessary for the *notional* system to function. The activities of a named system are identified and expressed using *verbs*. The resulting diagram then shows the *logical dependencies* of the activities by the use of arrows which link the different activities.

The convention used in these diagrams is to place each of the activities within elliptically shaped boundaries to emphasize that what we are expressing is a representation of a *notional* system. That is to say that the activities named are not necessarily 'real-world' activities but the activities the drafter considers need to take place if the notional system is to function. The relationship between the activities is shown in such a way as to represent the logical sequence of the processes involved in a given course of action.

Drawing an Activity Diagram

As we emphasized in Chapter 1, the system, which in this case is represented by an activity model, must be carefully named. Then we begin to assemble verbs that relate to the activities that must be undertaken in order to enable the notional system to function. Once the activities have been identified we associate their logical dependencies using arrows to link the activities (see Figure 2.4). Sometimes this might mean moving the activities around to avoid overcomplicated line crossings (for neatness). Remember to define the boundary. In order to ensure the continuity of the system we include monitoring and controlling activities within the overall system boundary. It is usual, as a rule of thumb, to aim to limit the number of activities in each activity model to 7 plus or minus 2 (Miller, 1956).

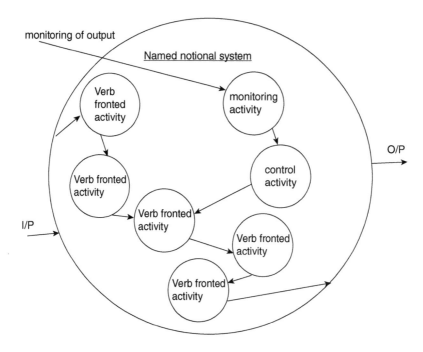

Figure 2.4: An example of an activity model

Requisite Variety

It is worth pausing at this point to consider what requisite variety means. Ashby, a psychiatrist and pioneer in cybernetics, is credited with the 'Law' of Requisite Variety (1958). In his book *Design for a Brain* (1952) he says '. . . that all processes of regulation are dominated by the Law of Requisite Variety'. He goes on to explain that '. . . if a certain quality of disturbance is prevented by a regulator from reaching some essential variables, then that regulator must be capable of exerting at least that quantity of selection . . .' (Ashby, 1978, p. 229). In simple terms this means that in order to bring about effective control over any situation the control mechanism must be capable of addressing as many different outcomes as it is possible for a situation to develop. So the more complex the situation the more difficult it is to predict its behaviour. We can reduce uncertainty by providing more information about it, as information reduces uncertainty and simplifies the system to be controlled. However, this requires the same level of variety in the control system as there is in the system to be controlled.

Take for example the erection of CCTV cameras to monitor an area considered to be at risk, say from unacceptable social behaviour. How many cameras do we need to ensure complete coverage of the area? Even where there are few obstructions, covering every eventuality is a tall order (see Figure 2.5). If we reflect on the LRV we need as much variety in the controller as in the thing (in this case it is human beings). Just ponder the ramifications of what this means for now but we will return to it in more detail in Chapter 3.

Black Box Diagrams (cont.)

In the first chapter we introduced the notion of Black Box diagramming and in this chapter we will take the idea a stage further. Although an advantage of Systems modelling is that each individual can express their needs or views unhindered by the approach itself there are some simple 'rules' that we need to bear in mind when creating our Black Box models which will help to extend the 'reach' of the modelling method. Remember that when we produce a Black Box diagram we are interested in the process not the detailed working that goes on inside the Black Box.

As with the first level Black Box diagrams there is no need to understand fully the processing being undertaken but when a sub-system is identified it needs to be carefully 'named' so as to reflect the way in which the inputs to this sub-system are transformed into the identified outputs. It may be that the activity of the sub-system is easy to name (e.g. research and development sub-system) but it is useful to move away from

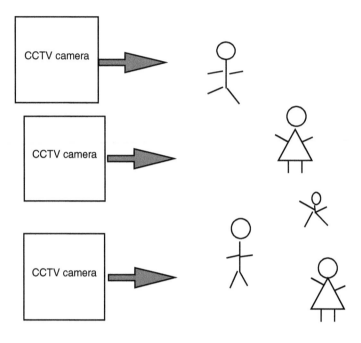

How many cameras are needed?

Figure 2.5:   Number of controllers needed to control a simple situation

the more traditional names (e.g. Customer Complaints Systems). The reason for this is that we often attach meaning to labels which is difficult to shake off. For example, a manufacturing system will have certain connotations whether we work within a manufacturing enterprise or not. Moreover, by thinking about what the system of interest is doing we can be more accurate in naming the activity. For example, a customer complaints department in an enterprise could be thought of as a system to *analyse* and *act* upon customer complaints which summarizes what task this department might do. Not all departments that deal with complaints are set up to do this of course as some are more concerned with protecting the image of the particular system – think about the way that specialized political staff react when complaints or criticisms are levelled at a senior politician in their party, or some commercial enterprises that want to protect the brand image at all costs.

If we return to the production of a Black Box (say a medical centre) we should identify all relevant elements of the larger whole, e.g. as shown below in Figure 2.6, and we can then go on to develop a more detailed Black Box diagram which will have a series of sub-systems that we think will make up the system as a whole, e.g. as shown in Figures 2.7 and 2.8.

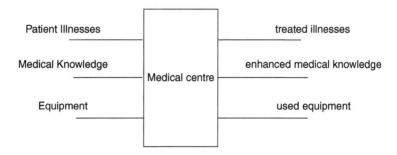

Figure 2.6:   Initial Black Box diagram

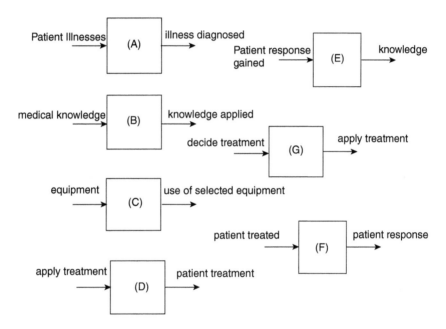

Figure 2.7:   Sub-systems

By investigating each input of this hypothetical example of a medical centre we have arrived at seven sub-systems which enable the medical centre to function. Our next step is to 'fit' them together in order to understand the relationships between the sub-systems and the system as a whole. This is not always easy, especially if the analysis has been a detailed one. The diagram is gradually built up by identifying how the output of one sub-system forms the input into a second and then the two sub-systems can be joined together as shown in Figure 2.8.

Whilst the representation of the system of interest is a function of interpretation, either as an individual or a jointly produced diagram, it is possible to make a mistake. For example, if the sub-systems are not at the same level of resolution you will find

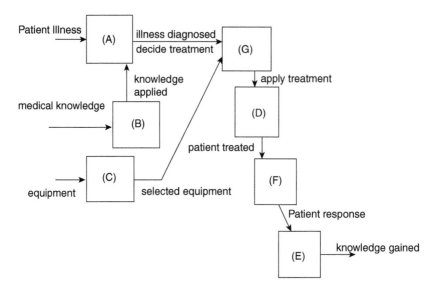

Figure 2.8:   Connecting the sub-systems

difficulty in connecting each of the sub-systems together, so decide the level of resolution that you intend to make the diagram. Also decide who the diagram is for and
what its purpose is – is it for communication? Is it for practical purposes or is it part
of a process of understanding? Typically the kinds of mistake that we find with Black
Box diagrams are as shown in Figure 2.9:

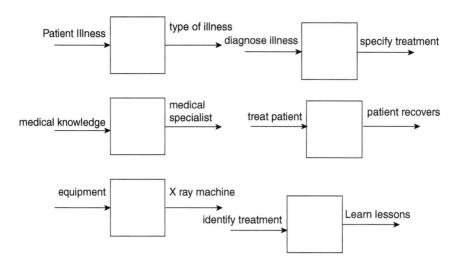

Figure 2.9:   Examples of 'correct' and 'incorrect' diagrams

In the above diagram there is a mixture in the level of detail which will lead to problems. If the input and output data have not been consistent across the descriptions of the different sub-systems then it will prove difficult to find corresponding outputs and inputs. The problem of maintaining a consistent level of detail across the analysis is one which is relevant to all systems diagrams and little advice can be given about how to avoid falling into this trap. All that the analyst can do is to be aware of the need to maintain the same level of resolution throughout a diagram. The ability to achieve this seems to increase with practice. When fully developed, the Black Box diagram is ideal for illustrating the relationship between the different processes being undertaken within a system. It is important to remember that the inputs and outputs identified for each sub-system may be either a physical input or a flow of information.

The production of a useful Black Box diagram means that the analyst will need to spend time investigating the problem situation that is to be represented in the diagram. The learning resulting from such an investigation is a valuable asset in the analysis process. It is not difficult to see that whilst a diagram can be used to represent a situation to another individual, the process of producing the diagram can be a valuable learning activity in itself.

Furthermore, a Black Box diagram provides a useful basis from which to represent an information system. Since the black box is concerned with 'Systems', which has at its heart communication and control, we may focus upon exploring this structure as the representation of the flow of data that supports the notional whole. Analysts may find this approach particularly useful when considering the role of Information Technology and its relationship to the systems to be served.

CHAPTER 3

The Practice

Using Models

In this chapter will draw upon some more of the ideas that we introduced in the previous chapters and show how these are combined to provide 'tools' to assist in gaining understanding of a situation of interest. In the previous chapter we discussed models and modelling and in this chapter we will add to this knowledge and introduce you to the notion of method and methodology. Please note this chapter is only intended to introduce you to the way that we apply some of the models and methods in Systems. We leave a more in-depth discussion about the underlying concepts and more advanced ideas until later in the text.

When you first became interested in Systems thinking you may have heard the terms method and methodology and wondered what we mean by these. For many, especially those new to Systems, these are somewhat confusing terms so it is sensible to begin this chapter by thinking about method and methodology and ask the question: is there a difference between the two? It is difficult to discuss them without thinking about the intellectual processes involved but the main aim of this chapter is to introduce you to some methodologies so we will confine ourselves to simple definitions and return to the more complex questions about logic and what we mean by logical coherence later in the text.

Method can be described as an orderly way of doing something. If you think about the implication of this it means that there is no such thing as THE method. We are taught ways of tackling problems usually without knowing where the ideas came from or on what assumptions they are based. So where do the methods that we are taught to use come from? In most instances we select them from a tool kit of methods which were taught to us at school or college and apply one or more to the situation of interest. Unkind though it might be, most of us rarely think about the impact that our choice of method might have upon the way that we model the situation as we are usually more interested in getting an outcome than worrying about the situation itself. How do we select the right method? Well this is a good question and more of that later, but suffice it to say at this point that an ill considered choice of method may create difficulties, especially where the problem involves human activities.

For a tool to be useful the user must be able to understand how its different components or phases relate and what kind of outcome can be expected. An important feature is that the tool should be coherent – the problem should not be distorted to fit the requirements of the tool. Western education is heavily influenced by the successes of natural science and as a consequence many, if not most, of the methods for inquiry that we are taught are those developed within the scientific paradigm. These may not be suited to the more complex issues that arise in the variety of social situations we might encounter. The German philosopher Gadamer (2004, p. 7) pointed out that '[t]he human sciences have no method of their own' and his view still has merit. Even when we are looking at social situations such as delinquency or malnutrition in a population, the tools that we use are frequently those taken from mathematics or statistics. But if we try to understand the causes of these problems we soon realize that some of our tools are inadequate. We find that the root of the problem is more complex than simply applying a formula to some observable actions. The so-called 'Credit Crunch' of the early 21st century had multiple causes. These included attempts to 'eliminate risk' through a complicated formula (which apparently few fully understood) applied by financial institutions to dubious credit transactions which unsurprisingly failed. Some analysts blamed collateralization, others access to easy money and the driver of large bonus rewards within the banking sector. For some it was the mispricing of risk in mortgage-backed securities and for others lax regulation. It is difficult to pin the failure of the financial system to one cause. The failure was not entirely because of a faulty statistical model but a combination of issues, such as individual ambition. Some have even tried to blame the biological effects of testosterone! Even in a field that appears to be open to quantitative modelling, such as financial systems, we can see that there are many unquantifiable dimensions.

In this chapter we are looking at the way that models, methods and methodologies are used. So let us begin by thinking about methodology. Methodology is about method, but it is not method. Methodology can be taken to be the study and description of methods when combined to be useful in a working context. Importantly, methodologies are not formulae but sets of methods. Unlike a technique, a methodology has no pre-scribed outcomes, but is characterized by being iterative. The prime expected outcome from a methodology is learning about the situation rather than a 'tidy' solution. In recent years within the Systems research community, efforts have been made to develop ideas which may be suited to developing understanding of complexity in human inter-action. In this section, some Systems methodologies are introduced but discussion of their origins and the underlying ideas and influences will follow later in the text (see Chapter 5). The aim of this chapter is to provide an outline of some approaches in sufficient detail that they can be put to practical use. You should be able to draw upon your understanding of the ideas expressed in the previous two chapters and use this knowledge to enrich the descriptions of methods and methodologies presented here.

Although successful application of a method or methodology discussed in this chapter will doubtless whet your curiosity to discover more about the underlying ideas, we have deferred an in-depth discussion until later chapters which are intended to provide you with some further insights and a road map for further study. The methods and meth-odologies described in this chapter will draw as much as possible upon the foregoing chapters to provide a clear link and an easy transition to using them.

Of course there are some constants that should be observed for every inquiry. One such constant that has been found useful, which we introduced you to in Chapter 1, is to begin by thinking about the extent of the situation of interest in terms of bound-ary and environment. It is sensible when beginning an investigation to decide where to draw a boundary around the system of interest – what is inside this boundary and what is part of its environment? (Of course, this requires us to ask the question 'From whose point of view?' The boundary that you might choose to draw may not appear appropriate from the point of view of your client.) This apparently simple task will help you to eliminate aspects which have no relevance to the problem situation. As you and your clients begin to understand the situation better so the boundary might move to embrace, or eliminate some system or sub-system. As you apply the method or methodology so your understanding will increase and the more reliance you may place upon your boundary and environment and what they contain.

Models and Modelling

We begin this section with two models of 'organization' which can be used as a means of gaining insights into a given situation. The first model we discuss is that developed from the writings of Sir Geoffrey Vickers. Vickers' work has been influential in Systems research and practice including the Soft Systems Methodology, but here we will consider what we call the Relationship Model. This idea, suggested more than 30 years ago, has a freshness and relevance to modern business and poignancy for the global economy and for companies who trade within it.

Vickers Appreciative Systems and Relationship Maintaining Model

Vickers (1970) pointed out that each human individual's experience of life is unique. We all make sense of the world around us through unique perception and sense-making processes. As we reflect upon our experience, we gradually develop individual sets of values and goals and these, in turn, colour our future perceptions so that we notice some things but screen out others. Vickers termed these our 'Appreciative settings' that make us uniquely who we are.

Relationship maintaining models retain the open systems perspective but represent a shift in emphasis from optimization and the maintenance of equilibrium between a system and its environment towards learning and adapting to maintain a relationship with a constantly changing environment. More important are ideas that are placed under this category of approach, which attempt to represent the system of interest and its environment from the perspective of those involved within the problem situation. As Winograd and Flores (1986) remarked that the majority of models of organization have been developed from within a framework of thinking which we judge to be functionalist and an historical legacy influenced by the concepts of scientific method. Using Vickers' ideas we are considering an organization as something ever-changing, not a fixed entity, and whose survival depends upon maintaining its relationship with its environment. (It is interesting to compare Vickers' discussion of relationship-maintaining systems with the theory of autopoiesis discussed by Maturana and Varela and by Luhmann – see Chapter 4). The idea is a simple one until one begins to think more closely about what is meant and how each part relates to another. We will leave this to one side for now and concentrate upon providing a general understanding and return to an in-depth discussion later in the text.

Vickers' discussion emphasizes the importance of an organization maintaining its relationship with its ever-changing environment. In relationship-maintaining models the emphasis is upon the methods suited to organizational understanding rather than the definition of an organization itself. A manager's primary task is not to define the goals and objectives of an organization: these change over time, but rather to understand how things are, or 'need to be', in order to maintain equilibrium or a 'satisfactory' performance (i.e. satisficing, Simon 1991). In this sense 'learning' about an organization is seen as a never-ending process. It is the exploration that takes place in determining the goals and objectives that is the important activity since this leads onto an Appreciation of that organization's activities.

The Appreciative System can be represented diagrammatically as shown in Figure 3.1 below:

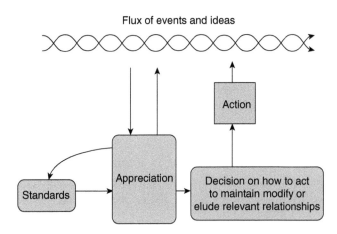

Figure 3.1:   Vickers Appreciative System, first produced by Checkland and Casar (1986)

At this stage of the text we will confine ourselves to a simple description of the idea and develop it in more detail later. Let's look at the key elements of the model. An enterprise exists in a turbulent environment. There is little which is static and we represent this here as a flux of events and ideas. The first task of those with responsibility for managing the enterprise is to be aware of or 'Appreciate' what is taking place, e.g. changes in the market, the economy or the impact of the tools available to management. A good example of the latter is the development of integrated information systems which have altered the way that an enterprise operates and even the way that we view an enterprise.

You may think that saying that an enterprise exists in a turbulent environment is obvious until we think about the number of organizations that have their mission statements displayed for all to see. But the idea of a mission statement suggests that success is achieved by striving to achieve the espoused goal with little consideration to the changes taking place every day. A mission statement is a statement that is effectively frozen in time and unless it is regularly updated once that goal has been achieved, it becomes irrelevant. It may be in recognition of this that many organizations now have 'vision' statements – expressing their values rather than their goals.

So what does relationship maintaining mean? Vickers argued that the prime activity for a manager is to maintain the relationship of the enterprise to its environment. A goal is something that is achieved and then we move on. It is not something that is set for all time. To survive, the enterprise must change to meet the changing environment in which it exists. In the relationship model the manager gains an Appreciation of the situation by considering what is taking place within the context of past experience and the standards or ideals of the enterprise. This enables consideration to be given to actions to be taken to modify or elude the relationship which has emerged. Of course this situation is 'never-ending' and is a continuous responsibility of those involved.

To be successful a manager should be less concerned with the prescription of '. . . one goal or even one series of goals; but in regulating a system over time in such a way as to optimise the realisation of many conflicting relations without wrecking the system in the process' (1972, p. 116). It is, Vickers argued, the influence of technology that has encouraged us to see decision making in terms of goal attainment. The ease of monitoring the attainment of a goal is easily achieved by technologically driven control systems, but these may not always be the pathway to success.

Relationship-maintaining models provide us with a means of maintaining a relationship with the environment, which is constantly changing. We believe that such a vision of an organization implies that we should represent the system of interest and its environment from the perspective of those involved within the problem situation rather than an outside observer. We are thinking of an organization as something that is not fixed, is constantly changing and whose survival is dependent upon the maintenance of its relationship with its environment. Vickers' ideas of relationship maintaining can also be useful when thinking about how each of us manages our own circumstances.

The Appreciative Cycle can be represented as shown in Figure 3.2:

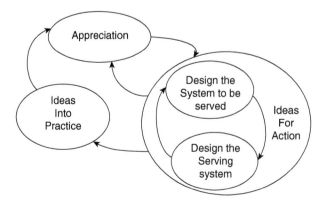

Figure 3.2: Appreciative Cycle (after Cooray, 2010)

The diagram depicts the way in which Vickers describes the cycle of Appreciation. It begins with our interests and concerns which, we should remember, are subjective and shaped by our view of the world. When our interest is triggered by some event we make what Vickers describes as a 'reality judgement', by which he meant where we select the facts we consider relevant to the situation. This selection is described as an Appreciation of 'what is' the case. Once we assimilate this we go on to consider 'what ought' to be the case for an ideal outcome. This is what Vickers refers to as making a value judgement that is based upon our 'Appreciative' settings, which change continuously. The outcome of this cycle is that we make an 'Action Judgment' where we consider the practicalities of the hypothetical relationship of 'what is' and 'what ought' to be the case. We decide 'what shall I do about the situation?' The important outcome of this cycle is that we gain a better understanding, or 'Appreciation', of the situation.

Whilst we can accept that the environment in which we exist continuously changes, common sense tells us that when the change is unexpected, especially if we feel that we have no control over likely outcomes, then we become uncomfortable. Experience shows that when individuals find themselves in a situation where they feel threatened then some form of resistance ensues. The kinds of change that have taken place over the past decade (and will continue for some time to come) have created a climate in which individuals expect to experience some form of insecurity. Many of the 'great' state enterprises from Railways and Education through to the Health Service and Defence have undergone significant changes and there is no reason to assume that the pace of change will not continue. The culture of change has prepared people to *expect* their circumstances to change and may provide an opportunity for managing change better than in the past. We will return to the notion of relationship maintenance later in the text. We now move on to another influential idea of organizational modelling, namely the Viable Systems Model.

The Viable Systems Model

The Viable Systems Model is associated with Stafford Beer. Beer became interested in Ashby's work on variety in dynamic systems (Beer, 1959) and reflecting on this, and other work in cybernetics, Beer realized that there was a deficiency when considering the nature of relationships in complex dynamic systems. The result of this reflection was the creation of what became known as the Viable Systems Model (VSM) (Beer, 1972; Espejo and Harnden, 1989). Through this model Beer was able to make possible a holistic view of the way a complex dynamic system such as an enterprise might work. It is interesting to compare this model with other views of organizational dynamics, e.g. Porter's Value Chain model (Porter, 1985). While the complexity of business activity may emerge quite clearly, Porter's model of the dynamics of that complexity does not emerge with the same transparency as is the case with VSM.

VSM has been used throughout the world and not just in business. Perhaps the best known and high profile project being its use in Chile during the Presidency of Allende (see Beer 1972 for an in-depth discussion and analysis). VSM is concerned with organizations which are viewed as complex dynamic systems. We can think of an organization as consisting of interrelated elements contained within a boundary defined by the interest of an observer. Outside this boundary are influential forces to which the system must respond, but which it cannot control (we refer to this as its environment). The system has emergent properties relating to a transformation it is designed to bring about. It also has hierarchy, i.e. it is composed of other, smaller, interrelated sub-systems.

In VSM, structures, relationships and flows are modelled to reflect the complexities of an organizational system. A viable system is defined by Beer as one that is stable within its environment, i.e. it can adapt its state at any given time to deal with the influences impinging on it through its systemic behaviour. VSM can be represented diagrammatically as in Figure 3.3:

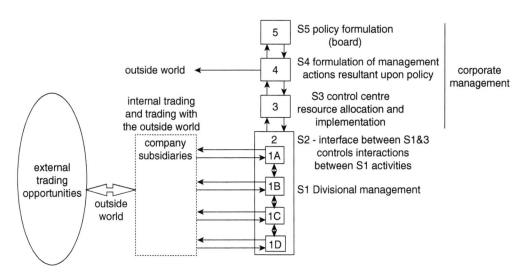

Figure 3.3: Viable Systems Model

VSM is so called to highlight the notion that viable systems have within their hierarchy systems that are also viable (See Figure 3.4). Each level in VSM is itself a system which has the same kind of configuration of the model shown in Figure 3.3 above.

A number of aspects of organizational behaviour are highlighted in VSM by reference to modelling of specific sub-systems.

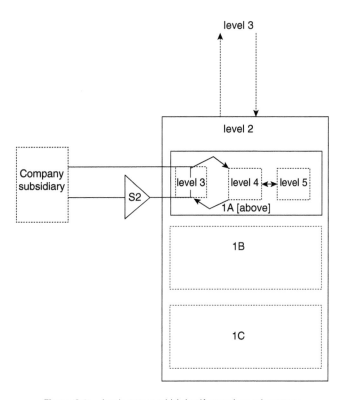

Figure 3.4:   A sub-system which itself comprises sub-systems

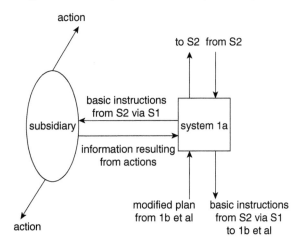

Figure 3.5:   Level 1 in VSM

Level 1: Primary activities needed to implement the key transformation that the system exists to achieve are referred to as System 1 (see Figure 3.5). These are recursive to the extent that all key activities must be implemented in a viable system. This is the level of the workforce, where things get done. In the case of a factory this might be the shop floor where components are made and assembled. If we were thinking

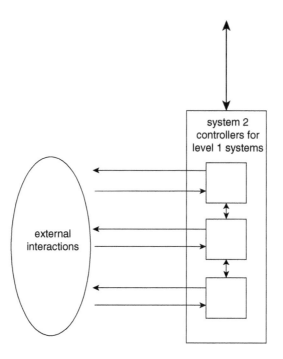

Figure 3.6: Level 2 – System 1 controller

about a multinational this might represent each of the companies that together make it up.

Level 2: Coordination of the activities inherent in implementing System 1 requires channels for communication between recursive sub-systems, in order for necessary information about the state(s) of this system to flow. This is modelled as System 2 (see Figure 3.6), but it should be noted that System 2 would oscillate aimlessly but for the function of System 3 which is to monitor System 2's actions.

Level 3: Cohesion between the various components of the viable system is achieved through System 3. This sub-system compares the System 1 performance to previously established measures. 'Algedonic' alerts (warnings of deviation) result from these comparisons when the system falls short of, or exceeds, capability. System 3 structures and processes are designed to impose control to correct deviations from target through action involving System 2 (see Figure 3.7). (See explanation of feedback control in Chapters 2 and 5.) Where homeostasis (stability) cannot be achieved in this way, System 3 processes seek recommendations from System 4.

Level 4: This sub-system gathers intelligence from the environment and generates suggestions for innovation and/or development. Where System 4 advice is needed,

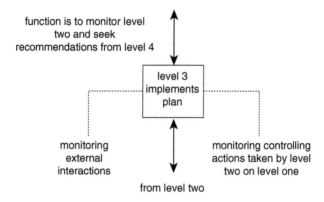

Figure 3.7:   Level 3 as a control centre

balance between different aspects at System 1 may be disrupted, or more resources may be needed in order to maintain the stability of the organizational system as a whole. In this case, policy decisions are needed from System 5, about direction to be taken and resources to be acquired or expended (see Figure 3.8).

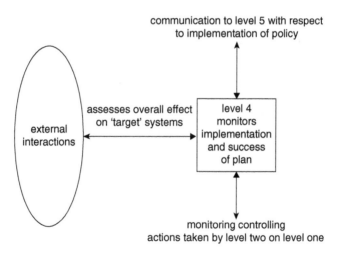

Figure 3.8:   Level 4 relationship to environment and Levels 3 and 5

Level 5: This is what Beer referred to as the 'Brain of the Firm' (Beer, 1972) (see Figure 3.9). It is from here that the whole complex system is controlled – decisions taken and instructions given to implement them. You will note that there is a link into Level 1 which shows that although this is the organization's 'brain' it is receptive to all aspects of the enterprise and not just the immediate level below.

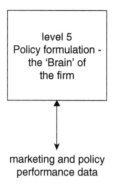

Figure 3.9:   Level 5 *The Brain of the Firm*

Soft Systems Methodology

Soft Systems Methodology (SSM) along with VSM is probably the most influential practical Systems approach developed for addressing complexity that has emerged over the past 30 years. Whereas for some VSM is a means of fitting organizational problems into a framework which can be used to design how the enterprise might work and to diagnose where things go wrong, SSM took a different approach where the accent is upon a process of learning about the situation and from this developing useful models. First we produce a desirable model (solution) and then, with the clients, resolve it into a feasible model; a basis for action, that all concerned are prepared to accept and implement. SSM, developed at Lancaster under the guidance of Peter Checkland, utilized the experience of a number of projects over a period of 30 years. These evolved into a powerful sense-making tool for gaining understanding of complexity. In 1981, Checkland published the fruits of this experience as a text. (A full account can be found in Checkland, 1981 and 1999.) SSM draws upon earlier work by Churchman (1971) and Vickers (1972), among others.

Over the past 30 years many people and organizations have made use of SSM to explore messy situations and learn more about them. The methodology has been refined through feedback from many such applications and is now described in two versions, known as Mode 1 (see Checkland, 1981) and Mode 2 (see Checkland and Scholes, 1990) which we will deal with in Chapter 5. Many applications of SSM have been developed including its use in developing Information Systems (for discussion, see Mingers and Stowell, 1990; Checkland and Holwell, 1998; Stowell and West, 1994).

The best known version of SSM is the seven-stage model, now referred to as SSM Mode 1, which we will use in this section of the text. It is a version most easily rec-

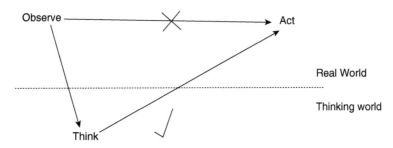

Figure 3.10: Real World and Thinking World

ognized and for some most easily taught. SSM Mode 2 relies less on a visual representation of the intellectual stages that the user goes through and more on understanding
of the concepts upon which it is based. SSM Mode 1 contains all the ideas of Mode
2, but in a form some find easier to grasp.

The idea behind SSM is an attempt to address some fundamental questions that any
would-be problem-solver faces. First, what is the nature of the situation of interest?
Many of us have been in situations where there are many strands to the challenges
that we face and it is necessary to tease out these various dimensions before any one
of them can be tackled to develop solutions. Before that we should consider the way
that we might address any situation of interest.

In Figure 3.10 we can see that we do not observe (e.g. an oncoming vehicle) and act
without thought. What we do is observe, think and then act. Checkland refers to this
process as 'above and below the line' activities. In this way we are able to differentiate
between the actions in the so-called real world, where we are conscious of events, and
the thinking world where we consider how we should react and in some cases act
instinctively, e.g. moving out of the way of an oncoming vehicle but avoiding other
dangers.

SSM Mode 1 is represented as follows (see Figure 3.11):

In cloud one, we are observing and gaining an 'Appreciation' of the situation of interest.
It is here that we try to find out as much as we can and represent it as a picture, called
a Rich Picture, (RD) to emphasize the richness of the information it contains (see
Chapter 1). As we indicated in Chapter 1 the picture should not be drawn in such a
way that it restricts thinking about the problem (or opportunity). For example, we
should not group all commercial department activities in one section, the production
department in another and finance in another. The Rich Picture is a snapshot of the
situation in which the interaction between structure and process is represented. This

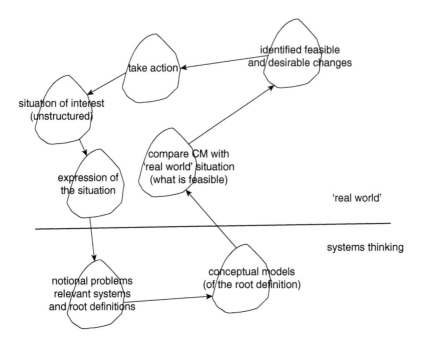

Figure 3.11:   SSM Mode 1 (see Checkland and Scholes, 1990, p. 27)

stage of the approach can take up to 25% of the time available for the whole project as it is at this stage that the practitioner or the researcher needs to gain an Apprecia-tion about the system of interest. Ideally this activity should be taken in conjunction with all those involved in the situation and should continue until there is agreement that it represents the given situation. It is important that the RP is as rich as possible. We have found that by involving those within the situation the RP is not only enriched but it also helps the participants to take ownership of the process.

In cloud two we are thinking about what we have learnt and expressing the Problem Themes (PTs) of the situation and then thinking about 'systems' that we consider relevant to them. It is worth remembering that there might be a number of PTs and it is a function of the level of Appreciation of the situation which helps in selecting one for further development. Of course there may be more than one chosen but too many might suggest that the practitioner/researcher is working at too low a level or even 'too real world'.

Systems relevant to PT are referred to as Relevant Systems (RSs). Just as there may be several important PTs, each PT will have more than one relevant system. Remember that the RSs are the name of a system relevant to the PT and not a solution. We can represent the relationship between them as in Figure 3.12:

problem theme 1
  relevant system 1
    relevant system 2
      relevant system 'n'

problem theme 2
  relevant system 1
    relevant system 2
      relevant system 'n' --> e.g. select this RS) --> produce Root Definition

Figure 3.12:   Problem themes and relevant systems

We then select a RS and define those RSs that we think are the most important in the form of a concise paragraph. This is called a Root Definition (RD). We define the Relevant System in such a way as to eliminate, as far as possible, any ambiguity. The development of the RD can be assisted by applying a simple set of ideas which go under the mnemonic CATWOE where:

C = Customers   referring to the customer of the system. There may be several customers so do not be afraid of having more than one, although too many might suggest the chosen RS is at the wrong level of analysis;

A = Actors   standing for the actors within the systems and once again there may be more than one;

T = Transformation   we believe 'T' is one of the two most important aspects of the definition to be considered. 'T' describes the transformation of an input into the desired output and it helps to clarify thinking about the RS;

W = *Weltanschauung*   we consider this to be the second important consideration. 'W' or *Weltanschauung* refers to the worldview behind the RD. It is an opportunity for the author of the definition to reflect upon why they have defined this system in this way and make that reason explicit. It is important that we make clear to others what 'system' we are talking about because if we do not it is likely that the listener will relate our description to a (usually unconscious) model of their own. Their model may bear little resemblance to the 'system' that we had in mind. For example, someone's description of their company's problems might well be interpreted by an accountant and a computer scientist in a different way; moreover the interpretation by another manager, a union representative or a production engineer in the same company might be different to the idea that the original individual had in mind. (This relates to the important point made in Chapter 1 that a system exists because someone perceives it to be of interest. It is a mental construct and not a reflection of some objective 'reality'.) If we are to be successful in describing the 'system' we must find a way of enabling all concerned to do so with the minimum danger of misinterpretation. It is easy for the parties involved to be thinking about their different needs and as such to be working from an undeclared model; and, in the course of discussions, they may unconsciously relate what is being said to their own previous experience of (what they perceive to be) a similar situation. So we ask, from whose point of view is the problem to be addressed? Different actors within a problem situation will hold differing perspectives as to how the situation can be defined and what sort(s) of outcomes would be acceptable. Then the question arises that we referred to in Chapter 1 – where should a boundary be drawn to define what is included in any analysis and what is to be considered beyond its scope? Here we can distinguish between the outside world in general (that can be safely ignored for the purpose of the analysis) and the particular aspects of the outside world that may have an influence over the situation (the environment that may be relevant to the systems we have defined). For example, these aspects within the Rich Picture contained within the boundary might also embrace elements of the environment which have an influence upon the situation, e.g. Government legislation.

O = Owners
referring to the problem owner(s) – those who have power to influence the continued integrity of the relevant system.

E = Environment
here we ask what is the nature of the environment in which this system will be operating – what kind of things will be exerting influence over it?

In the third cloud we model the activities that we think make up the system we have defined. This is a model of the activities that exist in the RD, either explicitly or implicitly. The activities should be verb fronted as they are depicting doing something. It is a common mistake to give each activity a noun or pronoun but we should describe the activities in the model to enable the reader to see what it is doing. Taken together, activity models provide a dynamic representation of the Root Definition. Please note that the process of turning the RD into a model should use the power of deductive logic and nothing else – we are not, at this point, modelling phenomena having real world existence.

We then return our model to the real world and use it as an agenda for discussion with those involved or, alternatively, we can use it as a comparison with what is actually happening in the situation. The comparison and discussion with participants lead to an agreed model of what is considered to be possible in the situation. The model and discussion represent another step in the process of learning which is fundamental to the success of SSM. Once all have agreed the resultant model we can go on to take action.

Summary

SSM is intended to support the practitioner/researcher to create a cycle of learning in order to explore messy situations. The methodology provides opportunities to define systems they perceive to be relevant, relating to key issues in the situation, to create idealized models of these systems and to reflect upon them in relation to the 'real world' as a means of generating an agenda for debate among interested parties. Following on from this activity it may be that some clearly defined problems have emerged, which are amenable to solution using 'harder' techniques. For example, a business might find that one of its problems relates to poor performance measurement. If so, it can look for a recognized management technique to solve this specific problem.

The Appreciative Inquiry Method (AIM)

The Appreciative Inquiry Method (AIM) was proposed in the 1990s (Stowell and West, 1990) and arose out of the lessons learnt from research undertaken into the methods of knowledge elicitation (West, 1991). AIM has developed over the years and examples can be seen in Stowell and West (1990) as part of the process of knowledge elicitation and in gathering of expertise in West (1992; West and Thomas, 2005; West and Bragança, 2011); as a means of gaining understanding of complex decision making in Smith's (2001) work in mental health; and in understanding management problems Stowell (2001–2009) in a number of Systems workshops within the Systems Practice for Managing Complexity network (http://www.northumbria.ac.uk/spmc).

The original incarnation of AIM was created from the learning experience gained during a research project where busy managers had little available time to discuss their problems (they were too busy tackling them). The lessons learnt from this experience were reinvested into what became the Appreciative Inquiry Method (AIM). In this case AIM was offered as a means of creating a non-intrusive method of knowledge elicitation that would help a busy individual to 'give up' their knowledge with the minimum of disruption to their day-to-day responsibilities. By adopting this approach it was possible to get close to the dynamics of the way each individual undertook their role responsibilities. Note that AIM should not be confused with AI, a management tool with a similar name, developed by Cooperider and Sravastra (1987).

Since then AIM has been developed as a means of gaining understanding of issues or questions raised about aspects of management concerns. In simple terms the Appreciative Inquiry Method was an attempt to provide a collection of tools, based upon the ideas of holism and subjectivity, that might be used collectively to support the process of exploring and making explicit an expert's domain of expertise. Strengths of using AIM include its ease of use and the possibility to surface tacit knowledge among participants. In this chapter we will describe AIM as originally conceived, as a method of knowledge elicitation, and go on to discuss developments which have added to its value as a sense making tool.

The version of AIM used as a method of knowledge elicitation was depicted as consisting of three phases and is represented by the diagram in Figure 3.13:

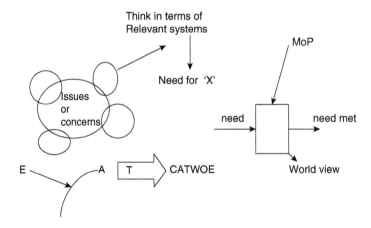

Figure 3.13:   General diagram of AIM

The first phase is the creation of a systems map (a kind of Venn diagram) by the participants that is a reflection of their understanding of the question relating to the expert's area of knowledge. In order to demonstrate what is expected the facilitator provides an example. The example is simple and can be provided quickly. The expert is then provided with paper and pen and asked to follow the same procedure. Their map is developed around the central question, which has previously been determined as core to the area of expertise. The facilitator will visit each of the participants (if there is more than one expert involved) for about 10 minutes (the average time that it takes someone to complete their map) to collect and discuss their map of the situation.

The second stage is concerned with the description of the map elements as purposeful activities. The expert is asked to describe each map element using the CATWOE test from SSM (see p. 56 for ideas which we have found to be more enlightening at this stage). The CATWOE test is used to ensure that enough information is provided to develop the description of some purposeful human activity. This meeting takes on average 20–25 minutes. In the case of multiple experts the facilitator looks at each map that has been produced to see if there are any overlaps or areas of similarity. The facilitator will then produce a single map, called a composite map and return to each participant for their comment. The composite map consists of all the elements in each of the individual system maps and combining any areas of commonality. We have found in later developments of AIM that this stage is best undertaken with all participants assembled as a means of engendering a debate and to improve group understanding, although getting the whole group together at one time rarely happens in practice (see Figure 3.14 below and the worked example in Chapter 8 for the evolved AIM). The outcome of this activity is an agreed composite map. Ideally the composite map is enriched by selecting one or all of the sub-systems and defining what each sub-system is. This is usually achieved by producing a Root Definition in the form we have learnt to develop as part of SSM (see West and de Bragança, 2011).

Once the descriptions or Root Definitions have been produced the next task is to formulate an activity model. That is to say a set of verb fronted activities which together represent the definition (and nothing else). The third phase of AIM consists of the

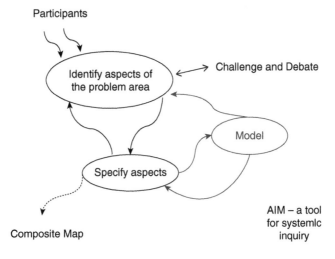

Figure 3.14:   AIM moving from individual to group settings

facilitator returning to each participant with the activity model, which is used to engender discussions about its feasibility. The outcome provides insight into the chosen area of expertise.

AIM as a Means of 'Making Sense of Things'

Since the original conception of AIM as a means of knowledge elicitation it has been developed further and is used to assist managers to understand the many difficult situations they face in their day-to-day responsibilities. Although the basic phases of AIM remain the same the refinements learnt though several PhD research projects and management workshops have helped to extend the idea into an effective way of making sense of difficult problems. The description of AIM that follows is the result of workshops and research projects in which lessons have been learnt about making sense of things using this approach. We have found that AIM used in this way assists managers to understand or *Appreciate* difficult issues they face and provides a means of addressing them.

In using this application of AIM we start with a central question or issue which has been established and agreed in advance by those concerned. The issue might be related to changes that an enterprise is to make or a question that has arisen from the way in which the enterprise is operating. For example, the central issue might be 'Why is the company losing its market share?' or perhaps 'How can we improve Management-Staff relations?' or 'What makes a good employee?'

Used as a means of addressing an agreed issue or question (we call this the proposition) AIM consists of three, but more often four phases because in this version we actively seek group participation and discussion and this can sometimes increase the number of encounters. As is the case for AIM when used as a means of knowledge elicitation the first phase is the creation of a systems map around the agreed issue or question. When using AIM in this way it is usually with a number of staff rather than a single expert as in the case of knowledge elicitation. In this case where we have a number of participants we have found it beneficial for them to be allocated to work in small groups. This will be followed at strategic points by plenary meetings for the group as a whole.

The first task is for individuals within their groups to consider the sub-systems which, for them, make up the central issue. Unlike the earlier version of AIM we ask each person to think about each 'sub-system' in terms of its Transformation and the *Weltanschauung*, the worldview, behind it rather than the whole CATWOE (e.g. see SSM, Checkland, 2006). Whilst Checkland points out that 'A bold sparse statement of T could stand as a Root Definition . . . but would necessarily yield a general model' (Checkland, 1981, p. 22) it is good enough at this stage as our purpose is to engender a cycle of learning. This process will help the participants with their thinking and also enable them to answer any questions about their map when discussing it with other members of this group. Once individual maps have been completed each sub-group then combines the maps produced by each participant to arrive at a single map. We have found that the point of this step is intended to generate a discussion within the group in the spirit of reaching what Gadamer (2004) called 'a fusion of horizons'. That is to say there is an exchange of ideas as a means of gaining an *Appreciation* of the situation of interest. This has been found to work well, for example, at a management workshop at the University of Northumbria in 2008 one of the facilitators noted: 'Once the group had put down some personal notes on W and T for their own models the discussion started' (Bednar, facilitator's notes, 8 July 2008).

It is important that participants discuss, without rancour, any differences between individual maps (we are seeking agreement, 'endoxa', from them). We advocate the use of the mnemonic PEArL as a means of understanding the dynamics of the group here (see below) as this might be where individuals seek to 'persuade' others to accept their point of view. We might reflect upon Gadamer's observation here when he points out, '. . . opinion has the ability to propagate itself and acts to suppress questions'. Opinion, for Gadamer, is the enemy of understanding (2004, pp. 359–361). What we are attempting at this stage is a form of Socratic dialectic, which is designed to create the environment for questions and enhance understanding of the participants about the 'systems' in their maps. For example, in another workshop, this time comprising members from social services, the facilitator commented: 'The group appeared at ease and willing to discuss conflicting views. They accommodated each other by either changing terminology to accommodate a group understanding or agreed to have two different subsystems' (Stowell, A., facilitator's notes, 9 July 2008). Such a free discourse meant that questions about each of the maps could be answered because the richness of the *Appreciation* gained within the sub-groups had been aided by thinking about just two of the elements of CATWOE.

On those occasions where it is not possible to get participants together the facilitators task is to develop the maps with the participants on a one-to-one basis. It is important that the facilitator does not interfere with the process and allows the participant, in comparative silence, to concentrate upon developing and representing their thoughts. In a group situation the group are asked to agree a single map representing the groups' view of the issue (see Figure 3.15).

The next stage is where the facilitator seeks clarification about each sub-system. Experience has shown that the maps can be a mixture of what the participant thinks the

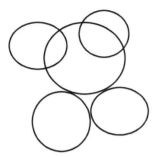

Figure 3.15:   Sketch of an Initial Systems map

situation to be and what they would like it to be. To address this Cooray (2010) found that by asking the client to describe the sub-system first in terms of *what is the case* (reality judgements), then *what ought* to be the case ('what ought' to be as being '. . . judgements of the significance of these facts . . .' to him/her and their society Vickers 1970, p. 150) it helps them to separate what is taking place presently and what they would like to happen. We then invite them to clarify what they mean by each of the sub-systems by asking them to explain the Transformation and *Weltanschauungen* behind each of their sub-systems. It is important to remember that the group composite map should show all the sub-systems from each member's individual maps. It is common for elements to be combined following group discussion as individuals often recognize that the only difference between some sub-sets is a simple matter of semantics. This process is a useful part of the learning exercise as the group begin to explore in more detail their thinking and understanding behind the map. This understanding is enriched when each group presents their map in 'plenary' to the participant group as a whole. We have found that a plenary session provides another opportunity for an open discussion about the situation of interest amongst the participants. The outcome of this session is to get the participants to combine the individual group maps into a composite map representing what the group as a whole think. The outcome for the plenary session is to produce a composite map for the whole group but it is not as daunting as might be thought. We have found that because AIM is focusing on a particular issue or question there are many overlapping points between individual maps; often the same sub-system but with a different name.

It is worth remembering at this point that the individual maps are often a combination of 'what is the case' and 'what ought to be the case'. We have found that by asking *what is the case* followed by *what ought to be the case* the participants provide a richer portrayal of their Appreciation of the issue. Once there is a clear agreement of the makeup of the 'issue' then the next task is to establish a composite systems map based upon 'what ought' to be the case. The facilitator's task is to ask the participants to consider each of their nominated systems in that context. This may mean that some of the sub-systems created in the first encounter will be removed and some added, i.e.

as the result of getting them to differentiate between *what is* and *what ought* systems maps. This part of the process helps the participants to gain a richer Appreciation of the issue or question posed. Experience in a project undertaken at a Government establishment showed that where the composite maps were sent out to each participant in advance of the meetings, it proved helpful in preparing the participants for the group, x discussions that followed.

Once an agreed systems map has been produced the participants meet again using the T and W for each sub-system to define what each of the overlapping ellipses means. Our intention here is to produce a root definition as we do in SSM. Availability of time will determine if this can be done collectively or if the facilitator should produce a rough draft off line that is taken for refinement in the plenary session. In the latter case we are seeking *authentication* of the definition produced by the facilitator from the group (Champion and Stowell, 2003 pp. 27–28). Once all participants have *authenticated* the definition the final task is to produce a model of the systems that make up the view of the central issue or question. It is not unusual for the model to be in the form of an activity model (see Figure 3.16) although other systems diagrams may be more appropriate, e.g. influence diagrams, feedback models, Black Box diagrams. We have found that the activity model can be used as the basis for developing other models, for example, Cooray's (2010) research into client-led design of information systems where Stowell and West (1994) and later Stowell and Champion (2002) used an activity model to develop relationship and class diagrams as part of a technical specification for the design (see Chapter 8 for a worked example).

We mentioned above that we have found the mnemonic PEArL (Champion and Stowell, 2001, 2003; Stowell, 2009a) to be an aid in helping both the facilitator and the client fully appreciate the situation as it unfolds. PEArL is described in detail in

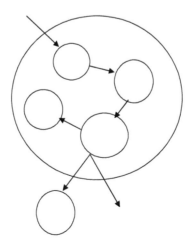

Figure 3.16: Activity model

Chapter 7 but in summary, PEArL stands for the following: P = Participants; E = Engagement; A = Authority; r = relationships; L = Learning. PEArL enables the researcher and client to be explicit about who is included within and excluded from the situation of interest. Cooray (2010) found it particularly useful when using this incarnation of AIM. We have found the mnemonic to be useful in two ways. The first is at the start of a project as it can be used as a means of thinking about the boundary and participants that are likely to be involved in the situation of interest. Second, when used within AIM to help participants think about and describe the 'systems' they consider relevant to the central issue. During the AIM process we have found that using PEArL helps the facilitator and the client to explain their reasoning behind each sub-system contained in their systems map, for example by asking about (P in PEArL) for each activity in the systems map. Consideration of the A and r helps surface the power relationships (A & r in PEArL) that are thought to exist between the participants (Stowell, 1989, 2000; Checkland, 1999). It helps all concerned to be aware of the importance of group dynamics upon the outcome and the process of producing models from the final systems maps provides all the participants with an *Appreciation* of the situation of interest and the basis of an 'action judgment' (Vickers, 1970).

By involving the participants fully we find it helps them take ownership of the outcome. In this use of AIM we have found it is a powerful means of gaining a deeper understanding, or Appreciation, of the situation of interest. It is from the Appreciation that the action judgement emerges. That is to say the 'What shall I do about it?' (Vickers, 1984, p. 240) for action emerges.

The use of AIM as a method of 'making sense of things' is shown in the following diagram (Figure 3.17):

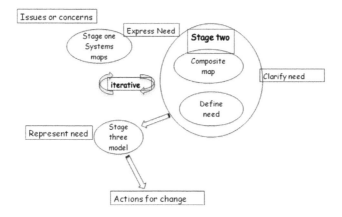

Figure 3.17:   Schematic diagram of AIM as a management sense-making tool (Stowell, 2012)

Summary

The above provides descriptions of AIM as a tool for knowledge elicitation and AIM as a tool for managers to help them make sense of difficult problem situations. In both cases when applying AIM, each individual participant produces a systems map that is the first step in a cycle of learning which AIM represents. The map is focused upon a central element, which has been agreed in advance to be the core issue or question to be addressed. The elements surrounding the central element consist of thoughts that the individual has regarding the declared worldview. In the version of AIM used for knowledge elicitation CATWOE is used (part of SSM Mode 1) to prompt the individual to think about the surrounding elements in a deeper manner. In the second use of AIM this activity is truncated to using W and T but aided by the use of PEArL. Of course just like any 'system' the map is recursive and, if needed, any of the surrounding elements can be taken separately as a central theme and another systems map be produced for it. This process could be conducted in an iterative manner until the participants have a richer understanding of how their declared *Weltanschauung* was formed. Studies where AIM is used as a means of gaining understanding, or Appreciation, of management problems (Stowell and Cooray, 2006; Cooray 2010) have shown that when conducted in a group environment there is an atmosphere of 'challenge and debate' which results in participants coming away with a deeper understanding of the central theme than is the case when AIM is conducted on a one-to-one basis. By bringing everyone together it means that each individual should be prepared to justify why the particular *Weltanschauung* was formed and face the challenges posed by other participants, but more of this in the later chapter.

AIM has proved itself to be a useful management tool and valuable to the researcher and practitioner alike.

Client-led Design (CLD) – Client-led Information Systems Creation (CLICS)

This method was developed as an aid to the development of organizational information systems. The initial stages of the framework use either AIM or SSM to help participants to go through a cycle of learning about the situation. When CLD was published it is true to say that the idea of using a 'soft' or 'interpretive' approach, such as SSM, for IT development was not new: others had tried, e.g. Wilson (1981: Miles, 1985: Stowell, 1985; Avison and Wood-Harper, 1990). But using soft ideas as a means of empowering clients to *lead* the design process was. There were several attempts at that time which were developed to give greater client involvement and this desire continues today including: Stowell (1995: Mingers and Stowell, 1997; Guo et al., 2000; Peppard, 2001;

Champion and Stowell, 2005; Cooray, 2010). In software engineering there are also attempts to involve the end-user in the development process. The best known of the lightweight methodologies, XP (extreme programming), focuses on building a person-to person mutual understanding of the problem environment through what they describe as minimal formal documentation and maximum on-site interaction (Highsmith, 2000). The inclusion of the end-user in the development of the software underlines the importance attached by software engineers to obtaining a successful end result. It is also not clear from the methods used if the design process is requirements or product driven. But we feel that by using the underpinning ideas of Soft Systems in the design process it helps in the transfer of the responsibility of design from the IT specialist to the development group as a whole. This is achieved by their involvement in gaining an Appreciation of the situation leading to greater understanding of the various tensions that have to be met. For example, managerial requirements and technical requirements which, at times, may appear at odds.

One of the earliest attempts to produce a seamless approach to user driven IS design was that by Stowell and West (1994) who suggested developing an activity model which was then to be used in conjunction with data flow diagrams. Their intention was to continue the development by using Structured Data Flow Diagrams (SDFD) in the same 'spirit' as the Conceptual Models (CM) in SSM. By approaching design in this way they argued that the difficulty of translating CM into a technical specification diminished, leading to the prospect of client-led development becoming a real possibility (Stowell, 1990; Stowell and West, 1994; Prior, 1990). There were critics who pointed to the incompatibility between the CM and an SDF diagram (e.g. Mingers, 1990; Wood, 1992) on ideological grounds. However, the counter to this criticism was that there is only an incompatibility if the use of the soft approach is seen merely as a front-end to the subsequent development of the SDFD, and is viewed as a separate exercise to be undertaken by a technical expert. The idea of client-led design (1994) and then the improved Client-Led Information Systems Creation (CLICS, 2005) is based on the belief that a partnership should be developed in which the client brings to the working arena a knowledge of their environment, culture and working practices whilst the IS professional brings along knowledge of appropriate means of facilitating inquiry and technical knowledge.

We believe that the process of inquiry should serve to increase the practitioner's own awareness of the situation and their role as facilitator/teacher (about the approach). The major difference between this approach and other methods, which aspire to *participation*, lies in the transfer of responsibility from the problem identification stage and information system development, the latter task traditionally being taken on solely by the IS professional. It should be noted that neither CLD nor CLICS which followed is a methodology but rather a framework for thinking based upon the interpretive para-

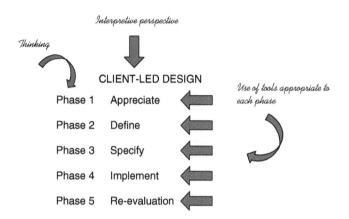

Figure 3.18:   Phases of Client-led Design as a framework for thinking (from Stowell and West, 1994)

digm. The process of thinking of CLD is described in five phases (see Stowell and West, 1994, p. 31) but these should not be considered as a set of discrete steps but as part of an iterative process (see Figure 3.18).

Facilitating a Client in Leading the Design Process

Despite the expectation of these early ideas there are still instances where a subjective method of inquiry has been used as a front-end to information system design and it has failed. It seems that when the practitioner reached the technical development stage the subjective account that enriched the inquiry became engulfed by the functional requirements of technology. The whole development process seems to be dominated by the need to produce a technical specification (Mingers and Stowell, 1997, p. 5). The translation of the *system of information* as described by the Conceptual Model is taken over by the technical specialist and used independently to develop the computer-supported information system (Stowell, 2008). One problem is that the approach can become an exercise in generality and any benefit of clients'/practitioners' *Appreciation* gained from the early stages of the development process is lost.

It is the *Appreciation* gained by the 'team' (practitioner, IT specialist and clients) that helps to guide the information system development process. This process has the advantage that the development of the information system can then be considered by both technical staff and the group as a whole in its widest context (see Figure 3.19) rather than be considered as a set of discrete steps in which the form of the information system is determined by the technology (see below and Stowell, 2008).

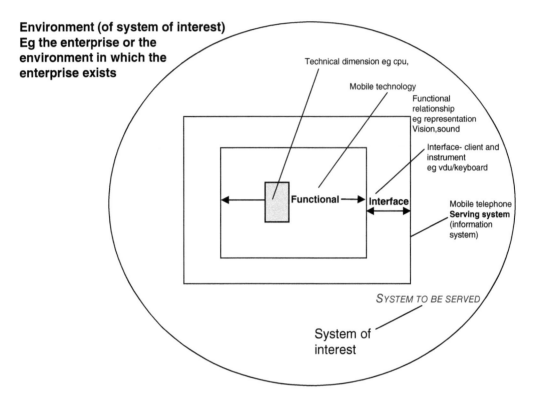

Figure 3.19:   A notional Information System

In CLD, the idea was that the practitioner should seek to become a 'facilitator' of the IS investigation, analysis and design process but consider themselves as a part of the team including company representatives (managers and staff) and IT specialists all of whom have valuable contributions to make. The notion of CLD means that each participant becomes an equal partner within the team and their involvement is simply based upon the kind of contribution that they can make, reducing the dominance of the IT specialist. By developing the IS in this way there is a possibility for real change since the recognition and subsequent acceptance (or rejection) of the proposal will come from the team rather than be imposed from outside or determined by the requirements of the technology. (See discussions within Stowell, 1990; Stowell and West, 1994; Guo et al., 1999; Champion and Stowell, 2005; Stowell and Cooray, 2010) The notion of CLD is developed further from the research of Champion and Stowell, 2003) and called CLICS to underline the developments. A diagram of the CLICS framework is included in Figure 3.20 and a worked example using CLICS is included in Chapter 8 (see also Champion, et al., 2005).

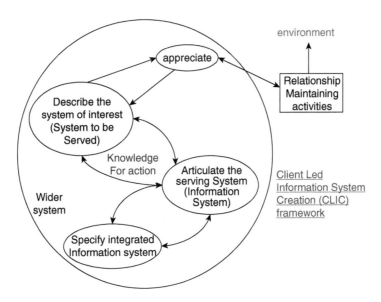

Figure 3.20: CLICS' framework (Champion, Stowell and O'Callaghan, 2005)

The most noticeable difference between the two diagrams (the idea of *client-led* design remains) is that we differentiate between the serving systems and the system to be served (Winter et al., 1995). This allows the participants to consider all the activities that together make up their information systems and then consider which of them can be assisted by some form of technology. Once the information systems have been defined ideas for action are generated.

By repeating the process in this way (Figure 3.16) we are able to view the activities involved in the design and development as a whole. Engaging all participants, technical and management, in the development and design process the relationship between the 'information system' and the various parts that contribute to it (e.g. technology) are seen as making up the system as a whole rather than being seen as a set of discrete elements. A worked example of the CLICS' framework is given in Chapter 8.

System Dynamics

The ideas behind SD were first developed by Forrester (1961) for use in corporate and industrial management. Forrester felt that the mathematical techniques used to address complex management problems were deficient and that an approach which enabled these situations to be viewed holistically was more appropriate. Since then many applications have been developed, including Urban Dynamics (Forrester 1968), Vensim (Ventana Systems, 1988–2009), Powersim (2006). Applications in relation to global problems were considered by the Club of Rome in 1970, resulting in simulations designed to model socioeconomic systems and their problems.

System Dynamics places a very emphatic focus upon structures and processes in systems and involves an implicit assumption that these are the key factors influencing behaviour. It has been subject to criticism in that it tends to divert attention away from other factors that may influence dynamic behaviour in the 'real world'. Of course it also involves the assumption that there is a 'real world' susceptible to objective description that is reliable. Those who suggest that the different worldviews people hold can lead them to create different descriptions of 'reality' reflecting their particular perspectives are likely to find SD rather limiting as a means of analysis (see, for instance, the Soft System Methodology).

As we have seen in earlier sections, a system is perceived to be an interrelated set of elements forming a coherent whole within a defined boundary. Systems exhibit behaviour relating to the interactions among their elements and can be seen to change from one state to another. We introduced you to this idea earlier when we looked at influence diagrams. System Dynamics focuses on those changes over time, as a response to perturbations, i.e. factors that influence system behaviour. In particular, the technique looks at cause and effect, i.e. internal feedback loops within a system and time delays that have an effect on the outcomes of system behaviour. In an earlier section, we looked at influence diagrams and later at control in systems and how feedback about deviations from planned output can be made to trigger an adjustment to inputs, in order to keep the system relatively stable. We also saw how positive feedback loops can cause the discrepancy from planned output to increase rather than decrease and can, at times, lead to a system becoming critically unstable. System Dynamics attempts to model feedback loops in relation to timing in order to examine their impact upon the system of interest.

The idea behind System Dynamics makes use of two particular types of diagramming technique. The first of these focuses upon causal loops: these are influence diagrams but instead of discrete 'a' influencing 'b' then 'c' influencing 'd' we now show how the whole System operates.

In Figure 3.21 the strength of the person causes 'acceleration' in the movement of the donkey, all things being equal. Causal loops can be loosely classified as systems that resist change of the vicious circle form. Let us look at a simple feedback system. We will then translate this into a causal loop diagram as shown in Figure 3.22:

Influence Diagrams
(Cause and Effect)

Accelerating
Motion

Pushing force

CAUSES

Figure 3.21:   Influence diagrams and causation

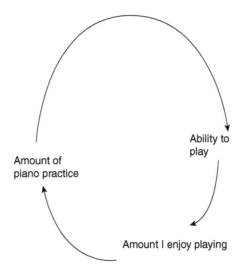

Amount of
piano practice

Ability to
play

Amount I enjoy playing

the previous diagrams can be translated
into a causal loop

Figure 3.22:   Causal loops

In SD we show the impact of the causes of perturbation in terms of positive and negative reinforcement of outcomes. So we might represent the process of studying with
the following causal loop diagrams but this time with positive and negative feedback
indicated (Figure 3.23):

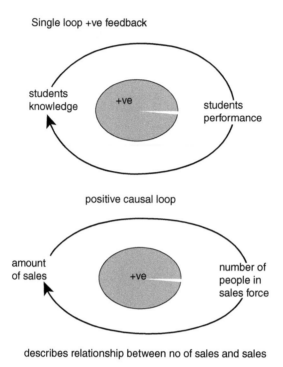

Figure 3.23:   Causal loops showing positive and negative feedback (After Roberts et al., 1997, pp. 33 and 36)

The second example focuses upon sales and the numbers of sales people. In this case the sales force is treated as an entity which can be augmented or depleted over a period of time. System Dynamics modelling can be used very simply by managers as a 'back of an envelope' technique but their strength is in the potential of computer simulation. Everyday software such as spreadsheets can be used to produce System Dynamic models, but it is more common for specialist software packages to be used to input equations underlying the dynamics of a system in order to run the simulation.

The causal loop diagrams are then converted into rate and level variables which describe the System represented by the causal loops. The rate and level diagrams are created for each of the causal loops within the overall system. Clearly the representation of complex situations results in more intricate causal loop diagrams and multiple loop diagrams than the simple examples shown above. We will return to these and the associated rates and levels diagrams later in the text.

It is worth noting that, as we discussed in the first chapter, it is also necessary in SD to define the boundary of the system of interest. Analysts can then attempt to define the entities that are of greatest importance and to describe the factors that will impact the flows of those entities. The ways in which information about these factors acts as feedback producing causal loops is then considered. Diagrams similar to those above are then drawn up and the underlying equations that determine flows are examined. A range of methods may be used to discover the actual parameters of the problem, e.g. surveys, consultation with experts. The equations can then be modelled using the simulation package. There are several SD packages available including Vensim, Powersim Studio 7, Altreva, myStrategy, and Consideo – but more of these later. There are also working examples available, e.g. http://portal.simulario.de/public/4/. For further reading and useful exercises see Roberts et al. (1997).

Total Systems Intervention (TSI)

TSI comes from a strand of the Systems movement known as critical systems thinking (not to be confused with critical systems heuristics). This area is characterized by three guiding philosophies: complementarism; sociological awareness and human emancipation. The first of these reflects recognition that sticking to one well-understood method in attempting to solve any problem that arises would be unlikely to result in success. Equally, a pragmatic, 'trial and error' approach, which does not seek sound theoretical underpinning, is unlikely to be successful except through serendipity. Instead, a deep understanding of different rationalities on which recognized approaches are based enables a would-be problem-solver to select an appropriate method to address particular problem situations. At the same time, an awareness of the wider socio-political context within which the problem situation is experienced enables those who wish to address it to take into account relative acceptability of one approach rather than another to the involved participants. Such awareness can be helpful in choosing a method that will succeed. Finally, critical systems thinkers consider problem situations from a perspective of desire to bring about beneficial change, empowering interested individuals and organizations to fulfil their potential.

The objective of TSI (see Figure 3.24) is to create a learning system about problem situations from which to generate an approach to solution. Total Systems Intervention proceeds on the basis that it is possible to envisage a 'System of Systems methodologies' (Flood and Jackson, 1991, p. 48). This is conceptualized by evaluating the strengths and weaknesses of many differing methodologies for diverse situations and systemic contexts. First, a typology is created, which groups existing systemic methodologies. Groupings are derived according to the assumptions (or dominant metaphors) underpinning them about the systems to which they relate and the participants in those systems. For example, the underlying assumptions of Operations Research appear to be that system behaviour is stable and relatively predictable and that there

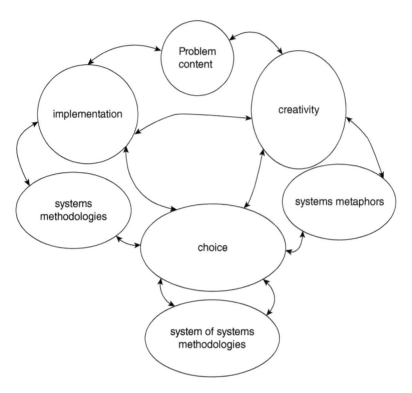

Figure 3.24:   Schematic diagram of TSI (from Flood and Jackson, 1991 p. 55)

is consensus among participants about goals and values. Thus, TSI proceeds through three phases reflecting seven principles derived from a critical systemic philosophy. The first may be described as the Creative Phase, in which organizational problem-solvers are encouraged to make use of systemic metaphors to produce a vision of their problem situation and desired outcomes. The output from this phase is the creation of a 'System of Systems Methodologies' appropriate to the context. Next, a phase of selection among these methodologies (Choice Phase) drawing upon knowledge gained from consideration of metaphor, engages the problem-solvers. This clearly involves linking the assumptions underpinning particular methodologies with the relationships subsisting within the system of interest. Those metaphors that emerged most strongly during the Creative Phase will clearly influence choice. The outcome of this phase will be a selected methodology, adapted for use by consideration of the metaphors applied to the problem situation by participants. The final phase is Implementation of the selected methodology to bring about transformation of the organization in which the problems are located.

It is worth bearing in mind that consideration continues to be given to the potential of other methodologies to assist in the problem situation. For instance, the Soft

Systems Methodology might be employed to unravel a mess of entwined problems, before a cybernetic approach is applied in order to solve each emerging puzzle.

Critical Systems Heuristics

In the earlier chapters of this text we have discussed the importance of identifying the boundary before work begins on the project. Werner Ulrich (1988) researched this important stage of problem appreciation and offered what he calls Critical Systems Heuristics (CSH). Ulrich provides twelve questions through CSH that can be used by participants to reflect upon their boundary judgements and the value systems behind their suggestions (see Figure 3.25). Ulrich's concern was to develop a means of helping to provide insight into the way that groups interact when confronted with the problems of agreeing a boundary. He considered that the process of drawing boundaries may, in

Boundary questions *see a more detailed discussion in chapter 6
Who is/ought the client?
What is/ought to be the purpose of the system?
What is/ought to be the measure of success?
What is/ought to be the decision taker?
What conditions/components are/ought to be controlled by the decision taker?
What represents (ought) the systems environment?
Who is/ought to be the designer of the system?
Who is (what kind of) expert is involved?
Who will/ought to guarantee that the design will be implemented and be successful?
Who will/ought to represent the concerns of those most affected?
Are (and in what way) the affected able to emancipate themselves from the experts?
What world view underlines (or ought to) the design of the system?

Figure 3.25:   Summary of Ulrich's 12 questions, after Midgley (2000, p. 141)

practice, act to constrain the ethical stance and the values of those involved. If you recall we suggest that a situation of interest for an individual, conscious or unconscious, is defined by a notional boundary and created by each of those involved. We know from our earlier discussions that where that boundary is drawn and by whom can significantly affect the outcome, but at the same time getting agreement about what the boundary should include or exclude is problematic. Ulrich's CSH engages systemic thinking in what he calls the service of reflective practice and research. He says that by so doing it 'allows us to identify invalid claims by uncovering underpinning boundary judgments other than those intended (or pretended) by the proponent. Therein resides its critical power' (Ulrich, 2003, p. 6). The approach makes the creation of a boundary a prime consideration because by making the process explicit it allows participants to question and debate boundary claims by others. In other words Ulrich, like Stowell (2009a) places great emphasis upon dialectic as a means of establishing boundary in such a way that there is an equality of opportunity to express opinion. But more of this discussion later. A summary of Ulrich's twelve questions is provided in Figure 3.25 but it should be noted that this is a summary and a more in-depth discussion of the questions and the implications of individual influence and power upon boundary definition will be found later in this text (see Chapter 6).

The Socio-technical Approach

Readers from the field of management or information systems may have been introduced to Systems concepts through the idea of socio-technical design. This derives from work of the Tavistock Institute after World War II (see Chapter 4) and features particularly in the work of Enid Mumford relating to socio-technical design of work systems. Although this work dates back to the 1970s, it established principles for participatory design that are still relevant for the 21st century. Mumford often courageously entered into territory that was not readily accessible to a woman, e.g. factories and coal mines, and her work was often constrained by the intensely political environment of industrial relations, in which individual consultation and participation were wholly foreign to contemporary views about management roles and responsibilities. Mumford harnessed socio-technical principles developed by the Tavistock Institute in developing the ETHICS (Effective Technical and Human Implementation of Computer-based work Systems) methodology for participatory work design (Mumford, 1995). Her aim was to enable design of systems that would enhance both work satisfaction *and* productivity in tandem. The methodology involves a number of steps which guide and support groups of people to establish a dialogue about technical requirements for a desired work system and also factors influencing enjoyment of work activities (see Figure 3.26). It includes a number of tools and techniques intended to support indi-

ETHICS

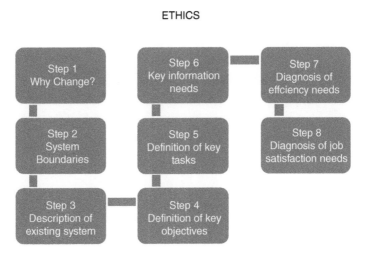

Figure 3.26: The ETHICS Methodology

vidual stakeholders to reflect upon, reorganize and redevelop their activities to meet new challenges in changing environments. The focus of ETHICS is on the real people whose experiences shape the work environment. It has inspired many subsequent researchers into participatory design (e.g. Stowell and West, 1995; Stowell and Champion, 2000). For a more detailed discussion of ETHICS, interested readers are referred to *Designing Human Systems – The ETHICS Method*, which is available online at http://www.enid.u-net.com/index.htm.

Concluding Remarks

This chapter has presented, by way of introduction, the idea of methodologies – sets of methods combined for use by practitioners in particular working contexts. The expected outcome from a Systems methodology is learning about a problem situation, and the intention is to use particular tools and modelling techniques in order to explore systems of interest on an iterative basis. We have provided brief descriptions of a number of examples of Systems methodologies, with a discussion of ways in which their associated tools and techniques may be applied in practice. It is most important that we recognize that a methodology is not a recipe to be followed slavishly, nor is any methodology a guarantor of success in structuring and solving problems. However, when applied mindfully, by reflective inquirers, the methodologies described here can provide powerful vehicles for exploration, expanded understandings, sharing of ideas and creative thinking.

PART II

SYSTEMS THINKING

C hapters 4 and 5

In this section we build upon the basic ideas introduced in the first three chapters. These chapters are designed to help the learner to increase their knowledge and improve their Systems practice. These chapters are intended for the student of Systems studying approaches useful for organizational intervention. Areas of application are useful in helping managers to address the many challenges they face in a highly competitive and global market. These chapters also make ideal reference material for students studying approaches to organizational inquiry and design methods.

CHAPTER 4

Thinking about Systems

Introduction

In earlier chapters we have defined a system as a 'whole' and one which is perceived by an observer when s/he considers that certain components come together in an organized and purposive way within a defined boundary. It is important to recognize that when we use the word 'system', we are referring to a system that is an intellectual model of some aspect of the world which is useful to us (the participant), but we must remember that it is an intellectual construct and may not be reflective of the real world. We often refer to it as a 'notional system' in recognition of the spatial and temporal nature of the choice.

By now you will have begun to understand that when we refer to something as a System it is because we choose to see it as such. This idea can be a difficult one to grasp because many of the phenomena we usually refer to by using this term are not soft, but hard systems, i.e. they appear to have a distinct existence of their own. To take one example, the transmission 'system' in a car comprises gears and levers each with physical forms and shapes that together form part of an engineered artefact. Here too the concept of 'system' may be a convenient label reflecting the perspective of the engineer. Pirsig provides an example of the way in which we perceive things in the classic novel *Zen and the Art of Motor Cycle Maintenance* (1974, p. 72) when discussing a motor cycle drive train, he says '. . . there is a knife moving here . . . an intellectual scalpel so sharp and so swift you sometimes don't see it moving. You get the illusion that all those parts are just there and being named as they exist. But they can be named quite differently . . .' In this paragraph Pirsig reminds us that what we see is what WE see and may not be what others see at all. The example shows us that both hard and soft 'things', let's call them systems, can be seen to be mental constructs so the notion of System applies not just to ideas but to physical things too.

In the 21st century, we are surrounded by a man-made world offering us many facilities, activities and objects that have been conceived through the application of creative thinking. Designers and engineers have continually used their ingenuity to produce new artefacts and processes that have enabled us to do things we could not do before – from making a cup of espresso through to probing the surface of Mars. These artefacts began as mental models in the minds of their creators and were designed through a process of reflection upon the mental models from which they originated and the possible interactions between components that could lead to (different) desired outcomes. Designed objects often go through an evolution of improvement as creative minds reflect upon the experience of using them. 'As reflection triggers change in use, and such change triggers further reflection, a spiral comes about. Lived human experience, and reflection upon that experience, seems to shape a double helix' (Bednar and Welch, 2007, p. 273). Vickers (1965, p. 15) refers to a two-stranded rope in which the history of events and the history of ideas develop in an intimate relationship, each influencing the future of the other. Thus, it may sometimes appear to us that events and artefacts that we perceive around us have an external 'reality' of their own, but it is important that we recognize human thinking and perception as the engineer of what we choose to label as 'systems'.

In a social context when we interact, or reflect upon interactions, we perceive the emergence of systemic qualities. A system's 'existence' is essentially a description of systemic qualities perceived by an observer – whether this person is a creator or user of that system, or is reflecting experiences more generally. (We discuss some philosophical ideas on the way that we might think about the world in Chapter 6.) But once we identify what is for us a system of interest we must think about what appears to be part of that system and what does not.

Boundaries and Perspectives

In the earlier chapters we have introduced you to the notion of boundary and how each person's perception of where that boundary might lie may be different, sometimes very different. Since systems exist only as mental constructs, any observer is obliged to conceive not only the emergent properties of the interactions inherent in the system viewed, but the boundary between the system and the environment within which it acts, i.e. to choose to see a distinction between what is regarded as part of the system and what is not. As we have discussed earlier (see Chapter 3) boundaries are a matter of choice and boundary critique forms an important part of reflection upon social systems. Ulrich reminds us to consider from which particular stance, or *Weltanschauung*, a system appears to have the characteristics in question (Ulrich, 2003, p. 6). Clearly, any observation is made from the point of view of an individual who observes. Any system investigated must have boundaries, spatial or dynamic and 'strictly speaking, spatial boundaries exist only in naïve observation and all boundaries are ultimately dynamic' (Bertalanffy, 1968, p. 215).

Every person has a unique perspective (or set of perspectives) of their own, shaped by their entire life experience. This is what Vickers refers to as Appreciative settings (see Chapter 3). Viewpoints may vary depending upon the role an individual is playing at a particular time and the values that are relevant to that particular context, but such situations might create difficulties. Consider, for instance, the choices a Minister for Education might make about what is best for 'all children' in a country. Comprehensive schools may seem to offer the best prospects to 'all children' but not for a Minister's own child whom she might chose to send to a selective or fee paying school. Like most parents the Minister will consider the particular qualities of the school and the aptitudes and aspirations of the child. We might argue that it is possible to hold both perspectives simultaneously and present them such that they appear equally reasonable in context, but they might not be seen this way by others. Sending her children to a private school, whilst advocating comprehensive schools as best for the general population, might suggest that the individual Minister is able to hold apparently conflicting views about the same subject, by adopting different perspectives; but it might also be viewed by others as hypocrisy (Macintyre, 1996).

Where did these ideas come from? Capra (1996) points out that Systems thinking has been a product of simultaneous observations in several distinct disciplines during the first half of the 20th century. Its emergence was championed by biologists, developed by Gestalt psychologists, and found its most emphatic expression in the work of quantum physicists. The advancement of General Systems Theory was initiated by the biologist, Bertalanffy, economist, Boulding, physiologist Gerard and the mathematician Rapoport, who together founded a Society for General Systems Research (later renamed International Society for the Systems Sciences). All of these pioneers were guided by a recognition that the discrete disciplines (as enshrined in separate University departments) did not provide all the answers to human questions.

Capra goes on to suggest that we may need to go beyond a holistic, or systemic view of phenomena as we experience 21st century life, to embrace an 'ecological' view. He uses this term in its widest sense to signify an awareness that '. . . recognizes the fundamental interdependence of all phenomena and the fact that, as individuals and societies, we are all embedded in (and ultimately dependent on) the cyclical processes of nature' (Capra, 1996, p. 6).

Taking Capra's example, we may perceive a bicycle as a system, i.e. a functioning entity comprising a number of interconnecting parts from which personal transport emerges. An ecological awareness gives us a richer perspective, observing the bicycle in its physical and social environments. This incorporates awareness of the materials from which it is made; the sources of those materials and the processes by which they were derived; how and where the bicycle was designed, manufactured and marketed; what potential riders are seeking in their use of the bicycle; its impact on the environment in which it is ridden and the society in which the riders live; and so on. The relevance of this view depends upon the individual perspective of the observer – in this case someone with environmental concerns. Someone working in a bicycle repair shop, on the other hand, will probably choose to draw a boundary around the working (or not working) artefact as the system of relevance for their immediate purpose. Capra's point has become increasingly significant to us in our daily lives, as we are made aware of the finite nature of the Earth's resources and fears about the impact of our activities on climate. We are urged by environmentalists to 'reduce, re-use and recycle' in our consumption of resources (see Stowell, A., 2012).

Environment

As these examples show, when thinking about boundary we also need to consider the environment in which the system of interest resides. Despite our best efforts we should remember that the environment within which living individuals and organizations interact is in a constant state of flux. Change is experienced, not as exceptional but a normal function of existence. The pre-Socratic philosopher Heraclitus is quoted as saying that 'On those stepping into rivers the same, other and other waters flow', which we take to mean that a person cannot step twice into the same river, since both the water and the man will be different as time passes. For Heraclitus, change is the natural order of things but people fail to notice the constant change taking place around them (for a short discussion of the contribution of Heraclitus, see Crowe, 1996). Classical Systems thinking (Churchman, 1971) determines that a system cannot influence its environment but the environment can influence the system. However, when thinking about the environment in which our system resides we also need to apply common sense.

By now we are aware that to identify a system, its boundary and environment are complex tasks, and we can recognize that this is a major step towards avoiding a superficial assessment. We should consider the options and (preferably together with those involved) make a decision about where to begin, remembering that as we learn more about the 'system' so too the boundary will alter.

Hierarchy

At this point, we should reflect upon the way in which we choose to draw boundaries around systems perceived to be of relevance (see Chapter 2 onwards). Earlier, we considered the distinction between a system and its environment. Now we can see that that environment may be perceived as a wider system of which our chosen system is a smaller part – a sub-system. Similarly, sub-systems of the system we have chosen to define may be thought of as systems in their own right – the chosen system can then be perceived as their environment. As we go through iterations of this process, we can see that systems nest in hierarchical relationships.

Checkland (1981) points out that the different 'layers' in a systemic hierarchy require different levels of description. He illustrates this with an example from the natural world:

> Thus in the language of chemistry, any arrangement of the bases in DNA obeys the laws of physical chemistry. But it is constraints upon the ordinary chemistry of the base-sequences which produce the specifically biological property of genetic coding, an emergent property which marks a transition from the level we call 'chemistry' to that called 'biology'. (1981, p. 81)

An individual reflecting upon the world may find it relevant to develop a mental model of a system, set in its environment, as an integrated, purposeful whole. But the reflections may lead to a deeper examination of a part of the system, which is itself a coherent and purposeful whole, i.e. what was earlier perceived as a sub-system now becomes a system in its own right. In this sense we can think about a system, indeed all systems, as being hierarchal with each being a part of a hierarchy of systems interacting within a wider system of which it forms a component part (see Figure 4.1). An example of hierarchy, and one relating to the food chain, is provided by the BBC home web which says:

> In order to gain one pound in weight, a seal has to indirectly consume 10,000 pounds of tiny marine plants called phytoplankton. The 10,000 pounds of phytoplankton are eaten by 1000 pounds of tiny marine animals called zooplankton, which in turn are eaten by 100 pounds of small fish such as herring or anchovies, which provide food for 10 pounds of larger fish, which are eaten by the aforementioned seal (BBC web page fact of the day – 29th June 2010).

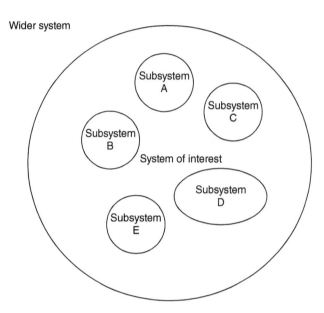

Figure 4.1:   System, wider system and sub-systems

Clearly in nature there are practical examples of the hierarchical relationship between the tiny creatures and those at the top of the food chain.

Another example is that of transport. As a system we can think of it as sub-systems that together make it a whole. The sub-systems are many: there are personal transport systems (which themselves may also have many sub-systems such as motor car, bicycles, horses and so on), public transport systems such as rail and air, virtual transport systems such as video conferencing and many more. Each of these sub-systems could be taken separately and the components that make them considered separately but we learn that we must recognize them as part of a wider system. We might also consider transport in terms of wider systems such as population exchange, spreading disease and many other possibilities.

Entropy and Negentropy

Earlier in this chapter we considered Heraclitus' observation that our world is in a constant state of change. If we accept that, we may then ask what is the impact upon the 'life' of a system? It cannot last forever as it is in a constant state of change. At this point we return briefly to Bertalanffy (1901–1972), who was one of the founders of modern Systems better known for his theory of Open Systems. This is important to the way that we think about a system. In simple terms, what Bertalanffy questioned was the second law of thermodynamics. Entropy, which works to a defined end, does not explain the world around us because, he argued, it relates to a closed system whose '. . . tendency towards maximum entropy or the most probable distribution is the tendency to maximum disorder' (Bertalanffy, 1968, p. 38). Consider a fire as an example of a closed system. Once ignited, it will continue to burn only as long as there is fuel remaining and oxygen present. Once these conditions no longer hold, there is a tendency for the system to experience maximum entropy (the fire goes out). Bertanlanffy goes on to point out that all living systems are open systems which maintain themselves through the import of information which may arrest the tendency for disorder. This idea was an important contribution to general Systems theory that had a significant impact upon Systems thinkers in general and cybernetics in particular. Bertalanffy's ideas provided the means of thinking about systems not as things confined within fixed and immovable boundaries that would not allow anything past (try to think of examples of closed systems) but as systems that allow 'resources' to pass across their boundary. At the time Bertalanffy did not have the mathematical techniques available to him which were capable of expanding his ideas about thermodynamics and proving his theory of open systems.

However, some years later in 1967, the Nobel laureate Prigogine did have these techniques and was able to refine the idea in terms of self-organization as what he called 'dissipative structures' (Prigogine, 1967; Prigogine and Nicolis, 1977). A dissipative structure is a way of describing 'systems' that are not in equilibrium. Our world and universe is, as Heraclitus observed, changing all the time, but such systems not only maintain themselves in a stable state, far from equilibrium, but they may even evolve. Prigogine called these systems *dissipative systems*, because they are formed and maintained by the dissipative processes which take place because of the exchange of energy between the system and its environment and because they disappear if that exchange ceases. They may be said to live in 'symbiosis with their environment' (Prigogine and Lefever, 1968). In cybernetics the idea is to 'measure tendency of any closed system to move from a less to a more probable state' (Bullock and Trombley, 1999).

People, as part of social groups within any organization, need to make decisions about maintaining its relationship to its environment as a response to entropy. That is to say we need to make a change if we are to avoid collapse (think about the number of companies over the past few years that have collapsed because they failed to embrace change). We call the effect of this action negentropy, in other words we are avoiding entropy. Negentropy is the difference between open and closed systems. Open systems allow the import of 'resources' whereas closed systems do not. By allowing 'resources' into the system it can alter its relationships according to the changes taking place in its environment. So we have an argument for sustainability but at the same time the problem of constant change.

In the case of an organization (remembering our previous discussion) problem definition and re-definition are needed if it is to perpetuate itself and achieve relative stability
within its environmental constraints. The constant re-evaluation of the situation and
how perceived problems might be addressed is required leading to a continual demand
for resources in the shape of 'new' ideas.

Let's move on now to thinking about what we mean when we identify a 'system'.

Purposeful and Purposive

We usually define systems in terms of some *purpose* that they serve, that is to say
something that *we as observer* describe as having a purpose. We can draw a distinction
between behaviour that is *purposeful*, i.e. system behaviour that results from an act of
will by some engaged actor(s) – conscious human action is involved – and behaviour
that is *purposive*, i.e. system behaviour to which an observer attributes a purpose
(Checkland, 1981, p. 119). Ackoff (1999) considers a distinctive aspect of 'purpose'
when he discusses the difference between 'mechanistic' and 'animate' systems. For
him purposeful behaviour involves an element of choice. But in this respect he distinguishes purpose from function. Like Checkland he thinks systems that are animate
are also purposeful since they act consciously and they can choose a particular behaviour. It is important not to be confused about this distinction. Some systems might
appear to be 'animate' and be said to serve a function (or can be perceived to have a
goal) but are not 'purposeful' as such, e.g. we might consider a human heart
to serve a useful function, and it appears to beat of its own accord, but within Ackoff's
definition it is purposive rather than purposeful as it does not *choose* to beat or
not beat.

The concepts 'purposeful' and 'purposive' have particular relevance for Systems practitioners as we soon begin to have conflicting thoughts about the nature of a system.
In extremis this reflects a personal observation, which may not accord with the observations of others, and the acceptance that some things 'exist'. It is for instance difficult
to disagree that such things as business enterprises exist only in the eye of the beholder.
Let us turn our attention to the nature of 'organization' which we touched on briefly
in our earlier discussion (see Chapter 3). This is an area where Systems thinking can
have a significant contribution, although it is here too that confusion can arise if those
adopting an interpretivist approach fall into an unconscious trap of taking on functionalist analysis. When engaged in the practice of Systems thinking within an organizational setting and working with other stakeholders, very great care is needed to avoid
this trap.

Goals and the Appreciative Cycle

In Scientific management (Burrell and Morgan, 1979, pp. 126–130) the techniques used frequently refer to the importance of the achievement of goals. Within this paradigm '. . . the world of work is treated as hard concrete reality characterized by uniformities and regularities which can be understood by cause and effect' (Burrell and Morgan, 1979, p.130). Vickers (1970) criticized the adequacy of goal seeking as a model of both human behaviour and organizational aspirations, arguing that life consists of experiencing relations rather than seeking 'ends'. He goes on to challenge the cybernetic paradigm, which is implicit in goal seeking, preferring a model as a cyclical process in which experience generates norms and values.

Vickers expressed his understanding of the unconscious thinking behind individual decision making by what he called 'Appreciation' (Vickers 1983a, pp. 54–58; 1983b, pp. 67–74). He described Appreciation as 'the activity of attaching meaning to communication or the code by which we do so, a code which is constantly confirmed, developed or changed by use' (Vickers 1970). Checkland (1999) expanded upon this by describing an Appreciative system as '. . . a mental evaluative act, a cultural mechanism which maintains desired relationships and deletes undesired ones'. Appreciation then is an iterative process, which Vickers calls the 'Appreciative Cycle'. This cycle begins with the interests and concerns that each individual might possess. As we have highlighted earlier we realize that our interests and concerns are largely subjective and inter-subjective and are shaped by what Vickers describes as our Appreciative settings. Appreciative settings are our values, beliefs, standards and experiences. Our interests and concerns are internalized and represented in the form of a 'situation' (Vickers, 1983a) and from this we make what Vickers calls 'reality judgements' which we do by selecting perceived 'facts' that we consider to be relevant to the current situation. Of course these 'facts' are subjective and are shaped by our Appreciative settings. In other words a reality judgement is the way that we appreciate 'what *is* the case' (Vickers, 1983a, 1983b) for the current situation.

Once a reality judgement has been made we then go on to consider 'what *ought* to be the case' (Vickers, 1983a, 1983b) for the given situation or in other words we consider 'facts' relevant to an *ideal state* of the situation based on our Appreciative settings. Vickers calls this the making of a value judgement. Value judgements are made based on an individual's 'Appreciative settings'. Our Appreciative settings will develop as we learn from challenges to our judgements or from those that are confirmed by experience and it is this ability to judge and reflect upon past judgements that contributes to our understanding of the world. Our Appreciative systems are mental processes and our Appreciative settings change continuously with different cycles of Appreciation;

'. . . the standards, models and values in the model are never absolute; able to survive unchanged over a long period of time. In fact, they are themselves the product of the previous history of this process' (Checkland, 1999). The outcome of reality and value judgements is a set of *hypothetical* relationships deemed significant enough to maintain/modify/delete in the given situation.

The third aspect of the Appreciative process is an action judgement where the practical feasibility of implementing the hypothetical relationships is investigated. 'The action judgment is involved in answering any question of the form *what shall I do about it?* when "it" has been defined by judgements of reality and value' (Vickers, 1983a, 1983b – author's italics). The results of an action judgement are the selected relationships that are deemed significant enough to keep, change or remove from the current situation. We select the relationships from among the hypothetical relationships that followed from making reality and value judgements. In other words as a result of each single cycle of Appreciation, the individual's Appreciative settings might be modified (Stowell and Cooray, 2006) which would change the manner in which she makes judgements in the next Appreciative Cycle.

Vickers' concept of Appreciation gives explicit recognition to something of which we are all aware as we attempt to negotiate our daily lives – that is to say that much of our behaviour is experienced as 'muddling through' rather than pursuit of goals. Vickers regarded an Appreciative system as one that is constantly revised or confirmed by three needs; 'First it should correspond with reality sufficiently to guide action. Second, it should be sufficiently shared by our fellows to mediate communication and Third, it should be sufficiently acceptable to ourselves to make life bearable' (Vickers, 1983a, p. 55).

Most of us, living in complex, developed societies, are attempting to achieve a life balance. For instance, if we pursue success in our careers there may be a price to pay in terms of opportunities to engage in family activities. Alternatively if we put family life before anything else we may constrain our careers. The ways in which we tackle such dilemmas are a reflection of individual, personal values that are continuous and messy – we cannot act as goal-seeking beings even if we wish to. The same is true when we are part of an organization as change is incremental. Lindblom suggested it to be evolutionary rather than revolutionary, and achieved through many small, often unplanned moves (Lindblom, 1959).

A Chance to Reflect – Summary

As you have seen, the identification of a System is not at all straightforward. Whilst it is true that a 'system' owes much to individual perception and context there are still conventions (rather than rules) that turn what critics might call 'anything goes' into a framework for thinking which challenges and reflects upon the way in which we look at our world and perceive its problems. Two observers will perceive a hill in a different way depending upon the position they occupy. The observer at the bottom of the hill will see it differently from an observer at the top (Crowe, 1996). Pirsig's (1974) example of a motorcycle gear train which we quoted above further underlines the point that any perceived system should be considered only as a *notional* system since it is the observer who defines it and it may not really exist as such in other people's minds.

If we extend this notion and apply it to making sense of the world in which we live it soon becomes difficult. Checkland (1999, p. 102) argues that 'it would be insightful to take the apparent chaotic universe to be not a set of phenomena (whose laws can be established by the reductionist experimental approach) but rather a complex of inter-acting wholes called *systems* . . .' But how we make sense of our world is easier said than done. In Checkland's book *Systems Thinking Systems Practice* (1981) he provides some examples of creditable attempts of the past. For example, he cites Jones (1967) who suggested the world could be considered in terms of: Manual, Mechanized, Auto-matic, Collaborative man-made systems, Mechanical sub-systems, Administrative, Voluntary, Environmental, Biological, Physical and Symbol Systems (Checkland, 1981, pp. 102–103). He refers to Boulding's hierarchy of real world complexity (1956) as an attempt to provide an account of the world by arranging it hierarchically. His table (see Checkland, p. 105) begins with Structures and Frameworks such as crystal structures and bridges, through Clockworks, Animals, Man to transcendental systems, arranged hierarchically. Although a superficial glance at Boulding's attempt might be easily dismissed, its credibility requires closer examination as it does provide food for thought provoking the question 'if not why not, what is wrong with it?' Jordan's Taxonomy also provides a challenge to the way that we might wish to think about the world. The reader is encouraged to look at Checkland's summary and follow it up with a closer examination of the work itself (Checkland, 1999, pp. 100–122).

Each of these ideas on 'what is a system' and how the idea might be used to explain the world deserve further consideration. However, as we have argued above that the world might exist differently than we first imagine, how can we make sense of it without imposing our preconceived ideas upon what makes it up? (After all, isn't that exactly what we might have done by choosing to ignore the early Systems thinkers' attempts?) When trying to make sense of the world our choice will be determined by our Appreciative System and all that this implies. For some, the scientific paradigm of order and structure provides a good basis for understanding. For some Systems think-ers, social and political philosophical argument motivates but for others only a meta-explanation will satisfy. We have no advice to give here as it is a personal choice and journey, but as far as this text is concerned, we have chosen to adopt an interpretive take on Systems thinking and for that reason in the next section we advocate Checkland's idea of a System which he characterized by the notions of Emergence, Hierarchy, Communication and Control (Checkland, 1981, p. 75). The second reason for selecting Checkland's definition of a system is that it attempts to provide a neutral vision of what a system can be taken to be and allows the observer to translate this into a description which makes sense to them. In the previous section we have addressed Hierarchy and we now turn our attention to Emergence, Communication and Control as a means of helping us to gain understanding of Systems thinking.

Emergence

When elements interact in a certain way something emerges which is different from the individual components in combination. It is important to remember that human activity systems 'cannot be seen as reflective of real world systems, but as mental constructs that allows us to examine and argue about aspects of the world we perceive around us' (Checkland, 1985, p. 765). Different ways of perceiving 'emergence' are possible in relation to human activity systems. We can look at emergent phenomena from two perspectives. First, we observe something that emerges that could not have been predicted from the component parts. For example, many people will associate high quality with the name Rolls Royce. If we examine the formation of this engineering company we could not have predicted that the outcome would become part of the lexicon of our vocabulary. Rolls Royce has become synonymous with quality outside that of manufacturing motor vehicle or aero engines. We hear people refer to something as a Rolls Royce job by which they imply that this (whatever this might be) is of high quality. Second, we could look at an emergent property in terms of what it was designed to do and what actually emerged, which was not predicted, but is the result of the interaction between the component parts, i.e. before and after. For example, the development of the cell-phone has resulted in different patterns of social behaviour, e.g. acceptance of someone walking in the street talking in a loud voice as the normal behaviour of a person using a cell-phone, rather than an odd form of behaviour. Some commentators blame the ability to text on a cell-phone as having a damaging effect on the ways in which we use language and also upon social interaction. When thinking about any system, it is not just the transformation taking place that we need to consider but what are its emergent properties too. But applying a clear definition to 'emergence' is much harder than the simple descriptions we provide here.

An emergent property of an enterprise might be something that is of great value to the company that may not be possible to engineer or create easily, but can be damaged. Consider a business enterprise irrespective of what it might trade – an important emergent property of any business it that it is trustworthy and honourable. If we think of the Banking sector (and maybe a bank known to you) consider how you would describe its emergent property following the financial difficulties that have affected many millions of people across the globe. What has emerged is a general view that, by all accounts, is not very complimentary about the sector and yet to most of us our local bank has not changed much of what it was before the crash. Is it possible for banks to return to being thought of as the reliable and trustworthy institutions that they were once considered to be or will the emergent property which has arisen from the economic difficulties, which many blame on greed, stick?

The notion of emergence is not new and not something invented by Checkland but his idea that this is an essential part helps to identify a system. The idea of emergence can be traced back to Aristotle (McKeon, 1941) who is reputed to have said that 'the whole is greater than the sum of its parts' meaning that when certain components are connected together the outcome is more than that of each component. But there are many who have debated its meaning including Mill (1843), Popper (1977) and Checkland (1981). The editors of the *New Fontana Dictionary of Modern Thought*, Bullock and Trombley (2000) describe an emergent property as the property of some complex whole which cannot be explained in terms of the properties of the parts. Whilst it is complex we can all think of examples of emergent properties from our own experience and despite this complexity the notion of emergence then enables us to identify something from amongst surrounding chaos and give it a name that is meaningful to us. But it is interesting to note that there are numerous examples of an emergent property of something which is shared by many, often with people who have had no direct contact with each other yet share a similar view.

Moving on, the second feature that characterizes a system is that of hierarchy. We discussed the notion of hierarchy above but, to recap, it can be summarized as follows:

Hierarchy

It can be said that all systems exhibit hierarchy in that every system is part of a wider system and is made up of sub-systems. The identification of the system and the sub-systems relates to the particular viewpoint or *Weltanschauung* of the observer. Consider a coffee house. Of what system is it a part? We could consider it to be a part of a chain of coffee houses which in turn is part of the portfolio of a business. If we consider the coffee house from the other direction, downwards, we can think about espresso machines, cups and saucers and so on (see Figure 4.2).

We can also think of a coffee house in other terms. We could think of it as part of a system providing a particular flavour of caffeine, which in turn could be part of a system of non-alcoholic refreshments. Coffee houses can be thought of in terms of other kinds of system too, say as part of social engagement systems, where people meet to exchange

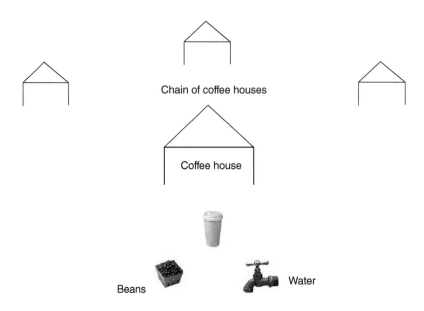

Figure 4.2:   Coffee cups through to coffee houses

ideas and socialize. If we think of them in this way we could think about smaller elements of social systems which allow people to engage in social interaction, such as conversations, emails and so on. The key feature in the identification of a system and its sub-systems is to preserve the logical coherence which binds these systems and their sub-systems together. Clearly how we describe these systems is a function of our individual points of view. (Remember our earlier discussions about the importance of recognizing why and how we describe a particular system of interest?)

There are examples of hierarchy in nature; consider, for example, the food chain. One has only to spend time observing a natural habitat, such as woodland, and the relationships between predator and prey soon become apparent.

The next feature of a system is that of communication.

Communication

There are several ways of looking at communication ranging from an engineering perspective through to one based on sociological theory. Littlejohn and Foss (2008) offer a theoretical framework of communication theory as being:

1. Mechanistic: Where communication is seen as a perfect transaction of a message from the sender to the receiver.

2. Psychological: Whereby communication is considered as the act of sending a message to a receiver as well as the feelings and thoughts of the receiver upon interpreting the message.
3. Social Constructionist (Symbolic Interactionist): In this case communication is seen as the product of those interacting who share and create meaning in which truth and ideas are constructed or invented through the social process of communication. This involves the interaction between human beings and free sharing of thoughts and ideas.
4. Systemic: Here communication is seen as being new messages which are created via 'through-put', or what happens as the message is being interpreted and re-interpreted as it travels through people.
5. Critical: In some respects a Foucaultian perspective in which communication is a source of power and oppression of individuals and social groups.

Communication is not about transmission but of transmission and reception. Communication is a two-way process that requires a shared understanding of the 'code' used and can only be said to have taken place when the receiver receives something that is meaningful to it. For example, in human communication the phrase 'you can say that again', as a means of agreeing about some assertion, is difficult to grasp by someone from a different culture even if they are familiar with the language, as it requires absorption of the culture and of the context in which the expression was uttered. Communication is of course not just the transmission of words it can also be non-verbal communication too. For Vickers the mental activity associated with receiving the 'code' he called 'Appreciation' and the associated meaning attached to the 'code' as the Appreciative setting (Vickers, 1983a, p. 43). Luhmann (2006, p. 252) considered communication networks to be the constitutive element in autopoietic social systems, of which organizations are examples (see the discussion on autopoiesis below). Communication may be between system elements in the course of their interactions, or between the system and its environment or between autonomous systems co-evolving through relational behaviour. Messages may take many forms, e.g. electrical impulses, coded messages or human speech.

Closely related to communication is the concept of information. Information has been defined by Bateson (1972) as 'a difference that makes a difference', a definition which is useful when considering system behaviour. A message from one element of a system to another, which is interpreted in a certain way and leads to a change in system behaviour, may be regarded as information. Interpretation of messages depends upon an ability to attribute meaning to signs and symbols, e.g. 'language'. However, this would be of little value if it was not possible to send the message contained in those signs from one entity to another. Thus a system requires appropriate channels to conduct messages. Communication takes place when some piece of data (the message) is conveyed by some means (the channel) from one element (the originator) to another (the receiver) who attributes meaning to it. Often the originator and receiver of messages will be human beings. As social animals, human beings continually receive messages from the environment, some deliberately transmitted by other people, some arising naturally or as a by-product of relational behaviour.

Human sense-making processes are employed to interpret those messages in relation to our own behaviour. Sometimes this happens very directly, e.g. when you speak to someone who is with you in the same room. Your voice travels to their ear through the air in the form of sound waves and the message is received and interpreted. Sometimes the process is not quite so direct. This message is being typed into my computer. The process involves thinking about the message, expressing those thoughts in English – but the computer only understands binary code. The message typed at the keyboard, using English syntax, is being stored and processed in the form of 0 and 1 signals. The software is able to interpret certain patterns of 0 and 1 as representing the letters of the alphabet which are reproduced on the screen, using ASCII code. Once satisfied with the words that appear on the screen, the command is given, e.g. to print or to transmit to another computer system. The 'message' is again encoded into 0 and 1 signals for transmission. It is reproduced on paper and you are now reading it, taking in the information via your eyes to your brain, which interprets the symbols on the paper as words capable of carrying meaning (see Figure 4.3). Perhaps the meaning you are attributing to those words is similar to my own, or perhaps it is somewhat different.

What seemed a fairly simple process, which we take for granted every day, actually emerges as a combination of logical, physical and psychological steps. Many factors can interfere with the successful transmission of the messages, which will then impact upon the behaviour of any system to which they are relevant. Use has been made of a variety of models to describe communication processes within systems. For example,

---

This message is being **typed** into my computer. The process involves **thinking** about the message, **expressing** those thoughts in **English** but the computer only understands **binary code**. The message typed at the keyboard, using **English syntax**, is being stored and processed in the form of **0 and 1** signals. The software is able to interpret certain patterns of 0 and 1 as representing the letters of the alphabet which are reproduced on the screen, using **ASCII code**. Once satisfied with the words that appear on the screen, the command is given e.g. to **print** or to **transmit** to another computer system. The 'message' is again **encoded** into 0 and 1 signals for transmission. It is reproduced on **paper** and you are now **reading** it, taking in the information via your **eyes to your brain**, which **interprets** the **symbols** on the paper as words capable of carrying **meaning**. Perhaps the meaning you are attributing to those words is **similar** to my own, or perhaps they are somewhat **different**.

Figure 4.3: Example of human communication

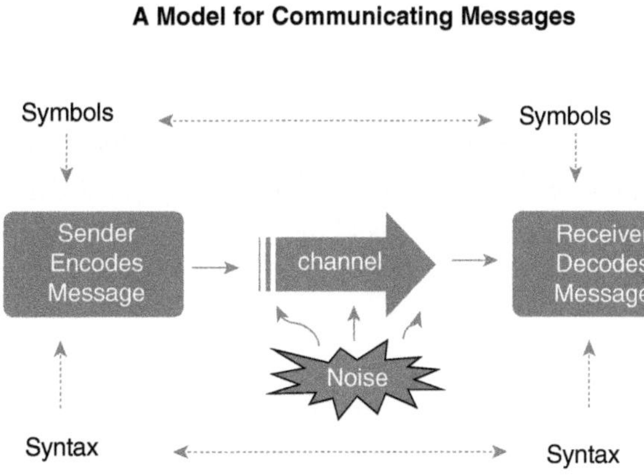

A Model for Communicating Messages

Figure 4.4: The Shannon-Weaver Model of Communication

a conduit metaphor is often used to suggest 'flows of information' from one person to another. Discussions have often been related to a model developed by Shannon and Weaver (1949) (see Figure 4.4). The Shannon/Weaver model has been 'borrowed' from a technical environment. However, as these authors themselves point out, great care is needed when it is considered in relation to communicative processes between people, since it is a message which travels through a channel and not a piece of 'information' which would require human interpretation to create it. It is possible to establish channels, coding methods and syntax in which signals can be transferred from one person to another. However, these signals are not, themselves, meaningful information. 'Messages' may represent something that is meaningful to a sender, but cannot be meaningful to a receiver except through a process of interpretation that is dependent on that receiver's own previous life experience (Langefors, 1966). This point also reflects Vicker's view about Appreciative settings, mentioned above.

Within complex social systems, failures in communication and control can have very serious consequences for the human actors involved. Examples of this can be found in some of the well-publicized cases in recent years in which children have died through neglect and/or abuse despite concerns about their situation among welfare agencies. This is often expressed in the Press as a failure of modern society to protect its most vulnerable. However, Batty (2003) reports a number of cases, including one from as far back as 1945, in which a child died after: 'There had been confusion between the two local authorities responsible for the boy's foster placement, conflicting reports by childcare staff about his wellbeing, staff shortages and miscommunication' (Batty, 2003, np).

This example clearly demonstrates that human communication systems require design for use, just as technical artefacts do. Attention to effective communication channels, communication practices and timing of feedback are needed from the designers of human social systems. Indeed, thinking about systems is vital to all human life. Checkland points out that a system needs some form of communication if it is to function (Checkland, 1999, p. 83) and goes on to say that 'Systems thinking . . . could not do without the idea of information, although its precise definition raises some problems which are not yet solved' (Checkland, 1999, p. 89)

Control

In any kind of system there must be a means of controlling it. Without this the behaviour of the system is unpredictable, random and erratic, in short it is not recognizable as a system. Checkland argues that '. . . in any hierarchy of open systems, maintenance of the hierarchy will entail a set of processes in which there is communication of information for purposes of regulation or control' (Checkland 1999, p. 83). Control in systems relates to a need to bring about desired behaviour. Much of the traditional theory relating to control (cybernetics) is connected with the idea that system behaviour is goal seeking, i.e. that the desired outcomes are known and defined. As we have seen, these ideas have been subject to much criticism when attempts are made to apply them to Soft, rather than Hard System contexts. (See Vickers, Appreciative System in Chapter 3.)

As we have suggested, control is necessary to deal with entropy. Entropy is a state of increasing probability and decreasing order (Bertalanffy, 1968, p. 150). In other words a system (remember this applies to a closed system) will reach a state of equilibrium and decline, towards chaos (or, more simply, the tendency is for things to go wrong!). Controls will be needed for every individual variable that could have an impact on the outcome of the system's behaviour. It is recognized in cybernetics that every distinct dimension of a complex system needs to be controlled in a way that is appropriate to its characteristics. This is known as the Law of Requisite Variety (Ashby, 1963 – see Chapter 2). It is easy, for instance, to imagine that a car with brakes but no steering wheel would be difficult to drive – direction and speed each needing distinct and appropriate controls (Ashby 1963).

This text is designed to aid the practitioner and researcher in their use of Systems ideas as to how a business organization can be viewed as a system. Monitoring in business is vital since, however successful a business is, there will be influences tending to make it go wrong in the longer term. Aspects of the environment will change – prices of materials, customers' tastes, the activities of competitors. These things are not under the direct control of organizational management and cannot be held constant (remember Heraclitus? See p. 76). Thus, a business may be making a profit this year, but will not necessarily continue to do so next year. Equally, internal aspects of business activity, e.g. the activities of staff, the functioning of equipment, may not always perform exactly as expected. It will be necessary for managers to monitor the business on a continuous basis and to make adjustments in an effort to keep it running smoothly – they must seek to maintain the relationship of the business to its environment. Both self-organization and emergence are characteristics of complex adaptive systems – see Holland (2006), in which he describes such systems as:

> . . . a dynamic network of many agents (which may represent cells, species, indi-viduals, firms, nations) acting in parallel, constantly acting and reacting to what the other agents are doing. The control of a CAS tends to be highly dispersed and decentralized. If there is to be any coherent behavior in the system, it has to arise from competition and cooperation among the agents themselves. The overall behavior of the system is the result of a huge number of decisions made every moment by many individual agents. (Holland, 2006, p.1)

Some systems can be designed to be self-regulating (cybernetic). A familiar example is that of a central heating system in your home. There is usually a thermostat which measures the temperature in the room, compares this to the setting and switches the heating system on when it is too cold and off when it is too hot. This happens without any intervention from you once you have set the required temperature. This type of self-regulation is called closed-loop, feedback control (see Figure 4.5). 'Closed-loop' because no outside intervention is necessary, 'feedback' because information about the output of the system is required to trigger remedial action (see Chapter 2).

In many problem situations, 'negative' feedback is required. This involves detection of a deviation from planned output and adjustment to inputs to bring about a return to plan. Sometimes the effect of a control loop may be that of 'positive' feedback so inputs

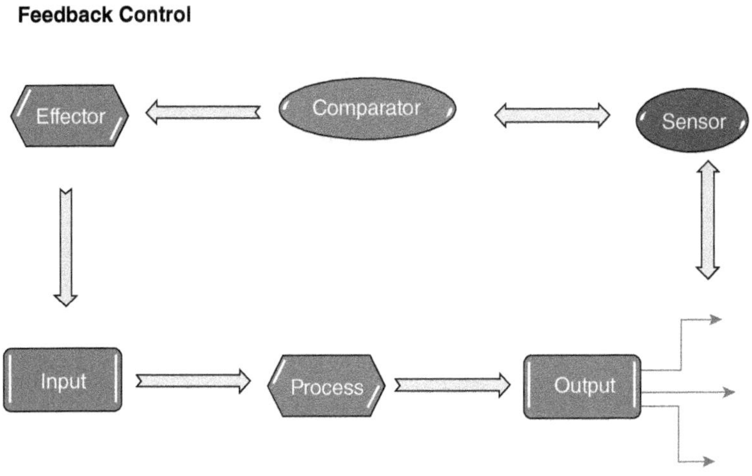

Feedback Control

Figure 4.5:   Close-loop feedback control in a system

are adjusted in such a way that the deviation from planned output increases. This effect may be desirable if, for instance, the profits of a business have exceeded expectation and the result of positive feedback in the system is that they continue to grow but the whole system becomes unstable; negative feedback will restore equilibrium. The effect of positive feedback alone is often disastrous. Consider a business that is doing badly which attempts to correct this by cutting costs. A cut in the market research budget leads to the business missing an opportunity that its competitors seize upon. The result of the supposed 'corrective action' is that, in the following year, its position is even worse!

This problem of time lag and oscillation round a desired state brings about the need for a different type of control mechanism, which is usually referred to as 'feed forward'. Here, very careful predictions are made about the nature, size and frequency of inputs needed to maintain a constant, desirable state in the system. This is, of course, the approach adopted to regulate a life support machine. Adjustments are made to inputs on a continuous basis in response to monitoring, so that the output never can deviate from requirements. An observer might see this as a series of very short, rapid feedback loops. An example of feed forward control could be the preparation of a cash flow forecast. Managers use this to ensure that the business never does become insolvent by planning inflows of cash (from say, overdraft facilities) to cover periods of heavy outflow.

The final aspect of control we will discuss here is one often referred to as preventive control. Security systems often involve this type of control which involves taking steps to ensure that entropy cannot set in at all, rather than taking corrective action when it does. Consider the security system of a factory. At night, a burglar alarm is switched on which detects any movement in the factory and triggers an alarm bell that rings in the local police station. This would be an instance of feedback control. The system is effective in triggering investigative action if, say, an intruder has broken into the factory. However, as an additional measure, steel shutters have been fitted to the windows and doors, which are rolled down at night and locked. This is a form of preventive control because it attempts to make it impossible for intruders to enter in the first place.

In the previous section we have discussed Systems ideas from an interpretivist point of view. We now turn our attention to another important idea in Systems but this originates from biology and as such has echoes from the early Systems thinkers.

Change, Communication and Control

The environment within which living individuals and organizations interact (and experience use of created systems) is in a constant state of flux. Change is experienced, not as exceptional but as normal. The reason people and organizations need to make decisions is in many respects a response to entropy (i.e. the status quo is not an option). Relationship maintenance will need to be a constant feature if an organization (as an autopoietic, social system) is to perpetuate itself and achieve relative stability within its environmental constraints. At the same time, 'muddling through' requires a con-stant re-evaluation of problem solutions and this leads to a continual demand for 'new' ideas, i.e. to find new solutions to problems or possibly to create new, more interesting problems to which 'solutions' can be sought (Popper, 1934). Having said this, it is interesting to note that the majority of projects to engender organizational change appear doomed to failure. Kotter (1995), for instance, reported a study in which he examined one hundred top management-driven 'corporate transformation' efforts. He found that more than half of these efforts did not survive the initial phases and few were deemed by stakeholders to be very successful (Kotter, 1995, p. 59). More recently, the IT Governance Institute commented on many surveys suggesting that up to 70% of large-scale investments in IT-enabled projects have failed to bring a return to the enterprise (ITGI, 2008, p. 7). We can speculate that the nature of the intended trans-formation, and the strategies intended to bring about the desired emergent properties, were in need of clarification. Senge et al. (1999, p. 6) comment on such phenomena by suggesting that understanding success factors in sustaining change requires us to adopt the same thinking processes as biologists in order to understand the nature of growth processes (forces that aid our efforts). But we also need to understand the forces and challenges that impede progress, and to develop workable strategies for dealing with these challenges. We need to appreciate 'the dance of change,' the inevitable interplay between growth processes and limiting processes (Senge et al., 1999, p. 10).

In other words, in order to bring about desired change in a complex adaptive system such as an organization (see below) we need to embrace systemic thinking.

Risk and Failure

It seems unfortunate that, for many people, perceptions of interconnectedness and Systemic properties such as emergence and hierarchy in the world around them first arise when something goes wrong. When something in life fails to meet our expecta-tions it is often obvious why – if my car fails to start in the morning, it may be because a lead has come loose somewhere under the bonnet. At other times however it is not so easy to pinpoint the cause of our disappointment as investigation uncovers a number of contributory factors. The more complex the situation in which we experience 'failure', the more difficult it can be to intervene in order to put matters right. Some of the approaches to modelling of Systems that we discuss in these chapters can be helpful in gaining insight into the situation.

'Failure' is experienced at many levels, illustrating interconnectedness in both the natural and man-made worlds (see, e.g. Sauer, 1993). An example of this was the Deepwater Horizon oil spill in the Gulf of Mexico. The initial failure was a mechanical one – a drilling well exploded beneath the sea. In addition to the tragic loss of life and serious injury among those working near to the explosion, a range of further consequences ensued. A pall of smoke some 30 miles high filled the sky and an estimated 21,000 gallons of crude oil per day began to leak into the sea from an untapped well head. The resulting spillage (approximately 1.6 million gallons over time) had the effect of killing aquatic life in the vicinity and smothering coastal wetlands of the southern United States. As the companies involved in drilling attempted to find engineering solutions to cap the leak, lawsuits commenced (some 300 as at August 2010) by injured parties for a wide range of areas – fishing, tourism, boat hire, waterfront property management. In June 2010, BP, as the principal oil company involved, agreed a preliminary figure in the region of $20 billion over several years against potential compensation claims. A complex and costly investigation into the causes and effects of this catastrophic event has been launched. Interested readers can find details at http://www.deepwaterinvestigation.com/.

Many instances of 'failure' we encounter result from the interactions of people and technology, which we can think of as failures of a socio-technical system. For example, from time to time we hear of people suffering harm when a medical procedure goes wrong as a result of equipment or drugs being applied wrongly by poorly trained or careless practitioners. When this occurs, we are sometimes faced with searching for a solution: how can we deal with the aftermath of the failure in order to minimize its impact? Consider the effects of a terrorist attack on London Transport on 7 July 2005. The authorities immediately needed to make sense of what was happening (an explosion could be an accident resulting from a gas leak, an isolated bombing, or the first in a series of attacks). Then they needed to coordinate rescue of those who were trapped, care for the injured, extinguishing fires, evacuating and safeguarding the public from possible further incidents in the area. Later, deliberation was needed about prevention of such incidents in the future. Systems modelling may also be helpful in determining strategies to prevent failures becoming critical, or, of course, in seeking to determine who or what is to blame for a failure. In business organizations, a whole area of management has developed in relation to perceptions of failure. This is called Risk Management, and professionals in this field devote themselves to classifying, assessing, preventing or dealing with the risks inherent in any aspect of industry, commerce or public service.

Of course, the idea of failure depends upon a person's perspective – if the England Test Cricket Team 'fails' to win the Ashes, this means that the Australian Test side has been successful. Failure is characterized by goals not being met or being met but accompanied by unacceptable side effects (Bignell and Fortune, 1984). It is for the person who chooses to draw a boundary defining a System that has failed to define what she means by failure in context. Judgements of this kind are undertaken in different ways depending upon the nature of the System of interest and may involve detailed measurement, e.g. deciding whether a company has failed may require the expertise of a team of insolvency experts, or it may simply be a matter of taste, e.g. when an audience decides whether to applaud the cast of a play when the curtain falls.

The Systems discipline can provide useful tools for those wishing to analyse failure. For instance, a pass through the Soft Systems Methodology might be helpful in determining an agenda among stakeholders wishing to understand why a project went wrong and from whose perspective. On the other hand, modelling of causal loops as part of System Dynamics could be helpful in developing and understanding cause and effect. The emergency services do not wait for catastrophic 'failure' to occur before developing strategies to protect the public. Simulations and role plays are often conducted in order to explore what would be best practice in the event of a major incident, including coordinations between different services. Modelling of control loops and feedback can be an effective means of learning about System behaviour. Equally, it can be helpful to look at communication – within a potential problem situation or among a team who would need to respond. A model such as Shannon and Weaver's model of communication (Weaver and Shannon, 1963) could be a useful tool for reflection. However, care is always needed when modelling complex situations using any tools which might tempt us to simplify. Reflection upon modelling in order to learn about problem situations is likely to be useful in gaining understanding of systemic failure, but its predictive potential must be treated with caution as it is, after all, a simplification of the situation.

Autopoiesis

Maturana (1980) describes autopoiesis through a definition of 'living machines', in which he says:

> An autopoietic machine is a machine organised . . . as a network of processes of production . . . of components that (re-) produce the components which . . . through their interactions and transformations continuously regenerate and realise the network of processes . . . that produced them (Maturana and Varela, 1980, pp. 78–79).

In other words a system is said to be autopoietic if the components of which it is composed interact with each other in such a way as to continually (re)produce and maintain that set of components and the relationships between them. Such systems are by definition deterministic – their purpose appears to an observer as given, not chosen. Autopoietic systems are, by their nature, closed systems – they generate no output beyond their own continued integrity. Within an autopoietic machine, there may be (and indeed very often must be) sub-systems perceived to be allopoietic, i.e. that have a purpose other than continuation of their own integrity. For example, a human being could be regarded as an autopoietic machine but the human digestive system, for example, takes in inputs from the outside world and processes them to produce energy. It is thus an open, allopoietic system.

Although Maturana and Varela were careful to restrict use of the term autopoietic to the realm of biological systems, it is possible for a non-living system, such as an organization, to be seen as autopoietic within its boundary, i.e. it is a homeostatic system whose critical variable is its own being. We can perceive that such systems are self-referential in that they continually reproduce themselves. They are not, of course, living, conscious beings. It is not 'life' that is continually (re)produced but 'meaning'. Luhmann (1990) elaborates upon this point as follows:

> Social systems use communication as their particular mode of autopoietic repro-
> duction. Their elements are communications that are recursively produced and
> reproduced by a network of communications and that cannot exist outside of
> such a network. . . . Their unity requires a synthesis of three selections, namely
> information, utterance and understanding. (1990, reproduced in Midgley, 2003,
> p. 67)

Such a system constantly creates and recreates itself within its autopoietic space in the context of interactions with its environment. Any structural element of the system may change radically over time, but the existence of the system is maintained. Within the context of an organization, the individual people of which it is comprised may be observed as allopoietic sub-systems, i.e. their interactions make up inputs and outputs to organizational processes and are therefore purposeful in that organizational context. However, those living individuals, viewed as individuals, are autopoietic in their own right. An organization can be said to be part of the wider environment with which the individual system must interact in maintaining its ontological integrity – the sole ultimate goal of the living autopoietic system. (Note: It is interesting to reflect upon this in comparison with Vickers' relationship maintenance model – see Chapter 1). If the theory of autopoiesis is accepted, then the goals of the disparate individuals cannot be identical, or congruent with the expressed goals of the wider organizational system, at any given time.

Beer contributed a preface to Maturana and Varela's essay on Autopoeisis (1980) in which he pointed out the importance of this theory for human beings as social animals.

Much previous recorded debate on the nature and behaviour of living things, going back over centuries, has focused on higher orders of meaning. Some explanations were religious, attributing a higher purpose for nature to a deity. Some were philosophical, looking for explanations such as a need to ensure survival of a species through transmission of DNA. Only with Darwin's theory of natural selection was the search for higher purpose challenged in favour of the impact of serendipity. However, Maturana and Varela have chosen as their focus the idea of living things as *autonomous* machines, whose purpose is solely to maintain their own integrity. In this context, the medium may change but the autonomous individual remains – it may be that few cells remain of the body with which you were born; cells continually die and are regenerated, but the pattern which is uniquely 'you' remains.

Humberto Maturana turned his attention to interactions between autonomous living systems in his address to the September 2004 SPMC Workshop in Oxford. He pointed out that, as the structure of a living system changes, so too does the medium – congruently and spontaneously. Two living systems interacting together will change together congruently. Coordination of behaviour takes place through a flow of interactions, which we call *languaging*. Coordinations of behaviour are conserved through generations of autonomous living systems as languaging, i.e. flows of meaning within which sounds and gestures participate. Thus, not only is existence conserved but also congruence with circumstances. We might refer to this as *drift*. Maturana made use here of an analogy with a boat – a boat drifts as long as the shape of the boat and a floating state are conserved. A change in the integrity of the boat or its environment also changes the relationship. He pointed out that this represents a law of conservation for biology, where none traditionally existed.

In the matrix of human existence, relations are embedded so that some are seen and some are not seen within the space of existence. Maturana discussed examples of ways in which we experience emotions. In his view, emotions are not in the 'feelings' but in the flow of associated interactions. Pain may be biologically generated and inevitable, e.g. contact with fire results in pain for the individual. However, where pain is culturally determined it can be changed. Maturana suggested that we are not genetically programmed to feel pain of a kind that arises culturally. Pain is experienced as a denial of self-respect, and this can be changed through recovery of self-love which cures it. He went on to discuss emotions as relational behaviour, pointing out that different words we use to denote emotion reflect the relational behaviours they entail. Interference in the way we see behaviours can arise from prejudice, expectation, etc. For something to be seen it must belong to the history of coherence and must be allowed to be or the flow of interaction will be different. Prejudice introduces an element not naturally occurring in the history of the relation. Taking love as an example, he suggested: 'An observer says that there is love in a relationship when s/he sees a behaviour through which another arises as a legitimate other in living in that relation. (A legitimate presence in a relation is one which requires no further justification)' (Maturana, 2004).

In contrast, to be asked to be 'realistic' or 'objective' actually suggests you are being instructed to do as you are told. For Maturana, there is not one objective reality but many realities, all with corresponding operational coherences (see also the discussion of hermeneutics in Chapter 6). As Beer points out, many social difficulties have arisen from a conception that the needs or wishes of individuals must be subordinate to the greater interests of the collective. He suggests that the theory of autopoiesis gives us back the legitimate right to focus on individual autonomy and self-determination as the heart of social action.

Socio-technical Systems

As we introduced in Chapter 3, one area of interest in Systems concepts has derived from what became known as the socio-technical approach to working practices. These approaches grew out of work conducted in the Tavistock Institute, originally focused on medical/therapeutic applications to help servicemen to resettle in civilian life after World War II. Participants included well-known names such as C.G. Jung, R.D. Laing and Kurt Lewin. Founder members of the Institute, such as Eric Trist and Fred Emery, wanted to develop ways to harness tools developed by social scientists for the benefit of society. They began to utilize and develop what is now known as action research (see Chapter 7), espousing a view that there could be 'no theory without practice, no practice without theory' (Mumford, 2006, p. 320). Socio-technical design was envisaged as a means by which human intelligence and skill could be harnessed in conjunction with newly emerging technologies in the post-War period, to bring about radical improvements in work and in life. Practitioners saw two key values as essential: a need to *humanize* work through job design, and promotion of *democracy* in both the workplace and wider society. Gradually, a coherent set of socio-technical principles was developed (Cherns, 1976). Researchers considered that a work system should be seen as a set of activities coming together into an integrated whole, as opposed to a collection of separate tasks, i.e. as an open system, interacting with an environment that influences its behaviour as a consequence. The concept of group working became significant to its members (Pasmore, 1988). Socio-technical principles were in some degree a response to earlier reflections by Adam Smith about the potentially dehumanizing effect of work systems based on a strict division of labour (Smith, 1979, cited in Mumford, 1996). It was considered important that work be designed so that individuals would experience variety, stimulation, opportunities to make decisions and to learn, and receive recognition from the outside world for what they did (Emery,

1978). Emery developed a principle of adaptive strategic planning emphasizing the importance of shared organizational values, from which to derive organizational goals. Ideas of participative design prevailed; for instance, if work was to be democratic and enriching, so also should be the process by which work systems were designed. Mumford and Weir (1979) reflect that

> A work system that is designed to achieve objectives defined solely in technical terms is likely to have unpredictable human consequences. The reason for this is that technical decisions taken at an early stage of the design process will impose constraints on the organisation of the human part of the system (1979, p. 9).

A socio-technical perspective can help designers of systems to avoid a situation in which choices about technical systems taken at an early stage in a project influence the associated human system in unexpected and undesirable ways.

Concluding Remarks

In this chapter we have sought to expand your understanding of the ideas that we introduced in the preceding chapters. Some of the discussion may appear to be more theoretical than practical, but as you gain experience of the practice so you will find the need to increase your expertise and knowledge of the ideas behind the practice. We have found that by gaining greater insight into the thinking behind the ideas we begin to be able to improve them in practice. In the next chapter we will introduce some the thoughts that have been influential in modern Systems and a summary of the key ideas that individuals contributed to the practice.

5

Influential Ideas

Influential Ideas

Here we will discuss some of the ideas that have been important to modern Systems practice. Such an undertaking will necessarily leave gaps but this is a chapter that provides some background to the ideas discussed earlier. We group the contributions in terms of their relationship to each other rather than in a chronological order, although clearly each development has an associated history. The main ideas we discuss here include the work of Forrester, Vickers, Churchman, Checkland, Ashby and Beer. (For a useful history of Systems thinking we recommend Checkland's excellent book *Systems Thinking Systems Practice*, 1981 and 1999.)

Jay Forrester and System Dynamics

Forrester was an electrical engineer who was interested in the difficulties of modelling complex issues. He felt that methods used at the time (1968) were deficient and so chose to view complex systems holistically. Forrester argued that the way in which social situations function could be likened to a complex feedback system. (You will recall that in the earlier chapters of this book we discussed the notion of positive feedback, which forces growth and negative feedback, which is goal seeking.) Forrester used feedback loops and the notion of positive and negative feedback to model complex social situations because he felt that often the apparently obvious 'solutions' to social problems were apt to fall into one of a number of traps inherent in the nature of complex systems. Modelling offered a means of testing various scenarios as a means of aiding decision making (Forrester, 1968).

To give you a feel for how it works, we develop a simple example over the next few pages. This shows how System Dynamics might be used to develop a model of population growth. Leaving aside death and immigration/migration for the moment, the basic driver of population growth could be represented by a simple causal loop like that shown in Figure 5.1:

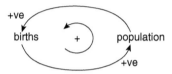

Figure 5.1:   Causal loop showing positive 'signings'

As you will remember from Chapter 3 we can create a diagram that shows the causal relationships between two, or more, events. In the above diagram we are showing that as the number of births grows, the population grows, and as the population grows the number of births grows. The next step is to put the ideas contained in the causal loop diagram into a more specialized kind of diagram from which it will be easier to derive the elements needed for a computer-driven simulation. To see how to do this, we will need to look at it in a slightly different way: . . . Let us consider the population causal loop diagram above. In this diagram we show the birth *rate* causing an increase in the population – i.e. an increase in the population *level*. Think of it in terms of a bath filling with water (see Figure 5.2):

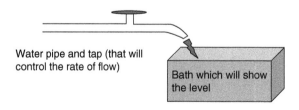

Figure 5.2:   Flow of water into bath

In System Dynamics we can represent the tap, the path and the flow of water by thinking in terms of the rate (of flow) and the level (accumulation over time). We can represent this as shown in Figure 5.3:

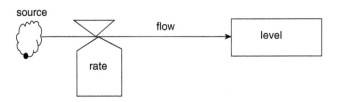

Figure 5.3:   The conventions of simple rates and levels diagrams

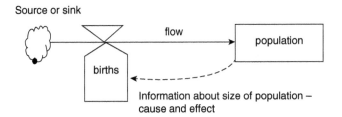

Figure 5.4:   Population as a rates and levels diagram

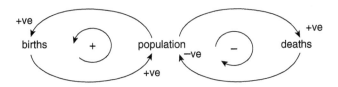

Figure 5.5:   Causal loop showing positive and negative 'signings' for births and deaths

You can see from the above diagram that there is a *source* from which emerges a *flow*. The *rate* of the flow is seen as being controlled by a valve and the output of the flow accumulates as a *level*. We can now use essentially the same conventions to convert our population growth causal loop diagram into a System Dynamics format (Figure 5.4).

Clearly the population growth shown here is unchecked. It acts as a positive feedback system which acts to reinforce the direction in which the system is going – the population will grow forever! We all know that in reality there are factors that act to modify this growth such as death and number of births. We can represent this by adding in an extra loop as shown below in Figure 5.5. Can you see how this will affect the behaviour of the system as a whole? (If you wish to remind yourself what the shape of negative and positive feedback looks like have a look in Chapter 2.)

Just as we converted the causal loop diagram in Figure 5.1 into the System Dynamics format of Figure 5.3, so we can convert this more complex causal loop diagram into the System Dynamics format, as shown in Figure 5.6:

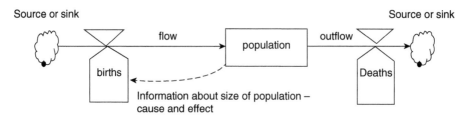

Figure 5.6:   Population with birth and death rates added

Notice that while the 'birth' loop describes a destabilizing positive feedback process (both arrows have positive signs) the 'death' loop describes a stabilizing negative feedback process. You might find Figure 5.5 a useful reminder of how the outputs of these two types of feedback differ:

Now that you have learnt how to move from a causal loop diagram with its associated positive and negative feedback we require more symbols to represent each kind of situation. Examples of typical symbols used in SD modelling are shown in Figure 5.7:

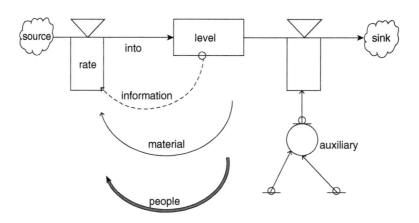

Figure 5.7:   Modelling conventions used in SD

In Forrester's approach to SD the resultant model using the above conventions are translated into a model which will be put into a form that will be recognized by the SD program.

SD has many components that can be arranged hierarchically. This can lead to the creation of very complex System Dynamics diagrams and hence very sophisticated computer simulations. The System Dynamics diagrams provide a bridge between creating a diagram by hand and a computer simulation. From modelling a situation of interest by using causal loop diagrams we can then translate them into a 'rates and levels' diagram. As you have learnt, 'rates and levels' are the basic building blocks of computer simulation for System Dynamics.

SD modelling requires that we convert the rates and levels model into an equation that represents what is happening in the diagram. Let us think of the population model in Figure 5.4 above. For simplicity let us say that the population is 400 and the birth rate is a constant 100 births per year (we did say this is a very simple model!). We then have to provide an explanation of what the population level will become over a time interval selected by us, the modeller. Let us say that we want to know the population level on an annual basis. Our equation will now look like this:

We begin with – Birth rate = 100 and Population Level = 400

This example is so simple that you can probably see immediately that if the population 'now' is 400 then the population in N years will be $400 + 100 \times N$. So if 'now' is, say, 2010, then the population in 2011 would be 500, and the population in 2020 would be 1400.

If we put this into the kind of equation that you might use in preparing a System Dynamics computer simulation, it might look like this:

$$POPE = POPP + (TI * BC)$$

where:
POPP = the present population
POPE = the population we wish to estimate
TI = the time interval (N in the example above)
BC = the constant birth rate

Similarly, for Figure 5.5, in which we added the death rate, the equation would be:

$$POPE = POPP + (TI * BC) - (TI * DC)$$

where:
DC = constant death rate

i.e. the net change in population is the birth rate multiplied by the time interval, minus the death rate multiplied by the time interval.

So if 'present' is 2010, and we want to estimate the population for 10 years' time (2020) and the death rate (DC) is 99, then:

$$POPE\ (2020) = 400 + (10 \times 100) - (10 \times 99)$$
$$= 400 + 1000 - 990$$
$$= 410$$

We can move on to the development of a model from the causal loop representation through to a simulation model (using Forrester's nomenclature) by using a number of building blocks such as summers, integrators, multipliers and trigonometric functions such as sine, cosine and so on to create the relationships between each of the parts of the equation. (For some useful examples of dynamics models see Roberts et al. (1997) and Pidd (2004).)

Forrester, Meadows and their colleagues (see Meadows et al. (1972) and Forrester (1973)) used an expansion of these ideas as the basis of their famous 'World Dynamics' model. In it, they attempted to model world problems from a System Dynamics perspective depicting the relationships between population, food, natural resources, pollution, capital investment and quality of life. The model was an interesting example of a very large and complex model which provided challenging and important outcomes.

Recent years have seen the development of useful System Dynamics software for personal computers, such as: Dynamo, iThink/Stella, Powersim and Vensim (a demonstration of the latter can be seen at http://www.vensim.com). The modelling methods used by these packages still follow Forrester's original concept.

Vickers and the 'Appreciative' Setting

In Chapter 3, we introduced the influential ideas provided through the writing of Sir Geoffrey Vickers. Vickers, after a long life in which he had been a highly decorated soldier, a lawyer and a public servant, spent his final years as a Systems theorist and a visiting professor at Lancaster University. His long retirement from public office was spent reflecting upon the lessons he had learnt from his various responsibilities and in trying to make sense of human decision making and action. One idea that we embrace in Systems practice is his notion of Appreciation. Vickers' 'Appreciative System' refers to the way that an individual gains understanding about a situation and its context leading to the formulation of policies and action (see Chapter 3). Vickers' ideas influenced Checkland who describes Appreciation as:

> . . . the observation of the actual and comparison with the norm that may or may not lead to action (Vickers, 1970) and is commonly thought to be an unconscious or tacit process (Checkland and Casar, 1986). However, it would seem that the

notion of appreciation relates not only to policy making but also to the social process in general (Checkland, 1999).

Vickers thought of the world in terms of tangible and intangible events, which he saw as an interacting flux of events and ideas. Appreciation is described by Stowell and West (1994, p. 114) as '. . . a continual process of learning for an individual (or group) through which the individual develops a personal view of, or appreciates, perceived reality as well as developing his/her own values and hence standards about that view of reality'. This view of learning about the situation of interest has resonance with the cycle of learning, which is a key idea in hermeneutics (see Chapter 6). Vickers saw Appreciation as our ability to select from the flux of events and ideas what is personally interesting, and relevant to us. The selection we make is the result of previous judgements that we made about *reality* and its associated values. In this way, Vickers argues, we gain an Appreciation of our world not only from our observation of its changes, but also via our own reactions, as we take action in order to maintain our relationship to that aspect of the world of which we are a part. This is a never-ending cycle in which '. . . an individual's view of reality and the value that the individual assigns to aspects of that reality change through personal experience' (Stowell and West, 1994, p. 114).

The Appreciative Cycle begins with our concerns about interests that are shaped by our Appreciative settings formed by our beliefs, standards and experiences. When we notice something of interest (shaped by what Vickers describes as our 'readiness to notice') we select from the environment the facts that we consider relevant to the situation. That is what he calls our Appreciative settings which act to '. . . create a pattern of concerns . . .' (Champion, 2001, p. 11). This is called our reality judgement. Once we have made this judgement we then decide what ought to be the case; our desired ideal state. We then make an action judgement based upon our contemplation about the situation within the context of our 'standards' in the form of the question 'what shall I do about it?', the outcome being to select the action considered significant enough to maintain, modify or remove the relationship. It is worth noting that our Appreciative settings are changing with each cycle (the flux of events and ideas) as we learn (after contemplation) and take action (Stowell and Cooray, 2006). These actions are not taken in a piecemeal fashion but as part of a continuous reaction to the dynamics of the situation.

As we saw in a previous chapter (Chapter 3) the idea of relationship maintenance is important and is relevant to modern thinking about a 'system' (whether individual or an enterprise). The prime outcome from the Appreciative Cycle is not action itself but a greater understanding of the situation (Ison, 2005). Checkland and Casar's work highlighted what Vickers considered to be the importance of relationship maintaining. This is an important distinction. Vickers is suggesting that decision making is better described in terms of relationship maintenance, than in terms of the goal achievement that is popularly suggested to be the main purpose of an enterprise. As Vickers explained, a system is a regulated set of relationships, and the key to its understanding is the way in which it is regulated.

> Thus we can sense, though we cannot yet explain or understand, a circular causal process by which the goals of society are set. They are continually under revision; factors which make for constancy are overcome by new demands, resulting from new experiences . . . This process cannot be explained without taking into account the verdict of the individual conscious mind . . . dynamic value judgements (which) are both a product and a cause of the ceaseless process of goal formulation. (Vickers, 1991, p. 36)

> . . . we do not seek or shun objects but relations with objects. No one wants an apple; he wants to eat it, sell it, paint it, perhaps just admire it, in any case relate to it in some way or other. The relation may sometimes be taken for granted; people who avoid tigers need not be pressed to say why. None the less, at the level of mental behaviour which I am considering, the distinction is usually important. (Vickers, 1983a, p. 16)

Stowell and West highlight the important distinction between goal seeking and relationship maintaining. They explain that whilst goals may be set and attained, for Vickers

> . . . they need to be carefully considered within the context of some desired relationship. Failure to consider this is likely to result in short term action and decision making which is not well considered in terms of the whole context of decision making and our attempts to manage (in its widest sense of the word) or control our perceived reality in order to attain a desired state of stability. (Stowell and West, 1994, p. 116)

It is worth repeating Stowell and West's (1994, pp. 116–117) paragraph on what Vickers meant by stability. He argued that it '. . . is likely to remain obscured in Western cultures until they rediscover the fact that life consists in experiencing relations rather than in seeking goals or ends. The intrinsic confusion about means and ends arises from the fact that no end can ever be more than a means if an end is equated with a goal' (Vickers, 1970, p. 128). They go on to say that for Vickers the successful management of any system, whether it be a business organization or an individual's personal lifestyle, does not consist in prescribing one goal or even one series of goals but in regulating a system over time in such a way as to optimize the realization of many conflicting relations without wrecking the system in the process (1970, p. 116).

Vickers highlighted three underlying problem areas for the goal/relationship maintenance issue (1970 p. 116):

1. The acceptance of goals as once and for all states to be attained, rather than a balanced state to be maintained over time as the overall aim of those who aim to manage and control;
2. The desire to simplify a situation by reducing multiple objectives to a single goal which in turn can be assessed by a single measure of success; and
3. The acceptance of effectiveness as the most important criterion for judging the appropriateness of alternatives to achieve a desired end.

In their section on Vickers' 'Relationship-Maintaining' Stowell and West (1994, pp. 116–117) provide us with a succinct account of Vickers' challenge to the belief in a once-and-for-all goal as a way of planning and maintaining control or in order to simplify a situation. They say that the major reason for defining a single organizational goal is its ease of quantifying goal attainment, and yet a goal-seeking view of organization is inappropriate. Vickers offered instead a view of policy-making and organization as the setting of governing relations or norms. He emphasized that the difference between this notion of relationship maintaining and the usual terms adopted (i.e. goal-setting aims and objectives) is not merely verbal but fundamental (1965, p. 31) as it is a means of avoiding the imposition of artificial barriers and (implicit) short-term thinking about organizational activities. They say that Vickers' contribution to the practice is that his ideas offer a basis for interpretive Systems thinking about organizations which uses language and concepts which are appropriate and consistent with the philosophy, ideas and sentiments expressed (see Chapter 4 above).

Vickers' writings provide the Systems practitioner with a number of intellectual tools which have been embedded in a number of methods of inquiry. These are discussed later in this chapter.

In summary some key thoughts introduced by Vickers' writings include:

i. A notion that the cycle of judgements and actions in human decision making can be seen as organized as a system;
ii. A separation of judgements about what is the case ('reality judgements') and judgements about what ought to be the case ('value judgements');
iii. A concept of action judgements stemming from reality and value judgements;

iv. An insistence on 'relationship maintaining' as a richer concept of human action than the popular but poverty-stricken notion of goal seeking;

v. A rich concept of day-to-day life as a flux of interacting events and ideas;

vi. The notion that readinesses can direct human action.

Vickers' ideas about the way in which we make sense of our world influenced the so-called 'Soft Systems' school. For a more detailed discussion of Vickers' work the reader is referred to *The Art of Judgement* (Vickers, G., 1965).

C. West Churchman, Boundary, Environment, Weltanschauung and Method

C. West Churchman's work has been influential in the development of modern Systems thinking and practice. Although his first love was philosophy, his contribution to the theory and practice of Systems has been significant. His view that philosophy should have meaning in the world had an equal resonance in his writings and teaching on Systems theory and practice. His research explored the philosophical foundation of Systems from which he drew a distinction between what we might call Hard and Soft Systems. Working at the time that General Systems Theory (GST) was emerging from the traditions of biological science, Churchman argued for the importance of recognizing individual perspectives of the world. For Churchman, the most important activity of inquiry was in the representation of the problems inherent in social situations. Unlike GST where boundaries were part of the structure of reality, Churchman's argument was that the identification of a system and its boundary related to individual or social constructs of their 'reality'. In this way, the participation of those involved in a situation was key to gaining understanding about it. This moved Systems thinking away from the model that says systems exist *out there* in the real world and our task is to find them, to the notion that a system is a personal construct that may, or may not, be shared by others.

What emerges from these ideas is the notion of boundary and the effect that an individual's view of the world has upon its definition. Boundary definition is a key issue for practical applications of Systems thinking. Consider some difficulties of boundary definition. If we take Churchman's argument literally and attempt to take all opinions into account then the identification of 'boundary' becomes an exercise in the unattainable. The idea of an absolute boundary requires that we gather all knowledge about a situation. In its extreme, such an exercise requires taking in all knowledge, which is an unattainable goal. The recognition of this impossibility means that the definition of a boundary and its surrounding environment is the result of a decision by someone or some people and with the decision comes the attendant question 'who is involved in making the decision and how was it made?' For Churchman boundary setting is the result of incorporating all stakeholder views and as a consequence there are no experts (in the traditional sense) as all views are valid and all add richness to understanding. At the same time Churchman recognized that the formulation of the problem and subsequent action meant that the worldviews, the *Weltanschauungen* (particular philosophies or views of life) of all participants and the role of the designer would be crucial factors in the final outcome.

Recognition of the importance of the effect of *Weltanschauung* upon human thinking is not of course new; Dilthey (1833–1911) developed a typology of the three basic *Weltanschauungen*, which he considered to be 'typical' (naturalism, subjective idealism and objective idealism – we will discuss influential philosophies in the next chapter). The acceptance of Dilthey's typology seems to challenge the ability of an individual to think objectively about a situation and yet it is unwise to ignore the importance of the various views of those involved. How do we address such issues?

Churchman has something to say here. His view of gaining greater understanding is described by the notion of teleology, in which all actions are thought to be the result of a predefined end (albeit sometimes an unconscious one). The importance and impact of teleology upon inquiry and design cannot be minimized as it casts doubts upon the possibility of gaining an uncompromised understanding about any situation. Churchman sought to explore this challenge by undertaking an examination of the history of the designer as the producer of knowledge. For this task he drew upon the writings of Leibniz (1646–1716), Locke (1632–1704), Kant (1724–1804), Hegel (1770–1831) and the work of his former teacher, E.A. Singer (1873–1954). Churchman's discussion of the characteristics of design, which itself has a hint of reductionism, suggests that it '. . . belongs to a category of behaviour called teleological, i.e. goal seeking . . .' (Churchman, 1971, p. 5); the designer's task then, is to identify the system as a whole and what makes it up; and this is undertaken by a process of enquiry.

For Churchman the outcome of the process of design becomes a selection between alternatives with the intention of achieving the desired goal. This is an important point as the design process involves communicating with other stakeholders, taking into account their thinking and then transforming thoughts into action. Churchman makes us pause for thought here because this means that the designer and those involved will only reach agreement if their respective worldviews are coincident or they can reach a consensus where there is sufficient resonance between them. In exposing this difficulty he indirectly raises the question of power and the ability of an individual or group to exert influence over outcomes.

Churchman also raises the question of method or methodology. He asks the question whether the method itself is neutral; does the chosen approach have an embedded pathway leading to an assured outcome?

> . . . if the inquiring system is Hegelian, it must have the ability to look at itself and this ability implies that the inquiring system can in some sense construct the opposite of its own image. That is to say, it has the capability of asking itself what an inquiring system would be like which did not function according to the basic principles of its own design. (Churchman, 1971, p.249)

We learn from Churchman several important points for the practice of Systems thinking. We learn about the difficulties of boundary definition, the effects of *Weltanschauungen* (and teleology) and the inherent dangers embedded in the approach adopted. Importantly he draws attention to a difference between reductionist-based approaches, which represent a journey from a defined problem to a comprehensive outcome, and an approach in which the process of learning is prime.

Soft Systems and the Work of Peter Checkland

Checkland's programme of action research over more than 30 years (Checkland, 1999) produced a method of inquiry which has proved to be one of the most influential ideas in Systems practice. Soft Systems Methodology arose out of what Checkland perceived to be deficiencies in systems engineering to address situations that involved social groupings – what he once referred to as human activity systems.

The approach that emerged over this period is known as Soft Systems Methodology (SSM) and is dealt with in earlier chapters. Checkland chose to name it a 'methodology', meaning 'the logos of method, the principles of method' (Checkland, 1999, p. A32). SSM has the benefit of a significant number of research contributions and intellectual argument, published in various learned journals over a period of more than 30 years. The approach has contributed ideas for practice not just through the use of the methodology itself, which has proved a valuable aid to inquiry, but because it has ideas that have been tested and developed which can be used in a variety of ways. There are examples of the use of this area of research in information systems, in management, education and social services.

In the previous section we discussed the contributions of Churchman to the practice of Systems and the difficulties he raised for the whole process of inquiry. Checkland's various research contributions have provided answers to some of these difficulties. Perhaps the most significant contribution of SSM to practice is the realization that interventions into 'problem situations' do not result in cast iron solutions, but are part of a process of learning, which is never-ending. In SSM we, the practitioners, adopt a Singerian notion of a never-ending cycle of learning (Singer, 1936). Churchman (1971, pp. 200–201) outlines nine characteristics, created out of Singer's notion of inquiry, which have some commonality with SSM. Of particular relevance is the first of the nine characteristics which Churchman summarizes, '1. The inquiring system has the purpose of creating knowledge which means creating the capability of choosing the right means for one's desired ends' (1971, p. 200). The impact of this message, made an explicit part of SSM, marks a distinct move away from an optimization model of problem *investigation* to one where the main concern is learning about the situation. What is made explicit in SSM is a message of inquiry that has been carried through into other 'soft' approaches (e.g. CLD, AIM, Chapter 4).

Peter Checkland points out in his 30-year retrospective of Systems thinking and practice (1999, pp. A33/34) that neither SSM nor any other methodology can bring about improvements to a problem situation for the user. To suggest this would be to miss the essence of the process of inquiry. A user, appreciating a methodology as a coherent set of principles, and perceiving a situation to be problematic, considers the question 'What can I do?' and generates a specific instance of the chosen methodology tailored to the perceived conditions of the situation of interest. The user then uses this specific instance of a methodology in order to promote learning. This learning may enable the user to bring about (or be a catalyst for) beneficial change within the situation. It may also bring about change in the user and his or her Appreciation of the methodology, so that any future inquiry based on the same coherent principles may be different. He goes on to report work by Atkinson (1984) who had observed many variations in the application of what users claimed to be SSM, bearing out Checkland's own view that methodology is adapted for specific use by the Appreciative settings of the particular user in context. Following from this, a number of people attempted to identify constitutive rules for the Soft Systems Methodology, including Checkland himself in his 1990 work (Checkland and Scholes, 1990). However, these attempts were never entirely satisfactory. Holwell (1997) argued that the 1990 rules were 'both too loose and not extensive enough' (p. 398) and suggested instead three 'assumptions' underpinning work purporting to be based in SSM. These were an acceptance of social reality as a continuously (re-)created social construct; explicit use of intellectual devices to explore, understand and act within the situation of interest; and inclusion among these devices of systems models of purposeful activity based in declared worldviews. Checkland goes on to comment that these three assumptions are key to 'deft, light-footed and flexible use' as they are internalized by experienced users. Thus he was able to distinguish between a somewhat tentative approach by novice users who follow the original seven-stage model very carefully, and sophisticated, internalized use in which specific adaptations of the methodology in context become more intuitive. This led him to identify two distinct archetypes for SSM: Mode 1 and Mode 2.

Our discussions of the Soft Systems Methodology up to now have largely focused on aspects of Mode 1, which is the typology for the methodology set out in Checkland's 1981 text (shown in Figure 5.10). Very many valuable inquiries have been conducted based on Mode 1 and continue to be so. It is not suggested here that Mode 2 has superseded or replaced it. However, Checkland has been at pains to point out that it should not be regarded as a recipe to be followed slavishly as a key to achieving improvements in a given context, but as the basis for creation of a learning cycle – a way of thinking about complexity in real situations. He has suggested that the best way to appreciate internalized use of SSM is through examples, and accordingly the 1990 text (Checkland and Scholes, 1990) contained a number of case studies illustrating very different adaptations to widely varying contexts (1999, p. A36). Thus the archetype for Mode 2 (internalized mode), although superficially different from Mode 1 as it appears in Figure 5.8, actually reflects the same underpinning assumptions or constitutive rules for inquiry to be regarded as SSM-based. Mode 2 highlights two streams of analysis: cultural and logic-based, proceeding side by side iteratively – one informing the other. The stream of cultural analysis involves reflection upon the situation through a number of lenses, e.g. social and political dimensions, and highlights the process as an intervention in the situation of interest (not simply an interaction between disinterested 'analysts' and engaged actors). A logic-based stream of analysis considers at the same time tasks and issues which appear to be key aspects of the situation. In both Mode 1 and Mode 2, a distinction is made between the real world in which actors experience the situation and the intellectual world in which relevant systems are

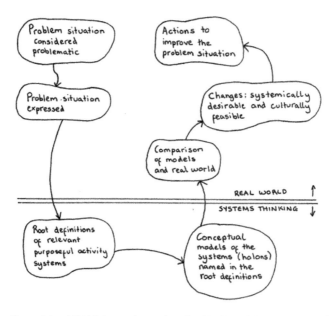

Figure 5.8:   SSM Mode 1 archetype (see Checkland and Scholes, 1990, p. 27)

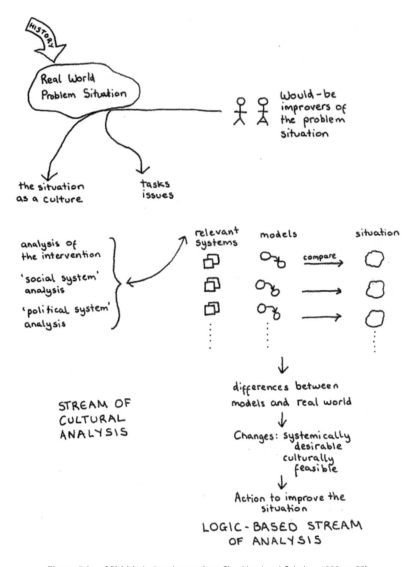

Figure 5.9:   SSM Mode 2 archetype (see Checkland and Scholes, 1990, p. 29)

modelled (because both modes are, in fact, articulations of the same methodological assumptions). In both modes, creation of learning about the situation is the desired outcome of the analysis, allowing reflection upon changes that appear to be both systemically desirable and culturally feasible. Action to improve the situation is then in the hands of the problem owners/actors themselves. The archetype of Mode 2 appears as Figure 5.9.

The importance of the influence of a participant's way of life (formal and informal) upon expressed views is made a feature of SSM through the mnemonic CATWOE devised by Smyth (1976) as a means of assessing Root Definitions. In CATWOE, the W stands for *Weltanschauung* which provides a means for participants to surface the thinking which lay behind their (in this case) definition. The point of this exercise is to provide a means of reflection and discussion as well as putting the definition into perspective. In this way SSM could be said to provide the means by which teleology may be taken into account.

While surfacing the *Weltanschauungen* involved in the production of Root Definitions and Conceptual Models we must reflect upon the way that SSM is used. For example, many believe that SSM is used to best advantage if all participants are involved in the development of the models but we then have to consider the problems of organizational power. This is addressed by the incorporation of the notion of power as a commodity (Stowell, 1989) incorporated within Analysis Three within the mode 2 archetype, which is concerned with the distribution of power in social situations (Checkland 1999, p. A20). Stowell considered power relationships as a fundamental part of the particular social culture, such that any change would bring about the exercise of power by participants as means of preserving the status quo.

Stowell is therefore looking for ways of gaining insight into how that power may exist within the participant group. He sees participation in terms of a 'game', in which the playing provides an opportunity for participants to unmask the 'truth' behind the interplay. This means that to effect change participants have to learn about the relationships involved.

This idea is also expressed by Gadamer who felt that experiencing the experiences of others is more a case of appreciating, through the medium of language, the interchange of the frames of reference of the observer and the observed. The idea has resonance with the notion of art and hermeneutics where both spectators and artists (actors) are all part of the same experience. Stowell extends this notion into the area of participation in which 'experts' and clients undertake to exchange ideas about the situation at hand, but all is not necessarily revealed. As Gadamer suggests, 'A man who is disguised does not want to be recognised, but to be taken for someone else . . . he plays another person' (Gadamer, 2004, p. 111). In other words the Soft Systems practitioner or researcher views the participants as actors. The inquirer's task is therefore to create an environment where those involved not only learn about the situation of interest (and the person behind the mask) but also, importantly, their position within it. Not only does this process require thinking about what ought to be, but also about what and how the present system operates.

It is here that Stowell's notion of power as a 'commodity' is useful as it helps those involved to learn about power as part of 'control' strategies used and managed within the participant group(s). This idea is appealing because it is the participants who are best placed to discuss the way in which individuals use their 'commodity' of power rather than a dispassionate observer. The participants are encouraged to think of power in terms of a 'commodity'. Commodity relates to *something* which is considered of value by organizational membership within the culture, or value-systems, of a given organization. It is the way that a 'commodity' of power used by participant(s) aids in the Appreciation of the dynamics of the group and the manner in which individuals attempt to 'transform' a situation that they may not want into one that they do. 'Commodities' can be both tangible and intangible things. Some tangible commodities may have a higher value in one culture than in another and some individuals may have a greater selection of commodities than others. The way in which individuals use their particular commodities can be blatant, e.g. from withdrawal of good will, to the subtle use of humour to criticize something. The Appreciation of the situation and the outcome of an inquiry will be influenced by the way in which power is exercised.

What the Soft Systems researcher is attempting is to use a method of bringing into public debate those 'commodities' which are taken to embody power as a way of managing their effect. The basis of his argument is that individuals attempt to control their environment through a dependency of some kind that an individual perceives others, or themselves, to have and that these dependencies are generated from a wide range of 'commodities'. By employing the metaphor 'commodity' as a means of describing power the inquirer can gain two advantages. First a better understanding of the problem situation can be achieved and, second, the metaphor can be used to discuss the impact of the way that 'informal power' is being used within the group.

The use of an appropriate metaphor may help to describe staff concerns about the way in which some decisions are being influenced by the way in which the group interacts. Bringing this concern out into the open may help to generate wider discussions and surface hidden, or sometimes imagined, manifestations of power. For example, a discussion in which the more vocal members of a group, carried away by the excitement of the discussion, may unintentionally suppress the participation of the more retiring members. These quieter members of the group may feel unable to make their opinion known and therefore not always feel in agreement with the outcome. Whilst it is easy to put this down to 'poor' chairing of a meeting it is not always that clear-cut. Members with a persuasive way of expressing themselves, or those who can raise a laugh, might use this ability to 'get their way' leaving the less scintillating members of the group at a disadvantage. The notion of commodity is now a part of the present incarnation of SSM. In Analysis Three in SSM Mode 2 Checkland incorporates the notion of commodity which he describes as working:

. . . with the fact that everyone who participates in the life of any social grouping quickly acquires a sense of what you have to do to influence people, to cause things to happen, to stop possible courses of action, to significantly affect the actions the group or members take. The metaphor of the 'commodities' which embody power is used to encourage discussion of these matters (Checkland, 1999, p. A20).

Stowell also uses the idea in the developed form of AIM through the use of PEArL where 'r' relates to power (Champion and Stowell, 2003).

SSM has had a significant effect upon Inquiry, some claim to the detriment of other approaches. But through the development of SSM by Checkland and the considerable number of researchers that made such important contributions we have a readily understood methodology that embodies a form of Systems thinking which can be described as having its philosophical roots in Phenomenology (Husserl, 1859–1938) and its sociological roots in Interpretivism (Schütz, 1899–1959) and Constructivism (Weber, 1864–1920) (see Chapter 6).

Ashby and the Law of Requisite Variety

Ross Ashby is credited as being one of the founding fathers of cybernetics and Systems theory. His contributions include the homeostat, the principle of self, the principle of regulatory models and (as far as this text is concerned) the most familiar, the Law of Requisite Variety.

Communication between an object to be controlled and the controller is a key idea in cybernetics and the flow of information between the object to be controlled and the controller is fundamental to effective control. Through his work Ashby demonstrated that effective control depends upon the ability of the controller to be able to match the changes to which the object to be controlled is subjected. (Although influenced by Shannon and Weaver (1949) here we refer to Ashby's notion of changes of state rather than to the basic unit of information as proposed by Information Theory.) In other words the controller must be capable of responding with as much variety as the effects of a changing environment have upon the object to be controlled. The more complex the system the more difficult it is to predict its behaviour and the more difficult to exercise control.

As with many so-called simple ideas, once expressed it appears to be obvious. However, as with many 'obvious' ideas, a closer examination reveals its importance. Consider the following example. Suppose you want to control anti-social behaviour, it might seem a good idea to install CCTV cameras in places where such behaviour takes place. Once installed the perpetrators' actions will be recorded for evidence against them should the situation arise. The perpetrator of course is aware of this fact so moves her/his actions out of sight of the cameras. The reaction is to install cameras to cover the new location. The perpetrator moves once again and so on. One strategy one might consider to respond to this reaction might be to cover the area with cameras. For example, in one 650-yard section of Holloway Road in London there are 29 cameras mounted on shops and lampposts, a church and a courtroom: a crime-ridden high street in north London has been branded the most spied-upon road in Britain after it emerged that it is watched over by more than 100 closed circuit television cameras (Beckford, 2007). Not surprisingly the perpetrators then adopt a new method to avoid detection: for example, cover their faces. Clearly such actions as these now require additional technology (or people) to address this development. The question now arises: at what stage will there be enough variety in the controllers to control such a situation as this?

Think about a simple situation involving five CCTV cameras and imagine that each camera has a small light which comes on when the camera is active. Each camera is 'looking' down a street that has been reported to have scenes of unacceptable social behaviour (USB). If any camera detects USB then there is an alert sent to the police who send out a patrol car to investigate, but no action is taken if activities do not fall into USB, e.g. noise but no violence. The cameras respond to a variety of activities but the main task is to identify USB; let us refer to USB by the letter (a). The perpetrator of USB can nullify detection by ceasing the activity; we will call their responses P1, P2, P3. We can consider the situation to resemble a competition between what the camera can identify as USB and the person causing USB. The cameras scan a range of activities, not all of which are in the category of USB. We shall call them (b), (c) and (d). We can represent the situation as shown in Figure 5.10:

Cameras	P1	P2	P3
C1	a	d	c
C2	b	c	d
C3	c	a	c
C4	d	b	a
C5	a	b	b

Figure 5.10: Showing the relationship between camera and perpetrators' 'action'

The cameras have a 'choice' of five actions, the perpetrators have three. We can see from the table that the perpetrator will always stop the USB (a) because no matter which camera is switched on the perpetrator can nullify the action. If C selects C4 then P can select P3 and stop the activity. If C selects C1 then P will select P1. Whilst this is a simple table the table can be extended but the outcome will be the same in that the 'game' is always in favour of P as the variety of moves open to C are easily countered by P. The conclusion we can make is that the outcomes cannot be less than:

$$\frac{\text{Variety in C}}{\text{Variety in P}}$$

In this example it is 5/3.

Ashby (1963, pp. 206–213) extends this idea and, taking up his argument (but within the context of the above example) we can now say that if P produces the same move irrespective of what the camera does then the variety in the outcomes will be as large as the variety in the cameras' moves – in other words the cameras are exerting full control. But if P has more moves available then the variety of outcomes is reduced. For example, if P has two possible moves the outcome is reduced by half, if there are three moves available then the outcome is reduced by one third; we can say that '. . . only variety in P's moves can force down the variety in outcomes' (after Ashby, 1963, p. 206). This is the Law of Requisite Variety (LRV) which says that '. . . only variety can destroy variety' (Ashby, 1961, p. 207).

Of course the inability to exercise complete control over a situation is predicted by Bremermann's Limit (Hans-Joachim Bremermann, 1926–1996) which effectively tells us what we may instinctively guess, that the systems to be controlled can easily generate more variety than the control system can generate. In practice this means choice. We either attempt to control everything or we select what not to control. One response to this is to try to control everything, e.g. the National Security Agency (NSA) apparently saves all the data from its unofficial eavesdropping for future use (Harris, 2006). As a security expert declared: 'If you can't find the needle, you have to take the haystack' (Harris, 2006). But if the controlee can always generate more variety than the controller, 'controlling everything' will never be truly effective. In that case, we will have to choose which aspects of the system to control and which to ignore. In other words we must simplify the model into one we can control.

What does the Law of Requisite Variety contribute to Systems practice (which after all is what this text is about)? At a superficial level it reminds the practitioner or researcher when carrying out an investigation into a problem area that any changes to the situation will mean simplification (or added complexity) of the means of control. In the workplace, we can exercise some control over the amount of information to be controlled by setting an agenda that is managed rigorously thereby limiting unexpected inputs. At a more interesting level we should consider the wider implications for our clients of the control system being installed. For example, the amount and frequency of data fed back to, say, managers may be too overpowering for them to process and take appropriate action or may provoke an overreaction and set up some form of oscillation in the system. Beer proposes that since controlling the whole is impossible, we should only attempt to control some of the system. He argues that thinking in terms of '. . . heuristics rather than algorithms is at once a way of coping with proliferating variety . . . instead of trying to organise it in full detail, you organise it only somewhat; you then ride the dynamics of the system' (Beer, 1981, p. 53).

In addition to the contribution to the foundations of cybernetics Ashby's work inspired other pioneers in the field, notably Stafford Beer. Beer's development of the Viable Systems Model has provided practitioners with a model of organization whether it is at a business enterprise or at national level. Beer provides the practitioner and researcher alike with a practical means of gaining understanding.

Viable Systems and Stafford Beer

Beer's argument was something like this: a manager's job is to control and as such s/ he wants information not data. In some respects, this seems to echo Vickers about maintaining relationships. However, Beer goes on to argue that our task is not to provide a data processing system but to design a system of control and control is the province of cybernetics (see Beer, 1981, pp. 16–17). He puts forward the view that '. . . what a system really needs is a way of measuring its own internal tendency to depart from stability and a set of rules for experimenting with responses which will tend back to an internal equilibrium . . .' (Beer, 1981, p. 27). This reminds us of Forrester's view of an enterprise as a machine rather than a social system. In his next assertion he provides us with a clear clue of the different approach to Vickers. He says: '. . . then there is no need to know in advance what might cause a disturbance...'. Beer provides us with a model, which, he says, represents the way that an organization operates. The key to the success of that model is its control system.

He argues that information in complex situations, such as an enterprise, is processed in a similar way to the way that the nervous system manages sensory input. These nervous interactions are achieved through the connection of a 'whole batch of inputs and a whole batch of outputs' (p. 30): a complex network. In order to understand the basis of Beers' Viable Systems Model (VSM), it is important to understand the idea of the 'anastomotic reticulum' because this, he argues, is the way that decision processes operate.

Management decision making involves a series of complex information processes that handle the large flow of data arising from many encounters with other managers, the variety of whose inputs adds to the complexity of decision making. The complexity is magnified when the system is considered as a whole. The result is that the way that each source of information led up to the decision is often impossible to discover. At best we may be able to identify some stages in the decision-making process. However,

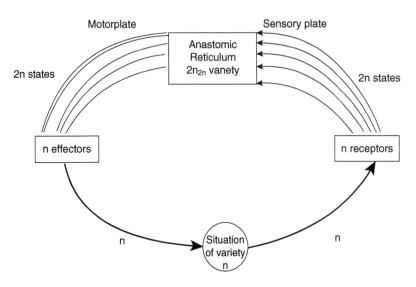

Figure 5.11:   Showing the input and output connected via the anastomotic reticulum (Beer, 1981, p. 47)

this decision process itself is a complex of inputs and assimilations of information from a multiplicity of sources each leading to different stages in the decision-making process. An analogy in nature is the way that a river may be fed with a number of tributaries making it impossible to detect which droplet of water came from where. In the human body, it might describe the separate parts of the circulatory system with various blood vessels branching to form a netlike structure. In medicine such a network is referred to as a reticulum, a network formed by certain structures within cells. Beer extends this idea by coupling it to the adjective anastomotic, which means connecting separate parts of a branching system to form a network, as blood vessels, or a river and its branches. This coupling, which he refers to as 'the anastomotic reticulum', acts as the control system (see Figure 5.11).

Let us think about the configuration of a system (cast your mind back to the Black Box idea we discussed in an earlier chapter). In any system we have one or more inputs which filter information into a place where it is collected (we will return to this) and then passed on to one or more outputs where we take action (passive or active). Of course the input and output capacity must be the same (remember Ashby's Law of Requisite Variety?). The connection between the input and the output is by means of the anastomotic reticulum.

Now if we reflect upon the practical implication of the Law of Requisite Variety we see that any control system generates so much variety that it becomes impossible to analyse it or to connect it to what Beer calls the anastomotic reticulum. The only way to make this work is to reduce the variety. Beer argues 'The brain of the firm just as a man's brain, has more potential states than can ever be analysed or examined by an enormous factor – an unthinkably large factor. Information then, has to be thrown away by the billion bits all the time, and without making nonsense of control' (Beer, 1981, p. 49). He also reminds us that we are unable to produce a conclusive optimum strategy, as not all alternatives can be examined. The only way to exercise control is by reducing variety. How does the system achieve this task – '. . . by organisation' (Beer, 1981, p. 50)?

At an elemental level we can argue that all decisions can be reduced to a simple Yes or No. There may be many variations en route to this final decision but at its end the logical pathway is to a simple binary switch between Yes or No or to put it another way 0 and 1. For example, if a situation has a variety of, say 32, we can say that in order to get an answer of 1 we only have to halve the number five times, that is 2^5. So we can say that using the binary bit as a basis we can represent variety as 2^n where n is the number of receptors or decisions we take to decide between alternatives. But this is to ignore the fact that things are not always symmetrical which this reasoning supposes. Social situations create complex issues and although we can devise a control system based upon this reasoning which appears to enable action Beer argues that we have to remember that we have to connect the input pattern to the output pattern. The anastomotic reticulum is where this is done. He says: 'If the variety of the situation . . . is n then the variety in the sensorium is 2^n and . . . the action needed has variety n then the variety of the motor plate is 2^n as well' (Beer, 1981, p. 46). He argues that the variety inside the network connecting the input (sensory) to the output (motor) is 2^{n2n}. This equation represents a large variety of actions to be controlled. To quote Beer (Beer, 1981, p. 47): 'Starting with a single possibility, we allow it to generate an alternative 0 or 1 . . . Consider a box with just two inputs and two outputs . . . this n = 2 generates $2^n = 2^2 = 4$ possibilities. They are 00, 01, 10, 11.' This creates a large number of possible combinations . . .' The answer is: 'the motor variety (4) raised to the power of the sensory variety (4), namely $4^4 = 256$' (Beer, 1981, p. 47). Of course, as Beer reminds us, a real control system generates so much variety that it is impossible to analyse it. In other words we have to reduce variety, i.e. simplify the situation if we wish to exercise some degree of control. Let us return to the problem of antisocial behaviour and to control discussed above. We have installed a number of CCTV cameras to monitor what is happening in a given area. How many cameras will we need, say, in an inner city area with nightclubs and bars? Leaving to one side what specific elements constitute unacceptable unsociable behaviour (USB), think about the variety that the cameras pick up. Common sense says a very large amount of data. We have a number of inputs that need to be translated, which in turn will transmit data to another part of the control system as a means of taking actions relevant to a variety of situations. Have another look at the diagram in Figure 5.7.

Accepting Beer's argument, imagine that to control USB we configure our control system in which we send an alarm if there is unsociable behaviour (ignore what this means, just assume for this simple example that something is happening which is unacceptable in a civilized society) or not. For this we have two inputs, incident or no incident, 0 or 1, which is then received for action to be taken, i.e. 00, nothing happening, 01 USB, what does our control system look like. Well, if we extend Beer's example of just one outcome, i.e. 1 or 0, we will have the following (Figure 5.12):

	0000 0000	1111 1111	 00
	0000 1111	0000 1111	 01
00 output	0011 0011	0011 0011	... ... 10 *input*
	0101 0101	0101 0101	 11

16 distinguishable states

Figure 5.12:   Possible states of the system (Beer, 1981, *Brain of the Firm*, p. 47)

In the above example we have 16 states for just one input but for the whole system we have 256 states!

Beer now raises the question – how do we organize and manage such complexity? In some respects, Beer's observations are similar to Vickers' once more. He points out that we cannot know what the future holds for us and we can only have a general idea of what effect the environment will have upon our enterprise. The enterprise exists in a turbulent environment. In order to attempt to manage such complexity the manager applies an algorithm, or general rule, as the basis of action. The general rule is derived from applying an heuristic, which will provide us with a way of behaving in order to achieve an end which cannot be precisely specified although we know what we want. We now have the difficulty of translating something that we cannot specify into some form of action. The input has to be made in a form that the anastomotic reticulum can recognize. Think about the kinds of inputs that decision makers in an enterprise receive: written reports, spreadsheets, and varieties of statistical analysis, opinions and general conversations. These have to be fed into the decision-making systems that manage the enterprise. At the risk of over simplification, the process could be akin to an eye examination. To make it more complicated, imagine having an eye examination in a foreign country where you and the examiner speak only a limited amount of each other's language. For example, you, the patient, will need to reply to questions about a range of things some of which are difficult to respond to in your own language, e.g. think about red, pink, orange or mauve and purple. Not everyone distinguishes these colours in the same way. We have to make some connection to the optician's questions and what we perceive. This is a complex situation as (i) the way that we perceive a colour may not be exactly the colour the optician sees and (ii) we have to translate what we see into a form of words that will enable the optician to form a diagnosis. The viability of this communication will affect the action taken. If the communication between optician and patient has been good then the patient will leave with the correct prescription; if not s/he may leave with the wrong prescription. The feedback mechanism that exists between the subject and the environment's response to its behaviour is referred to by Beer as the algedonic loop. Let us leave this idea and the anastomotic reticulum to one side for the moment and think about another aspect of the decision-making process.

We discussed earlier that the way we manage complex situations is to use some kind of algorithm based on an educated guess, an heuristic. However, as we have already learnt information comes to the decision maker in a variety of ways. The information often ends up in a summarized form that seems to capture the required action. For example, the CEO tells the finance director to 'cut costs'; the finance director then translates this into a number of different areas, take as an example stock control. The person in charge of stock then translates this directive into more specific areas such as reduction of certain items being held, purchase of cheaper versions, a review of delivery methods and so on. The initial directive is at a meta-level that in turn is connected to second order systems via its own algedonic loop. This means that if the lower level was unable to rectify the problem then it is passed to a higher level. This means that in each of the systems there are sub-systems that contain the same kind of arrangement as exists between the meta-level and the second order system. In other words, there are hierarchical systems of control.

Of course, in any enterprise, there are many sub-systems. The action of one sub-system may have a direct effect upon another. For example, continuing with the previous example of cost cutting in an enterprise; what the stores order or fail to order will affect a number of sub-systems, what the accounts department do will affect a number of other sub-systems and so on. The enterprise must be organized such that the action of each sub-system is fed back and each pathway is itself controlled. Beer then considers the way that stimuli, let's call this information, is used in the human body. He reflects upon the way that the information is passed to the various areas of the body from the brain down the spinal cord to the relevant area. Without trivializing Beer's excellent exposition on the relationship between a Neurophysiological model and the way that it might be used as the basis for managing an enterprise, what Beer called Neurocybernetics, suffice it to say at this point that this is the basis of what becomes the viable system. This is called viable because the '. . . ultimate criterion of viability must indeed be the capability to survive' (Beer, 1981, p. 226); it is applicable to any enterprise that is a viable system and capable of autonomy. For a complete discussion of the development of VSM the reader is recommended to read Beer's fine works and for the relationship between VSM and human information processing, page 99 of the *Brain of the Firm* (Beer, 1981).

The result of Beer's analysis and thinking about enterprise management resulted in a significant contribution to cybernetics and to the tool kit of Systems practitioners. In Chapter 3 we introduced the Viable Systems Model (see Figure 5.13) and how it might be used as a model for enterprises of varying sizes from a multinational with several

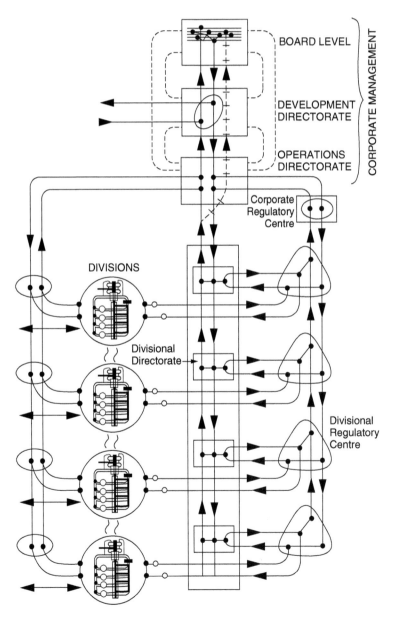

Figure 5.13:   The Viable Systems Model (reproduced from Beer, 1994, Fig 23, p. 131)

subsidiaries to a small company. For Beer, the most famous application of his ideas was when he was invited by President Allende to apply cybernetic thinking to the whole of the Chilean economy. This project, known as project Cybercyn, was organized by Beer through the creation of a complex network of computers, an electronic nervous system, which would run the economy and the text in which he introduced the notion of the Viable Systems Model, *Brain of the Firm* (1972), became the key document of the project.

Here we see Beer's depiction of the way he thought the human neurophysical system operated, with each level dealing with commands from the brain relevant to it.

The neurophysiological model of the human control system is translated into a model that could be used as a model of a viable system suited to the control of an enterprise (see Figure 5.14). In this model the action of the anastomotic reticulum is represented

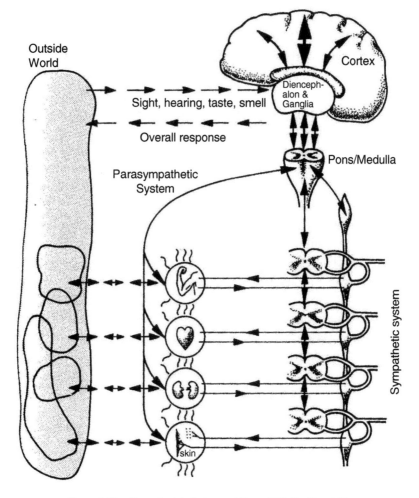

Figure 5.14: Neurophysiological control (Beer, 1994, Fig 22, p. 130)

across the whole of the enterprise, through the way that the decisions made at level four and five act as a means of formulating policies around decisions about what to take into account and what to leave out – effectively these decisions represent a reduction in variety. The resultant polices are communicated in a range of styles to the various levels across the enterprise as a means of exercising control. The form of communication is part of a kind of algedonic loop, which, in effect, are the channel filters that interact with the various communications sent to and received from each of the five levels. The communications in the form of reports pass back to level five. Should problems arise which will affect the enterprise as a whole then action is taken to change the behaviour of the system. But we have learnt that in order to have effective control our reporting system needs to be selective and information passed to level five which is appropriate for policy modification or affirmation.

Concluding Remarks

In this chapter we have provided some further elaboration upon influential work introduced in earlier chapters of the book. We have not attempted to deal with all of Systems practice, or provide a chronological history of the Systems movement, but to discuss applications of Systems concepts that we consider to be used extensively by members of the Systems community. We have looked at Forrester's view of social situations functioning as a complex feedback system for control, and how this grew into the field of Systems practice known as System Dynamics. We have given an overview of the influential work of Vickers, whose concept of an Appreciative system has underpinned much subsequent work, including the Soft Systems Methodology. The seminal work by C. West Churchman is discussed covering key concepts such as the setting of boundaries to define systems of interest in relation to their environments, and recognition that this crucially depends upon the viewpoint of the person whose interest is reflected. In this chapter we have built upon our review of Beer's model of a viable system that we began in Chapter 3. We have shown how complex systems such as organizations are in a constant state of flux and how Beer's model might help to design ways of maintaining internal control and find equilibrium. These have been the authors whose ideas have inspired two generations of Systems practitioners in their work. Many developments of these ideas have been generated through reflection upon their application in practice, but their significance and impact has yet to be surpassed.

PART III

THE CONTRIBUTIONS OF PHILOSOPHY AND THE SOCIAL SCIENCES

C hapters 6 and 7

These chapters are designed for the learner who wants to understand more about some of the origins of the ideas that underpin the methods and models discussed in the earlier chapters. These chapters suit those managers who wish to have a 'trail' to follow from the practice back to the theory and vice versa. The chapters are also written with the postgraduate researcher in mind who is learning about the framework of ideas which support a non-reductionist area of research.

CHAPTER 6

Philosophical and Sociological Influences

Introduction

Whilst this text is devoted to helping to improve practice it is inevitable that at some point we must turn our attention to some of the underlying ideas that are relevant to the approaches discussed within. Although many people like to refer to Systems as a meta-discipline, several of the methods and methodologies used in Systems practice do have their origins in other schools of thought. In earlier chapters we have looked at practical applications that have been developed within a particular philosophical frame of reference. These are examples of the application of ideas considered to be relevant across the disciplines. They illustrate the notion of an isomorphy of concepts that is at the heart of the modern Systems movement. Of course within Systems there are particular ideas about the way we make sense of the world that we need to think about too. In this chapter we will discuss some of the ideas relevant to the practical ideas that we use and provide a general overview of the Systems domain.

You will have learnt by now that Systems thinking and practice is in contrast to the way in which many of us have looked at things in the past, primarily because the methods of natural science and its intellectual tools of objectivity and reductionism dominate our education system, but are these Falsi Amici? This is not to criticize the methods of science and reductionism per se because they offer powerful intellectual and practical tools (it is after all why we enjoy so many comforts in the modern world) but such thinking is not always appropriate to all situations, particularly when the situation involves human activities. In this chapter we provide a brief overview of the evolution of modern Systems which is followed by a discussion of some of the key ideas that underpin some of the methods described in earlier chapters.

The Systems Movement

The beginning of modern Systems began in the 1920s when several scientists began to conceive of a General Systems Theory (to trace the ideas and development of modern Systems it is worth returning to the early work: Bertalanffy et al. c. 1940, 1950, 1956 and Sadovsky, 1991). The foundations of modern Systems theory can be said to be the result of collaboration between Von Bertalanffy, a biologist; Rappaport, a mathematician; Gerard, a physiologist; and Boulding, an economist. This collaboration resulted in a document announcing a Society for the Advancement of General Systems Theory, in the *Journal of Philosophy of Science* (1955, p. 331). Out of this came the International Society for General Systems Research which was formalized in 1956.

Before this, in the mid 1940s and early 1950s, there were a series of conferences that became known as the Macy conferences (1946–53). Participants at these conferences were leading scientists from a breadth of areas of study. In all there were ten conferences which have been defined under the heading *Cybernetics: Circular Casual, and Feedback Mechanisms in Biological and Social Systems* and sponsored by Josiah Macy Jr. The meetings that followed attempted to develop a universal theory of regulation and control that would apply across the disciplines. These were ideas that had resonance with the sentiments of Bertalannfy et al. It should be noted that it is not our intention to discuss in detail the outcome of these conferences or devote any space to the debate about the conferences and their contribution to cybernetics or Systems but to raise awareness of readers of this text of their place in modern Systems thinking. The conferences are important to Systems because their members attempted to engender discussions across disciplines and to break down the artificial barriers between areas of intellectual study. For those readers who wish to find out more about these conferences we refer you to the following web reference:

http://www.diaphanes.de/scripts/foreignrights/buch_englisch.php?ID=46

As a means of gauging the breadth of expertise we list below the names and area of specialism of the prime movers of the first conference:

Margaret Mead and Gregory Bateson, Anthropology;
Theodore Schneirla, Comparative Psychology;
George Evelyn Hutchinson, Ecology;
Julian Bigelow, Electrical Engineering;
Heinz von Foerster, Electrical Engineering;
John von Neumann, Mathematics;
Walter Pitts, Mathematics;
Leonard J. Savage, Mathematics;
Norbert Wiener, Mathematics;
Frank Fremont-Smith, Medicine;
Gerhardt von Bonin, Neuroanatomy;
Ralph W. Gerard, Neurophysiology;
Rafael Lorente de Nó, Neurophysiology;
Warren McCulloch, Neuropsychiatry;
Filmer S.C. Northrop, Philosophy;
Arturo Rosenblueth, Physiology;
Henry Brosin, Psychiatry;
Lawrence S. Kuble, Psychiatry;
Molly Harrowe, Psychology;
Heinrich Klüver, Psychology;
Kurt Lewin, Psychology;
Donald Marquis, Psychology;
Hans Lukas Teuber, Psychology;
Alex Bavelas, Social Psychology;
Lawrence K. Frank, Social Science;
Paul Lazarsfeld, Sociology.

The list of scholars indicates not just the wide range of disciplines but also the importance that this distinguished assembly placed upon these meetings. Details of the meetings can be found on the web at, e.g.

http://en.wikipedia.org/wiki/Macy_conferences

and

http://www.asc-cybernetics.org/foundations/history/MacySummary.htm.

For some this series of meetings was the foundation of modern cybernetics (Glanville, 2009). A perusal of the delegates at that first meeting reveals the names of many of the scholars who have had a direct influence upon Systems thinking and practice. At the meetings, especially the early meetings, the prime task was for the participants to find a means of communication because they came from such a wide range of specialist backgrounds. But the delegates did find a form of language that allowed individuals from the different fields to communicate about matters of significance. Useful references for an account of the meetings can be found in Pias, C. (ed.) (2003) *Cybernetics – Kybernetik: The Macy Conferences 1946–1953*, Diaphanes: Zürich/Berlin.

As we have indicated in earlier chapters, individuals born into the latter part of the 20th century have been involved in a system of education which compartmentalized our world into separate subject areas. This is so ingrained in us that it makes it difficult for some to recognize that these divisions are arbitrary. Checkland (1981, 1999) reminds us that it is not nature that divides itself into physics, biology, psychology, sociology and computing science, but mankind who imposes these divisions upon nature.

This section is headed 'The Systems Movement' but what is a 'movement?' The *Shorter Oxford Dictionary* says it is 'A series of actions and endeavors by a body of persons tending more or less continuously towards some special end' (Onions, 1980) and another definition is 'A series of actions and events taking place over a period of time and working to foster a principle or policy' (http://www.thefreedictionary.com/movement). The common denominator is that of working towards a special end or principle. If this is the case what is the principle the Systems community is working towards?

If we look back at Bertalanffy et al. and the Macy conferences there was a desire to find a common understanding; a desire to find an isomorphy of concepts which would span the different areas of specialism; a desire to find a 'oneness' within the processes of human inquiry. Systems thinking and practice is a conscious attempt to step outside artificial categorizations; it relates to all areas of intellectual curiosity and for this reason can claim to be a meta-discipline. It is an error to talk of 'Systems' as if it were a method of problem solving since this is to institutionalize the thinking and consequently clothe it in a straightjacket of intellectual demarcation (see Robb (1992) for an interesting discussion on the danger of institutionalizing Systems thinking).

Science and Systems

Now we get to the difficult bit! The status of science and its rationalistic orientation has a powerful influence over us – indeed as Winograd and Flores so aptly put it, it is '. . . the very paradigm of what it means to think and be intelligent' (Winograd and

Flores, 1986). Reductionist thought can be characterized by the following features: neutrality of methods/methodologies; objectivity in analysis; reality external to the individual; problem situation taken 'as given'; problem solving based upon optimization speed/efficiency/status. But when we are dealing with the complexity of human activities we find that this set of ideas creates a problem because human situations are complex and cannot be treated as rational. Judgements by humans are affected by and affect human experience. Humans appreciate value as well as fact. Our situation is ever re-forming with no eternal and universal laws of human behaviour. The analysis of any situation by the actors within will be different because each of our concerns is highly personal. Recognition of the validity of each interpretation implies the recognition of subjectivity which is at variance with the scientific model of objectivity.

Over the years the Burrell and Morgan (2005) classification of organizational theory and practice has been found useful to Systems thinkers. We must remember that the Burrell and Morgan diagram is a model of some ideas rather than a philosophical synopsis but it does summarize many of the ideas which Systems practitioners use when discussing different approaches to organizational investigations. For example, the relationship between subjectivity and objectivity is summarized nicely by Burrell and Morgan (2005, pp. 28–30) and in Figure 6.1:

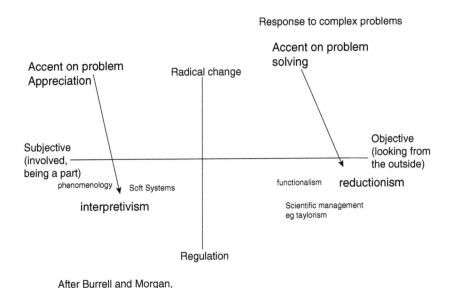

After Burrell and Morgan,

Figure 6.1: Burrell & Morgan's classification of organizational theory

One area where subjective appreciation is important is the business organization. It is not easy to gain insight into how an organization operates by observing it from the outside. To understand an organization we should seek to gain experience of how it operates by becoming a part of it: gaining subjective experience of its purpose. We can consider an organization as being made up by various social systems which themselves are in a constant state of change. The perception of a given organization by those that make it up will vary from a belief in its main task through to simply a means of providing an income and career. For those wishing to explore organizational behaviour then it is important that the tools used are capable of coping with the mixture of fact and opinion that exists within the interactions between individuals and social groups. The adaptive nature of organizations, in part the result of a reaction to operational and social exigencies, suggests that understanding of organizational change (which as an open system must happen because if it does not it will die) is best achieved by the involvement, the immersion of the inquirer in the problem situation. This proposition can be addressed through the adoption of the 'interpretive paradigm' as the intellectual theory underpinning inquiry. The idea of subjective experience being the basis of gaining understanding is a radical shift from the reductionist notion of objectivity.

The adoption of the interpretive paradigm is not without difficulty for both researcher and practitioner alike. Subjective involvement in a problem situation solicits criticism of bias and even lack of professionalism. But we must be aware that such criticisms are not exclusive to the interpretive or subjective methods of investigation as they are equally applicable to traditional methods of research and of practice. Aside from the hypothetical question whether there is any such thing as pure objectivity, even those that claim to be objective are susceptible to bias. It is not unreasonable to suppose that in some instances the orchestrator of an inquiry might unwittingly prevent undesirable consequences developing. The subjects of the inquiry have little or no control over the way that the activity is planned and conducted so too often the project is in the hands of the inquirer. The difficulty facing a Systems practitioner is a practical one because it requires being a part of the situation to become aware of events and to be able to explain them through perception and interpretation of actions. To acquire this kind of appreciation a practitioner needs to be able to adopt a framework of ideas, a philosophy, which provides and supports such interaction.

So 'What is a Systems Approach?'

Since the 1980s there have been attempts to 'classify' systems. We have referred earlier to the division between so-called hard and soft Systems approaches.

For those who categorize systems in this way, the term Hard Systems refers to the application of solid functionalist ideas such as System Dynamics; and Soft Systems refers to application of softer and subjective ideas such as AIM or SSM. Making a categorization such as this is met with dismay by many Systems thinkers and practitioners some of whom argue that hard Systems is a special case of soft Systems. There is merit in this view since what they mean is that investigating a system of interest may require the use of a model or a technique to help illuminate a particular aspect of the situation. Others have attempted to divide the subject into phases of development. For example, the suggestion of Midgley (2000) and latterly Leleur (2005) is that Systems ideas fall into distinct eras, with one idea being superseded by another. Whilst their categorization has some merit chronologically it is intellectually unconvincing. There are many questions to be raised about the motivation of these attempts, but to suppose that one set of ideas developed over many decades is exhausted and others have replaced them is open to question. It seems reasonable to argue that Systems thinking and practice have continued to develop over many decades and each new set of experiences have enriched rather than superseded previous thinking (see Stowell, 2009a).

For the purposes of this text we feel that the reader will benefit from an overview of some of the underpinning ideas which contribute to the way in which Systems practitioners and academics internalize and apply some aspects of the thinking. These ideas can be traced back into the main methods/methodologies we have described in earlier chapters.

Philosophy, Sociology and Systems

In the Systems community we hear people say that the practice feeds the theory and the theory feeds the practice. How then does theory feed Systems practice and what theory is it? Is it a single philosophy, is it a selection of ideas and is it possible anyway given the argument that Systems is a meta-discipline? There is some merit in the view that Systems should not stray into philosophy as most Systems practitioners are not philosophers and attempting to describe what we do in philosophical terms is open to criticism from those who are. But it is difficult not to acknowledge the impact that philosophy and sociological theory have had upon areas of Systems thinking and practice. For example we refer to scientific reductionism, interpretivism, functionalism, objectivity, subjectivity and hermeneutics. To this end in this chapter we will describe some important influences upon Systems without claiming it to be an expedition into philosophical discourse.

As we have said earlier in this text the importance of scientific rationalism in addressing problems and problem solving cannot be denied, but by now we should recognize that techniques found to be useful in the laboratory are often found deficient when used to address problems of a social nature. Objective inquiry and analysis, which is at the heart of reductionism, is not beyond dispute and the acceptance of the apparent deficiency of scientific rationalism for some areas of concern provides the motivation for what might be an alternative aporia but is the reason behind the discussion that follows.

We begin with an outline of hermeneutics because it is important to the thinking behind the account of action research described within this text. Hermeneutics also make a contribution to the way that we 'understand' our world. (For further reading see Gadamer (2004); Ricoeur (1988)).

Hermeneutics comes from the Greek *hermeneuein*, which means 'to translate' and from the Latin, *hermeneutica*. Hermeneutics is defined in the *Shorter Oxford Dictionary* as the art or science of interpretation, especially of scripture (Little et al., 1980, p. 956). Hermeneutics seeks to gain understanding from language, specifically written language, although in more recent times the notion behind (modern) hermeneutics extends to the ideas being used to gain insight into human events.

Traditional Hermeneutics

The intention of hermeneutics is the translation and interpretation of text that corresponds to its original meaning. Hermeneutics was developed from within Protestant theology in the 17th century as a means of gaining greater understanding of the scriptures. The first use of the term is attributed to Dannhauer (1603–1666) who proposed that three kinds of texts required interpretation: Holy Scripture, legal texts and the literature of classical antiquity (Mautner, 2000, p. 248). The purpose of hermeneutics was to provide both a correct and an authoritative account of the text that led to the criticism that '. . . hermeneutics was the art of finding something in a text that was not there' (Mautner, 2000).

A problem for hermeneutic interpretation is that words are polysemous, but the prime task is to produce an interpretation of a text that is unequivocal. In order to achieve this it became necessary to have a set of rules or techniques to produce an interpretation that can be said to reveal its true meaning. In order to interpret the meaning of a text the reader should be sensitive not only to the context of the message but the polysemy of words which mean that the interpreter needs to seek an unambiguous relationship with such words. The way in which this could be achieved meant that interpretation required each word to be understood via a set of questions and answers. A criticism is that this early sense of hermeneutical interpretation was restrictive because the route to interpretation concentrated upon the meaning of words rather than the whole sense of the text. The next significant development in hermeneutic analysis was from what has become known as Romantic Hermeneutics, so called after the German Romantics such as Herder (1744–1803) the poet and philosopher, Schlegel (1772–1829) the literary critic, and Novalis (1772–1801) the mystic, poet and philosopher; it was a period of thought which had a profound influence over the thinking and work of an important contributor to the development of hermeneutics namely, Friedrich Schleiermacher. The work and ideas of these poets, philosophers and mystics and the writings of Immanuel Kant (1724–1804) influenced Schleiermacher's intel-lectual contribution to the development of hermeneutical understanding.

Romantic Hermeneutics

Schleiermacher (1766–1834) was concerned with the nature of hermeneutic under-standing, which he described through the notion of the hermeneutic circle as the means whereby we gain understanding. He said that we '. . . understand the unity of the whole by the individual parts and the value of the parts via the unity of the whole' (Schleier-macher, 1998, p. 109 in Lawn, 2006, p. 46). Schleiermacher defines hermeneutics '. . . as the art of avoiding misunderstandings' (Gadamer, 2004, p. 185) because he recognized that understanding did not come automatically from reading a text – rather it was more likely to result in misunderstanding because of prejudice creating the anticipation of meaning. The key, he felt, lay in grammatical and psychological interpretation. Before Schleiermacher the translation of texts was either an exegesis of sacred texts (a critical interpretation or explanation) or a philology of classical texts (the study of written texts and establishment of their authenticity and their original form). The problem with this lies in the conflict between a grammatical interpretation of the text (which evokes the hermeneutic cycle of relating the part to the whole) and an attempt to understand the sense of the meaning that the writer sought to convey. There are practical difficulties too as we cannot gain understanding of the parts without understanding the whole. As Lawn (2006, p. 47) points out, Schleiermacher not only accepts this idea but also sees the circle (of learning) as ever expanding as the reader gains understanding.

Schleiermacher embraces the wider systems of understanding to include both cultural and historical context. Although his initial thoughts came down on the side of under-standing, where language is seen as an instrument for the means of communication, his later work attempts reconciliation between the two. Later researchers (e.g. Gadamer) criticize this attempt to reconcile the two because of the difficulties that grammatical interpretation implies. What he seems to be attempting is to gain understanding of the author's mind through what appears to be a form of reader/author osmosis. The difficulty with the idea is explaining how a reader is able to demonstrate that they were able to absorb the essence of the author's purpose.

Reaction to Romanticism

Dilthey (1833–1911) was critical of the romanticism of the previous work of Schleier-macher et al. (what we might call the German historical school); he sought an episte-mological basis for human sciences. Although influenced by the processes of science he distinguished between the concerns of the natural sciences, which he saw as hard science concerned with cause and effect, and the human sciences which he considered to be concerned with all branches of knowledge that are connected with the practicalities of human life.

The problem for hermeneutics that Dilthey raised is now concerned with connecting the text with its history, what we now call historicism. Dilthey sought a model of hermeneutics which reflected the way in which such models were being developed in the natural sciences. He moved away from Schleiermacher's concern with what we might now loosely call a form of psychoanalysis of the author, towards 'Verstehen', understanding through the recognition of the importance of the past and the way in which it shapes our understanding. His ideas evoke Schleiermacher's hermeneutic circle, but now through the way in which he linked our understanding of the present to its cultural past.

Dilthey's contribution to the hermeneutics tradition is by emphasizing the connection of the present to the past as part of our way of understanding. He expresses this by differentiating three classes of life: first, theoretical, e.g. concepts and judgements; second, practical, e.g. actions which are not meant to communicate anything, but reveal something about the actor and third, disclosure, e.g. expressions which disclose something about the individual (*Stanford Encyclopedia*, 2006 – web reference Plato. Stanford.edu/entries/Dilthey).

The way that humans gain understanding he referred to as elementary and higher understanding. To explain elementary understanding he called upon Hegel's elementary spirit, which embodies the everyday aspects of life. Higher understanding is required for hermeneutic analysis where inductive thinking supersedes elementary understanding, where the inquirer will call upon a variety of knowledge to make sense of the subject at hand. But this does not mean that it is limited to higher planes of contemplation as higher understanding also means the ability to focus. For example, higher understanding enables the reader to look at specific parts of a piece of work within the context of the whole and within the context of other work which may be of influence, of events which surrounded the author when the text or passage being studied was created, and events and influences surrounding the interpreter. Dilthey moved the emphasis of hermeneutics away from the psychological and grammatical emphasis of Schleiermacher towards the importance of cultural and historical influences.

Heidegger's Revolutionary Thinking and its Impact upon Hermeneutics

Despite attempts to move hermeneutic thought away from the criticisms of myth and dogma towards intellectual respectability it was still thought of as impossible, possibly due to the over-influence of Cartesian thought and methods of research in the natural sciences. It is to Heidegger (1889–1976) and his revolutionary ideas that we owe the re-orientation of hermeneutic processes. But first we must remind ourselves of the impact that Cartesian thinking had upon philosophy and the sciences.

Descartes set out to provide philosophical thought with the surety of natural science. He had argued that the only thing that is sure is that of being a thinking person, knowledge is an '. . . inner attribute of the individual knowing subject' (Lawn, 2006, p. 33). Descartes felt the need to rid himself of acquired beliefs and to find a means of satisfying curiosity that did not rely upon the processes of contemporary analysis. Descartes felt that personal contemplation of the physical and the mental 'reality' would challenge long held beliefs. This would lead to the realization that the only reality was that of one's own thought. From this realization he believed that investigation should rely on method. He was content that he had demonstrated that his method was apodictic; a clearly demonstrated concept. A simplification of Descartes' method is summarized as follows:

(i) Only accept what is true, that you know is the case – i.e. there are no doubts;
(ii) Break the problem in the smallest parts as necessary;
(iii) Address the easiest problems first; and finally
(iv) Make comprehensive lists to be sure that you have forgotten nothing.

The impact of Descartes' work was to provide a degree of certainty to the ways in which we gain understanding and was (is) influential upon the ways of inquiry. His ideas suggested that hitherto the foundations of knowledge were based upon opinions, speculations and unverifiable observations and as such offered little contribution to understanding and many opinions could be discounted as being mystical. Knowledge emanates from within and is sustained by reason alone which means, as Lawn neatly summarizes, '. . . any legal, religious, moral or political practices, which did not sustain themselves by reason alone, are immediately placed under suspicion as dark forces of reaction' (Lawn, 2006, p. 33).

Although Dilthey et al. had revealed the importance of history in the way that we gain understanding these ideas were still indebted to the methods of natural science. It is Heidegger who liberated hermeneutics from the search for a method parallel to the natural sciences to one that was defensible without the need to adopt the method of Descartes. Heidegger rejected both the epistemological and ontological constituents of Descartes' argument (see Cerbone, 2008, p. 33). His argument was that to have subjective experience of the world it must be preceded by something which itself cannot be subjectively interpreted as it is the thing which allows the subjective experience. He refers to this as *Da Sein*, sometimes referred to as a single word, *Dasein*. *Da Sein* means 'being here', 'here being', 'being there'.

Whilst *Dasein* means 'being' in the ontological sense it is both ontic and ontological, understanding of Being is itself a definite characteristic of *Dasein*'s being; '*Dasein* is ontically distinctive in that it is ontological' (Heidegger, 1967, p. 32). What he meant by *Dasein* being ontological is that it is '. . . being in such a way that one has an understanding of Being' (1967, p. 32), *Dasein* is always being engaged with the world. This argument is in contrast with Descartes' reasoning, which Heidegger felt to be flawed because it suggests that thought begins from introspection and is the basis of our knowledge. The Cartesian idea that thinking is an introspective act in which we turn in on ourselves in order to understand Heidegger rejected because he said that we could not be detached. We are '. . . presence-at-hand; in subsistence; in validity'. In *Dasein* (1967, p. 26) 'being' must be something of its own and different from other entities which it might seek to discover, '*Dasein* always understands itself in terms of its existence – in terms of a possibility of itself: to be itself or not itself' (Heidegger, 1967, p. 33). But the nature of Cartesian introspection means that as human beings we assume that we arrive with a clean slate, a tabula rasa, after which we develop understanding of the world. In order to be able to interpret our world Heidegger says that we need to be aware that certain things cannot be interpreted subjectively as '. . . they are the very things on which interpretations rely' (Lawn, 2006, p. 54). Lawn points out that the way in which Heidegger uses the hermeneutic cycle is because he thought that we use it in our everyday perception of the world. The way in which we have un-judgmentally absorbed the world that surrounds us is constantly working as we make sense of new situations (a similar point you might note is echoed by Vickers in his notion of the Appreciative system). Heidegger argued that we are 'there' as part of the world, being influenced and also influencing. It is through that existence that we are able to inquire about the world, which, in turn, reinvests itself in the way that we set about inquiring.

Heidegger's ideas were at variance with Husserl's phenomenology because he thought that Husserl's idea suggested a world in which we are able to remove ourselves from the entity itself and yet still be able to reflect upon it. For Heidegger understanding was not neutral (*Dasein* is not optional) as it is that which allows us to make sense of the world. We can describe Heidegger's idea as hermeneutical phenomenology, which as Cerbone explains '. . . makes explicit what is implicit, which thereby effects what was until then implicit, which then requires further interpretation, in this sense our route to understanding is circular' (Cerbone, 2008, p. 30). *Dasein* provides the basis of understanding, but how it understands is bound up in *Dasein*'s own being. It is on this point that Heidegger emphasizes the difference between the hermeneutic '*as*' and the apophantic '*as*' (Lawn, p. 56). The former refers to our involvement in the world, the way that we behave, whereas the latter is the form of our relationship to the world through language. The hermeneutic circle is the *interpretive* projection of *Dasein* upon the world in the form of individual projects and activities and the background *fore structure* that informs the projects and is in consistent movement with them (my italics, 1967, p. 67).

Heidegger's thinking moved hermeneutics away from the Dilthean idea of understanding the problem of the *other* to the problem of *being* in the world. He shifted hermeneutics from the problem of method (needing to understand the other) to that of *being in the world*. He breaks away from Cartesian logic through the recognition that the problem is not *being with* but *being in* the world and by so doing, as Ricoeur reminds us, Heidegger 'de-psychologises it' (Ricoeur, 1988, p. 56).

Philosophical Hermeneutics

As an erstwhile student and assistant to Heidegger, Hans-Georg Gadamer (1900–2002) was influenced by the arguments of his charismatic teacher. The fact that he was at first rebuffed by Heidegger is possibly the reason why Gadamer did not publish for many years. Although he became an established and respected academic in his own right the pupil–teacher relationship endured, much to the angst of many of his students. But it is Gadamer who continued to develop and enhance the ideas initiated by Heidegger into what became known as philosophical hermeneutics.

Gadamer argued that hermeneutics is properly known as the art of interpretation, because it is just that, i.e. interpretation, and as such we should remember that the process of interpreting means that we are a part of that we seek to explain. Gadamer's argument, like his mentor Heidegger, is that to view the world as if it can be observed objectively is not possible. To explain existence in an abstract form is to ignore the past and its part in the evolution of ideas and practices. He argued that human society functions through the tacit acknowledgement and acceptance of a common practice and purpose; it functions through evolving and continual development of social practices and not with reference to abstract theory. These ideas cast doubts on a major tenet of scientific rationalism, which assumes objectivity as the major plank in methods of gaining understanding. Gadamer's argument is that if what we observe is influenced by tradition, culture, physical characteristics and the like there can be no single explanation and no universally acceptable account. As a consequence we cannot ignore the influence of subjectivity and historicity. As a corollary of this the question 'what then is truth?' emerges.

Gadamer's major work, *Truth and Method* (*Wahrheit und Methode*), first published in 1960, is a description of the nature of human understanding in which the idea of Truth is addressed from what, some consider, relates to its Platonic origins (Lawn, 2006, p. 59). For Gadamer Truth corresponds to the way the world is and how we perceive it. Following on from Heidegger's notion of *Dasein* Gadamer was concerned with relating prejudice and tradition as part of the whole. Gadamer believed that it is tradition which is the basis of our prejudices which in turn creates the wherewithal of our understanding. This idea is a significant intellectual step in the development of hermeneutic thought as it challenges the idea of standing outside the ebb and flow of history. It is our immersion in the tradition to which we belong that defines our 'reality' and being in the world. An important distinction is being made here in that what we seek to understand is not, as Schleiermacher implied, a psychological act but '. . . a meaningful content which is immersed in a tradition of its own' (Thompson, 1983, p. 40). Gadamer's intention is not just to discuss the importance of historicity and culture but also the practicalities of the hermeneutic cycle.

Gadamer divides his text (*Truth and Method*, 2004) into three major sections. Truth as it emerges in the experience of Art, History and, finally, Language. First he addresses the problem of method and he begins by highlighting the influence of natural science over all other spheres of inquiry when he observes that 'The human sciences so obviously understand themselves by analogy to the natural sciences . . .' (Gadamer, 2004, p. 3). He then goes on to point out that the socio-historical world cannot be investigated using the deductive logic of the method of the natural sciences but at the same time he points out that the human sciences have no method of their own (we refer to a similar point made by Churchman earlier in this text you might recall). He questions whether method, based on inductive logic, is as important as other presuppositions. Aligning with the ideas expressed by Helmholz (1862) he draws attention to the importance of memory, authority and inference in gaining understanding and asks the question 'Does not what is scientific about the human sciences lie rather here than in their methodology?' (Gadamer, 2004, p. 7). This question is a dilemma for the human sciences because the reason for raising it is an indication that they do not fit into modern science and as a consequence create a problem for philosophy itself. Gadamer reflects upon understanding first through art.

Art: Gadamer says that trying to reconstruct what the artist had in mind is futile given the historicity of our being. What is constructed is not the original but a reconstruction based upon what the observer has absorbed from his/her history and culture. It is not possible to reconstruct the origins of the work of art because even returning it to its origins will not re-enact the original conception. What the artist created and what the observer makes of it, especially in a different time frame, will be different. By art we embrace both the visual and the enacted. Gadamer recalls Hegel when he says that the appreciation of art '. . . gathers all these individual gods and attributes of substance within one Parthenon, into spirit conscious of itself as spirit' (Hegel, quoted Gadamer,

2004, p. 161). Art then, he argues, forces us to reflect upon the aesthetics and history and it is '. . . the self consciousness of the spirit . . . comprehends the truth of art within itself *in a higher way* culminates in philosophy as absolute knowledge' adding that '. . . it is philosophy that carries out the hermeneutical task' (2004, p. 161).

History: Gadamer turns his attention to the role of history in relationship to romantic hermeneutics. Trying to gain insight into text through the dissection of language and, in Schleiermacher's case, understanding the psychology of the author too, results in using methods that are influenced by those of science. Hermeneutics, freed from the criticism of mysticism, now faces the difficulties that accompany scientific objectivity. Gadamer makes the point that we cannot ignore the influence of the past upon everything that we undertake. The exploration of historical facts he argues is a function of the questions themselves. He says that historical objectivism evokes the belief that the facts will speak for themselves but in reality they '. . . depend upon the legitimacy of the questions asked'. He goes further by saying 'When naïve faith in scientific method denies the existence of effective history, there can be an actual deformation of knowledge' (Gadamer, 2004, p. 300). This is strong stuff and a riposte for those who place great store in claims of scientific objectivity. Gadamer's point is that in interpretation there is a constant interchange between the past and the present as the reader attempts to make sense of the text. The point being made by Gadamer is that our knowledge comes from what we experience and learn, which is historical and, in acknowledgment of Hegel's notion of substance, it '. . . underlies all subjective intentions and actions and hence both subscribes and limits every possibility for understanding any tradition . . .' (2004, p. 301). It is here that we learn of what he calls the concept of horizon. Horizon is a range of vision that 'includes everything that can be seen from a particular vantage point' (2004, p. 301). The upshot of this is that someone without a horizon has no vision and consequently places most importance on what is immediately obvious to them. Someone with a horizon on the other hand has a greater appreciation of what surrounds them and what might exist beyond their horizon. What this means is that the views of the interpreter, the person who undertakes the unravelling of the matter, are not fixed as they are a part of what they seek to understand and influenced by the past in all its forms and the present – there is no neutrality, no objectivity. This is an important point as Lawn points out that what Gadamer is asserting is that there are '. . . no meanings external to current consciousness . . . meaning is always produced by a coming together of the immediate and the point of tradition one seeks to understand' (Lawn, 2006, p. 69).

Language: Gadamer's argument now turns to the importance of language to our understanding. Here he argues that language itself is what enables us to assimilate our world. He distinguishes between the world and the environment: it is language, he says, that gives our world definition. Humankind inhabits a world described through language which he differentiates from environment which is something shared by all living creatures. He says that the concept of world is created by humankind because '. . . language has no independent life apart from the world that comes to language within it. Not only is the *world* world only in so far as it comes into language, but language too, has its real being only in the fact that the world is presented in it' (Gadamer, 2004, p. 440). He says that *environment* is what is commonly used to define man's social existence in the world but considered in the wider sense, environment is somewhere that all creatures inhabit but the world belongs to man; '. . . man's relationship to the world is characterised by *freedom from environment*. This freedom implies the linguistic constitution of the world' (Gadamer, 2004, p. 441). It is only humankind that has a world within the environment, which is given shape for each individual by language. This is an important assertion as language is a social thing, created by interaction and a need for communication. We are referring not only to the attributes of man's creative ability and cultural credentials but to the spoken word. In short without language there is no world. Language for Gadamer, and Heidegger, is not merely to communicate, it is to exchange information in order to share what is held in common (Lawn, 2006, p. 82). This is not to be confused with a scientific approach to language such as Linguistics or Etymology. Gadamer is not saying that all is revealed through language rather that '. . . our understanding of the world is tentative, provisional, and never in a position to totally explain and understand being' (Lawn, 2006, p. 83).

This moves us on to the relationship between language and understanding. We do this through discourse, conversation, discussion, argument, and recognize the difficulty in gaining knowledge about something one does not know. Gadamer draws attention to the dangers that opinion has for the search for understanding. He says 'It is opinion that suppresses questions. Opinion has a curious tendency to propagate itself' (Gadamer, 2004, p. 359). He draws upon the Socratic dialectic which he says sets out to confuse the other discussant and as a consequence create the conditions for questions. In entering into a dialogue if understanding is to be achieved it is important that the participants do not talk at cross-purposes, and that the other person is on the same wavelength. Participants should be guided by the subject matter and this means that '. . . one does not try to argue the other person down but that one really considers the weight of the other's opinion. Hence it is the art of testing' (2006, pp. 360–361).

Gadamer follows the traditional view in that the spoken word has more authority than text. This observation also makes a distinction between the written word and the process of writing. The written word is considered inferior to the spoken word and Gadamer sees the task of hermeneutics as being to breathe life back into text in order to bring back the richness of speech and meaning. It is here that we begin to recognize difficulties. Because linking language, discourse and understanding, in this case to text, assumes a willingness between the participants to accept alternative views and a willingness to learn and exchange knowledge. Whilst it might be difficult to imagine a discussion about a complex narrative between two experts to provide the setting for a harmonious exchange of views, his assertion is not without credibility. Consider two friends dropped in a forest that they had played in 30 years before. They are given a route map produced when the forest was young and written in Latin and in Middle English. One friend understands Latin and the other Middle English. Their task is to find the shortest route out using the document and their previous knowledge of the forest. They would acquaint each other with the information contained in the instructions, discuss past experience and identify landmarks they knew as children and many other aspects that would enrich their appreciation of the situation. In a life threatening situation even though they may have different views about the best way to leave they would, eventually, agree on an exit strategy. The contribution of past experience and interpretation of the text will all serve to enrich their understanding. Whilst this is a somewhat trivial example it illustrates the way that two experts with a common purpose can enrich both their understandings about the matter at hand. The added complexity of different languages serves to illustrate the difference between the word as written, the translation and the context of the translation, in a sense the gap (*apechei*) between name and the utterance (*onoma* and *rhema*) (Gadamer, p. 409) The experiences and knowledge of the two experts become the currency of understanding, but only once they are internalized and appreciated by each person: this can only be achieved through discourse. It is appropriate here to reflect upon Gadamer's notion of a fusion of horizons.

Fusion of Horizons

Earlier in this discussion we referred to *horizon* as a range of vision that can see everything from a particular vantage point. Gadamer used that term because he felt that 'The concept of "horizon" suggests itself because it expresses superior breadth of vision that the person who is trying to understand must have. To acquire a horizon means one learns to look beyond what is close at hand – not in order to look away from it but to see it better, within a larger whole and truer proportion' (Gadamer, 2006, p. 304). Our horizon of the present is challenged by our appreciation of the past, and the fusing of these experiences provides us with understanding. In some respects this idea has resonance with the thinking behind Vickers' Appreciative System in which the mixture of experience and values, current happenings and the need to maintain a relationship with our environment provide us with knowledge for action. In this case what we seek to experience is a *fusion of horizons* which we work towards as we exchange knowledge with the 'other'. Gadamer has already pointed to the difficulties involved in discussion such as needing to keep an open mind and being prepared to accept other views. We have learnt that opinion is an enemy of understanding. One way to gain understanding is for the discussion to take the form of question and answer. What we seek in our discussion is to bridge the gap between what is said and what is understood by what is being said. We proceed by questioning what is being said in the form of Platonic dialectic. This is not to be confused with the Marxist idea of dialectic driven by contradiction and negation. Questions are at the heart of this discussion but the questions should be open so that the ensuing discussion is not about proving one or another is right but to gain insight. Gadamer's purpose was to provide a method and at the heart of this is dialogue with the intention that the discussants extend their horizons and through the encounter the horizons of the discussants are fused together. In this way we begin to understand what the 'other' is expressing and s/he will understand what we are expressing resulting in a fusion of horizons; 'To acquire a horizon means that one learns to look beyond what is close to hand – not in order to look away from it but to see it better, within a larger whole and truer proportion' (Gadamer, 2004, p. 304).

This brief discussion of Gadamer's philosophical hermeneutics will doubtless raise many questions such as those relating to the communicative aspects of art and beauty. But unless such questions can be articulated or written then they take their place alongside myth and the transcendental. The above is but a brief history of herme-neutics and is intended to trace the developments of 'modern hermeneutics' and no more. The intention is not to give an in-depth account of each argument – this can be found in the various references quoted within the above and listed at the end of this chapter – but a flavour of key ideas. Our reason for this is that hermeneutics and the thinking behind it, we believe, is important to Systems research and practice. We believe that a skilled action researcher will find some resonance with elements of hermeneutics described above and the less experienced researcher we hope will find that the discussion provides some guidance on the practice which, combined with one of the methods described earlier in this text, will provide a framework for action.

Interpretivism and Phenomenology

You will recall in various parts of the text we have referred to interpretivism and phe-nomenology as underpinning ideas behind some of the ideas and methods we have described. In many instances of Systems practice the ideas that we use recognize sub-jectivity and what effect that has upon inquiry and analysis. In this section of the chapter we will elaborate more upon these ideas touched upon earlier in the text.

Interpretivism

We have learnt that interpretivism is concerned with subjectivity and the need to understand the subjects' meanings. The category of inquiry that we call interpretivism relates to interpretive sociology and embraces phenomenology, symbolic interaction-ism, ethnomethodology and hermeneutics. Notable early contributors to this paradigm include Weber (1864–1920) and Durkheim (1858–1917).

The underpinning idea of interpretive sociology is that it rejects the claim that social acts and situations can be described through the use of reductionist methods. Interpre-tive sociology emphasizes the subjectivity of human perception and understanding. The approach '. . . emphasises that humans give meaning to social reality before decid-ing how they are going to act. These meanings must therefore be interpreted before social actions can be explained' (Bullock and Trombley, 2000, p. 442). Examples of the application of these ideas reveal themselves through the work of Checkland and his researchers at the University of Lancaster where so-called Soft, or interpretive, systems, have made such an important impact upon Systems thinking and practice over the past decades. Work by Checkland et al. created a means of applying the ideas and a tool for use in empirical research that acknowledges the importance of subjectivity whilst accepting 'reality'.

We can trace the formation of this kind of thinking to the writings of Kant (1724–1804), whose ideas in turn influenced Heidegger, Husserl and Gadamer and in the development of hermeneutics we discussed above. It is here that we need to reflect upon the ideas inspired, primarily by Kant, and the intellectual debate that surrounds phenomenology. We truncate the discussion here to those ideas that, hopefully, illu-minate the subtleties of what constitutes phenomenology.

Kant argued that our minds structure our experience of the world; we can never know the things in themselves (Jary and Jary, 1995, p. 346). Kant distinguished between phenomena and noumena. The former embody appearances which constitute our experience: noumena the things themselves and what we may think to be reality.

> Thus, on Kant's view, the most fundamental laws of nature, like the truths of mathematics, are knowable precisely because they make no effort to describe the world as it really is but rather prescribe the structure of the world as we experi-ence it. By applying the pure forms of sensible intuition and the pure concepts of the understanding, we achieve a systematic view of the phenomenal realm but learn nothing of the noumenal realm.'
> (Britannica, http://www.philosophypages.com/hy/5g.htm)

This idea leads us on to the development of the concept of phenomenology. Phenomenology is attributed to Husserl (1859–1938) who developed the notion of phenomenological reduction and pure phenomenology. The idea relates to the notion of phenomenology as philosophy; indeed Husserl considered all philosophical disciplines to be located within what he called pure phenomenology. He talks of phenomenological reduction by which he means suspending questions about the existence of the object and instead reflecting upon the experience that one has of it. Husserl says that his idea is a modification of Descartes' method (see above) '. . . by carrying it through purely and consequentially while disregarding all Cartesian aims . . . phenomenological reduction is the method for effecting radical purification of the phenomenological field of consciousness from all obtrusions from objective actualities . . .' (Husserl, 2002, p. 129).

But what does Husserl mean by reduction and pure phenomenology? These ideas mark an important distinction between his thinking and that of Heidegger. For Husserl phenomenology is about ignoring beliefs gained from our objective experience and what remains is the realm of pure consciousness. What we seek is to gain understanding of the shape, the *eidos*, of the thing in question: its essence. Husserl refers to pure phenomenology by which he means seeing the phenomena for what they are; '. . . by reflection as they are absolutely in themselves' (Husserl 2002, p. 130). This state of pure reflection is achieved by excluding objective experience of the phenomena; excluding every type of external experience, which he refers to as pure phenomenology; the science of pure consciousness. What Husserl is asking us to undertake is a form of eidetic reduction, which starts from concrete knowledge moving towards insight into the essence of the thing. This process involves neither induction nor abstraction, it is not dependent upon mental constructs or objective facts that are moved from perception into imagination, but the essence of the thing; the *eidos*, itself.

For some the above concepts may be difficult to grasp, or accept. For others they may raise questions about the inclusion of such ideas in a text purporting to be about the practice of Systems thinking. But to these we ask that you reflect upon the methods that you may have chosen to use, or may wish to use. In Soft Systems Methodology are we not suspending our knowledge of the real world when we work 'below the line' to develop our Root Definitions? In Appreciative Inquiry Method are we not attempting to ask the participant to describe the parts of which the central element represents the whole? When we attempt to create a composite map are we not asking the participants to authenticate it before we move on? Do we not attempt to tease out the undeclared as we use interpretive ideas to seek to understand individual commodities of power? This section of the text is included to assist us to get the best from these methodologies and ideas we chose to use.

If we return to Husserl's pure phenomenology, we might be tempted to write it off as lapsing into solipsism in that it appears that we can include anything that our imagination might conjure up. But his idea is that the phenomenologist moves '. . . from evidence in the perceptual sphere to evidence in the imaginative sphere'. . . and so doing '. . . he can arrive at the invariable and essential structure of the object' (2002, p. 130). How is this achieved? Husserl addresses this through his notion of empathy and its relationship to knowledge. What he means by empathy is putting oneself in the position of another, but this does not mean taking the position of the other but rather absorbing what it means to be 'other'. Gadamer sums up this idea well and provides us with another illustration of what he means by horizon. The meeting of horizons and '[t]ransposing ourselves consists neither in the empathy of one individual for another nor subordinating another person to our own standards; rather it always involves rising to a higher universality that overcomes not only our own particularity but also that of the other' (Gadamer, 2002, p. 336). What Husserl is saying is that we empathize not from our own experience of a phenomenon but by inhabiting it as 'other'. He says that we experience the world as an intersubjective world and we experience others as other subjects (Hermberg, 2006, p. 34). This is an important point and one that addresses criticisms of his ideas such as those of solipsism.

It is Husserl's notion of empathy then that defends pure phenomenology against criticisms of solipsism. Empathy is '. . . one's experience of another subject on the basis of something else – the Other's[1] body and behaviour' (Hermberg, 2006, p. 34). So what we are saying is that we empathize within the world through intersubjective experience. We experience other (people) as other subjects, empathy '. . . is that which makes possible an intersubjectively Objective world', '. . . The intersubjective world is the correlate of the intersubjective experience, mediated, that is through empathy' (*Ideas* 420, cited Hermberg, 2006, pp. 35–36).

In pure phenomenology what we are attempting to recognize is the essence of an Object. Aristotle referred to the essence of something as the 'what it is' or the 'what it was to be'. In a similar vein Husserl asks that we seek to recognize 'what it is' as part of the phenomenological experience. Take for example a mermaid. We cannot know what one is because they do not exist. They are a creation of imagination. However, we would know one if we saw one, but how can this be? What we attempt to do is to gain understanding of the shape of the thing in question; something that all will recognize. In this case what it is to be a mermaid. But this raises the question, if it is possible to arrive at such an understanding, and we are inclined to believe that it is, then does this not mean that this pursuit is similar to that of the scientist, namely

---

[1]Capital O is used within translations and critiques of Husserl's work to differentiate between objective, lower case o, as objects experienced and Objective being there for everyone (see Hermberg 2006, for a more complete discussion pp. 8–10).

the search for objective knowledge? Husserl acknowledges this but sets it apart by reminding us that our understanding of the world is achieved only through intersubjectivity; unless something is also experienced by other people there is a chance that it may be a mere illusion. He says: 'The naïveté of talk about objectivity which completely ignores experiencing, knowing subjectively, subjectivity which performs real, concrete achievements, the naïveté of the scientist concerned with nature, with the world in general, who is blind to the fact that all the truths that he acquires as objective, and the objective world itself that is the substratum in his formulas is his own *life construct* that has grown within him, is, of course, no longer possible, when *life* comes on the scene.' (Gadamer, 2002, p. 241): an effective challenge to the idea of objectivity. Husserl refers to life world, by which he means a world within which we are absorbed and is the pre-given of our experience. Our experience of the world relates to our subjective experience of it and as Vickers observed it is in constant state of turbulence. Husserl's notion of life world is, as Gadamer points out, the antithesis of all objectivism, it is a world '. . . in which we live as historical creatures' (2002, p. 239), it is a world which we share and involves interaction with others.

How does Husserl's phenomenology differ from Heidegger's and what influence did this have upon Gadamer?

Heidegger's Phenomenology

Husserl's notion of phenomenology says that we concentrate upon our experience as we experience it and leave to one side what may have created it or its relationship to the wider world (Cerbone, 2008, pp. 15–16). Let us remind ourselves of Heidegger's notion of *Da Sein* (*Dasein*) which was to influence Gadamer's thinking and his notion of philosophical hermeneutics. We recognize that their acceptance of the subjectivity of experience cannot be divorced from Kant's philosophy (*Critique of Pure Reason*, 1781) as Heidegger also uses the idea of 'empirical intuition'. For Kant this meant that we are directly acquainted with real objects and phenomena are mental contents. We should be mindful that this idea should not be confused with the Cartesian transcendental realism in which real objects are not considered to be mental contents but these are things that we do not experience. This is not what Kant is advocating, what he referred to as transcendental idealism is that we have subjective representation of such things and without the intuition we have for physical things.

Let us take as an example an object such as a miniature version of Rodin's sculpture *Three Burghers of Calais*. Imagine the model is placed in front of a viewer but it cannot be moved. The observer will see the front but can only imagine the reverse; other observers might have a different viewpoint and all observers will have varying amounts of knowledge about Rodin, the statue, the model, the era and so on. The physical presence of the model is real – it exists and can be appreciated – but everything else is a function of our thinking, our imagination and is open to subjective reasoning.

Heidegger's argument is that we do not come into the world a *tabula rasa* but develop an appreciation of the world, as Vickers (1983) suggests, as a continuous flux of events and ideas. However, Heidegger's contention is deeper than this. He argued that '. . . before we can actually interpret the world we need to be aware of the fact that certain things cannot themselves be interpreted subjectively as they are those very things on which interpretation depends' (Lawn 2006, p. 54). What do we mean by this? This is a complex argument but what he means is that we make sense of the world through three interacting factors: fore-having (loosely meaning prudence), fore-sight (something we see in advance) and fore-conception (the way in which we have decided to conceive it) (Heidegger, 2002, p. 191).

Unlike Husserl, Heidegger conceives an account of the world as something shaped by our 'being in' the world and in some respects inherited understanding, the '. . . world has . . . a pre-ontological *existentiell* signification' (Heidegger, p. 289) whereas Husserl perceives it as something which stimulates our senses as we experience it. He says that '. . . pure phenomenology draws upon pure reflection exclusively, and pure reflection excludes, as such, every type of external experience and therefore precludes any copositing of objects alien to consciousness' (Husserl, 2002, p. 129).

It is Husserl's phenomenology that has a direct impact upon the ideas and practice of Soft Systems Methodology, which has been said to owe its philosophy to Husserl and practice to Schutz (1899–1959) (see Schutz 1966, 1970).

Gadamer would not have considered himself a phenomenologist but there is no doubt that his thinking about phenomenology had some influence upon the development of his ideas. Gadamer's notion of philosophical hermeneutics owes at least part of its naissance to the intellectual positions occupied by Husserl and Heidegger. Gadamer's ideas along with Husserl have influenced both Client-led Information Systems Creation (CLICS) and the Appreciative Inquiry Method (AIM) which we discussed in preceding chapters.

Critical Systems

As we indicated earlier this chapter is limited to philosophical influences upon methods and methodologies described in the preceding chapters and in particular the influence of phenomenology and hermeneutics. But there have been attempts to incorporate ideas to Systems practice from other areas and to this end we now turn to an area of Systems thinking and practice referred to as critical systems. Although critical systems embraces interdisciplinarity this approach to Systems practice takes on a different world-view to the ideas that support the Soft Systems methods and methodologies.

First, we must differentiate between the common usage of the word 'critical' and that used within the critical systems community. The *Shorter Oxford Dictionary* defines critical as 'given to judging' (Onions, 1980) and in the *Dictionary of Philosophy*, critical theory is defined as being a '. . . theory determined by an interest in human emancipation and so committed to seeking radical change' (Mautner, 2000, p. 116). It is an important difference as I am sure that you recognize but it is also indicative of the different interpretation that the current proponents of critical systems use. On the one hand we are thinking about giving comments or making a judgement of something and on the other we are seeking to affect sweeping change. In the latter case it would seem that the thinking behind this idea is diametrically opposed to the preceding discussion in which we learn that phenomenology is about describing our experience as it is and independent from the influence of sociologists or politicians. Critical theory takes a view that the world is as it is because those that have power control the many without. The pillars of our society such as science and industry, it is argued, reinforce the status quo in order to sustain the dominance of the possessor.

The origination of the term critical theory within philosophy and social literature is not clear, as there are many claimants. But there can be little doubt that the term first appeared through the work and writing of Horkheimer in the 1930s and 40s, in which he and co-author Adorno (1903–1969) ventured an interdisciplinary theory intended to transform the theories of Marx and Hegel (Horkheimer and Adorno, 2002). But other claimants to the term include Popper (1972) who says '. . . The method described may be called the critical method. It is a method of trial and the elimination of errors, of proposing theories and submitting them to the severest tests we can design' (Popper, 1983, p. 16). But the predominant ideas behind the critical systems practitioners relate to the idea of radical change and to the stream of thinking that emerges from the Institute of Social Research[2].(ISR). At the risk of oversimplification the ideas that emerged from the ISR which gave rise to the notion of critical systems are those embedded in critical theory and based on the notion that the social world is unjust and should be changed.

The Development of Critical Theory

We can support the assertion that critical theory emerges in the 20th century from the Frankfurt school of neo-Marxism and includes writers such as Horkheimer (1895–

---

[2]Institute of Social Research founded in 1923 affiliated to the University of Frankfurt – the stream of thinking is also referred to as the Frankfurt School.

1973), Marcuse (1898–1979), Adorno, (1903–1969) and then moves on to what is referred to as the second generation theorists which includes the influential work of Habermas (1929 to the present). The present generation is represented by Axel Honneth (1949 to date) who is Professor of philosophy at the University of Frankfurt and director of the Institute of Social Research.

It is not the purpose of this text to add to the critical theory literature, but to explain, as simply as possible, the influence of these ideas upon some Systems thinkers and practitioners. Where possible texts and papers written by scholars of critical theory are consulted, as well as relevant publications of critical theorists and practitioners who have shaped these ideas.

Critical theory has been described as having a narrow and broad meaning and it is difficult to divorce the social aspirations from the interpretation of these ideas. For example, Moran and Mooney (2004) point out that the critical thinker Foucault, like Marx, no longer wanted to interpret the world but to change it. Indeed for Foucault power was always in the hands of the minority and his declared aim was to free history from the grip of phenomenology (Gutting, 1996, p. 263). Capra (2003) echoes this sentiment when he says 'Their ultimate task, according to Habermas, is to uncover the structural conditions of people's actions and to help them transcend these conditions. Critical Theory deals with power and is aimed at emancipation' (2003, p. 69). For the purpose of this discussion we will look briefly at the phases of thinking which represent critical theory and then focus on the ideas of what many consider to be the most influential exponent of critical thinking and who seems to have influenced those who incorporate these ideas into their Systems practice, namely Jürgen Habermas.

Frankfurt School

As indicated above the Frankfurt School can be thought of as being represented by three generations of critical theorists, the first generation being that of Horkheimer and Adorno. Horkheimer became the director of the Institute of Social Research in 1930 and was elected Professor of social philosophy at the University of Frankfurt in the same year. The pre-war and war years he spent in exile in the United States. The years spent in America confirmed his view that society accepted the status quo because the capitalist culture and industrialization acted to manipulate and control the population whose state of well-being was further reinforced through the fictional outcomes of contentment created by the movie industry.

During the time that he occupied these positions there were seismic social and political changes in Germany and eventually the whole world. It is against this backdrop and it has to be said through the influence of Marxism that Horkheimer's ideas of critical theory were expounded. For Horkheimer social theories merely reflected what were passed off as facts. He thought that the way of thinking about the world and the methods by which we shield ourselves from the undesirable effects of the environment are instrumental and a means to an end. For Horkheimer critical theory had to be critical, that is the theory should not just be about theory but lead to practice. (It is worth drawing attention to an interesting footnote in Midgley, 2000, p. 139.) In this case '. . . not just to bring about correct understanding, but to create social and political condition more conducive to human flourishing . . .' (Finlayson, 2005, p. 4).

Horkheimer saw the prevailing quest for knowledge as being calculating and instrumental resulting in the subordination of human beings to the needs of an insatiable economic system and to the endless pursuit of progress. There is, he felt, no reflection upon the cultural influences in which theories evolve and how their tenets are to be applied. During their time in the USA Horkheimer and Adorno (who became the Institute director in 1958) wrote the *Dialectic of Enlightenment* (1947), which became the guiding force for the emerging critical theory. In this publication they contend that human emancipation that is based on perceived benefits of scientific discovery, medicine and industry has in fact created a world in which inequality, terrifying weaponry and political suppression is accepted. Their answer to this apparent hypocrisy is that reason has become irrational and that emancipation can only happen through a '. . . radical break with merely "formal" rationality and merely "instrumental" thought' (McCarthy, 1988, p. 20). The essence of reason, they argue, is to control and dominate. They felt that the drive to harness nature created a scientific ethos that enslaved and that '. . . overcoming . . . scientism was the precondition for restoring Marxist theory as critique' (McCarthy, 1988, p. 20). For Horkheimer critical theory is not value neutral, it is diagnostic and remedial. The corollary to this is that the practices developed from this theory are de facto invasive too, which is in contrast to Churchman and Checkland's argument that the method of inquiry should be agnostic to the problem situation (see Chapter 5).

Habermas' Contributions

Habermas is considered to be a second-generation Frankfurt school critical theorist who has made a significant contribution to critical theory. His corpus of work in the form of numerous texts and papers are an important source of inspiration to critical thinkers and it is not possible to do justice to it in the short space we have allowed here, neither is it the purpose of this section of the chapter. We instead confine our commentary to areas that are related to methods reported in this text and pay particular attention to the notion of communicative action.

Habermas' initial work revisited Horkheimer and Adorno's concerns and although much is shared by Habermas, he felt that their critique of modernity and reason was too all-encompassing. For example, *reason* for them is thought to be instrumental: that is to say manipulative and domineering. He considered that this thinking would ultimately lead to a cul-de-sac as the thinking that they criticize can also be said to have enabled them to draw these conclusions. Habermas felt that human beings gain and use knowledge in more than one way and to this end he was concerned not so much with the possession of knowledge, but with how it is obtained and how it is used. From a social scientific point of view Habermas considers language as a medium for coordinating action and '. . . [t]he fundamental form of coordination through language . . . requires speakers to adopt a practical stance oriented toward "reaching understanding," which he regards as the "inherent telos" of speech' (Bohman, 2009). This is what Habermas refers to as communicative action and is what he describes when participants agree to cooperate and have mutually acceptable goals, '. . . in which there is ". . . an intersubjective communality of mutual comprehension, shared knowledge, reciprocal trust and accord . . ."' (McCarthey, 1988, p. 290) which can be described as communicative action involving consensus and understanding in what has been said. But there is a problem here; we question is this not merely reinforcing the way things are now? Are we really able to free ourselves from what might be considered to be constraints of the cultural mores of the society in which we belong? Habermas sees this as a problem of rationality because through rationality we reinforce the status quo. (*Rationality in Philosophy* refers to the exercise of reason; the way that humans come to conclusions. 'In practical sense adaption of means to an end' (Mautner, 2000).)

Communicative reason is intersubjective and relies upon a foundation of shared understanding. To achieve shared understanding we use language as the means by which we communicate our thoughts. This process Habermas describes as communicative action, '. . . communicative action succeeds insofar as the actors freely agree that their goal (or goals) is reasonable, that it merits cooperative behavior. Communicative action is thus an inherently consensual form of social coordination in which actors "mobilize the potential for rationality" given with ordinary language and its telos of rationally motivated agreement' (Bohman, 2009).

As a means of describing this process Habermas called upon the ideas of the English philosopher Austin (1962) and what he called the speech act. Austin made three distinctions of speech: locutionary, that is speech that has a direct conventional meaning; illocutionary, something we are to do, and perlocutionary, which refers to something we do because of something else. Habermas considered the illocutionary speech act to be the most important because this, he says, is the way in which individuals establish a relationship; it enables us to present a face of sincerity to those with whom we wish to engage. In addition to facilitating understanding the act of communicating serves as the means of socialization and social control. He asserts that the '. . . communicative acts serve the transmission of culturally stored knowledge . . . cultural tradition reproduces itself through the medium of action orientated to reaching understanding . . . social integration also takes place via this medium . . . Communicative acts serve the construction of internal controls on behavior, in general, . . . socialization processes takes place via linguistically mediated interaction' (Habermas, 2004, p. 63).

Now we need to consider how communication and control interact and what critical theorists consider as being legitimate control. Habermas talks of the legitimation deficit: the difference between justice and legitimacy. We can say that where there is bias towards legitimacy it is at some cost to justice; but what do we mean by justice? In this instance for something to be justified it is because everyone in the legal community agrees to it. This does not mean that the legal profession alone takes responsibility for a norm to become legitimate; it means that *all* who are concerned must have accepted it. Finlayson (2005, p. 116) says that what is meant by the legal community is '. . . anyone capable of lawful behaviour whose actions are covered by the law in question'. How then does the legitimacy fail or become deficient? Habermas argued that legitimation deficit is when the administrative processes fail to satisfy the normative structures that are implicit in his notion of legitimate justice. This is where the administrative processes become the instrument of the political and the dominant Social system. (For a full discussion of this complex argument see 'Legitimation Problems', McCarthy, 1988, chapter 5). There are three areas of influence over society which Habermas defines as: scientism, modern art and universal morality; of these the greatest social influence is that of religion. He suggests: '. . . through communicative action can the energies of social solidarity attached to religious symbolism branch out and be imparted, in the form of moral authority, both to institutions and to persons' (Habermas, 2004, p. 61). Culturally, society is influenced through the 'norms' communicated passed through speech.

Habermas sought a way of divorcing reason from the strictures of language and social communication and, in particular, a way of overcoming what he saw as the influence of religion over the way that individuals and groups act: what we might call a post-metaphysical way of action and reasoning. His concern was how individuals might engage in an exchange of views and reach understanding in a post-metaphysical society. So how does the listener interpret what is being said and how do those who seek to communicate free themselves from what Habermas considers being instrumental in reinforcing the status quo? Here he talks of the speech act (2004, p. 120) in which the speaker and listeners use a reference system relating to (i) the objective 'normative' world – in which true statements are possible, (ii) social world–interpersonal relations and (iii) subjective-world–real-world experiences of the speaker. Communicative action '. . . relies on a cooperative process of interpretation . . . Coming to an understanding means that participants . . . reach an agreement concerning the validity of the utterance' (2004, p. 120). This does not mean that the hearer has to validate each of the three conditions but uses the legitimacy of one to reflect upon the others. For example, if the speaker comes across as insincere then the listener will doubt the value of the utterance irrespective of the content relating to each of the other two. Communicative action is when a participant agrees to what is heard s/he implicitly accepts the other two components or contests what is being said.

So truth for Habermas seems to be a function of the validity of the utterance, as he says that '. . . the concept of truth combines the objectivity of experience with a claim to the intersubjective validity of a corresponding descriptive statement . . .' (2004, p. 72). In other words the acceptance of what the speaker has to say relies upon the hearer reflecting upon the validity of what is being said in terms of its claim to truth (objective world), the speaker's plausibility (social world) and the credibility of the speaker (the subjective world) thereby 'testing' the validity of its claim to be true. Thomassen (2010, p. 30) proposes that it is through self-reflection that emancipation is achieved, '. . . because they and their social context will become transparent . . .'. How does this work? If we reflect upon the earlier discussion, we said that norm legitimization depends upon universal assent so non-acceptance of what is said will provoke a response and as such incorporate other views. But there is a practical problem with this assertion as it assumes an appropriate and large enough audience can be found, enough time made available for all views to be aired and the expectation that it will result in a universal consensus. So it is no surprise that we learn Habermas refined his view of truth (2003a) in that '. . . truth is realist in holding that the objective world, rather than ideal consensus, is the truth-maker. If a proposition (or sentence, statement) for which we claim truth is indeed true, it is so because it accurately refers to existing objects, or accurately represents actual states of affairs' (Bohman and Rehg, 2009).

For practitioner and theorist alike there is an expectation that in any group situation it is rare to find an immediate consensus. There is, at best, a period of debate and sometimes head-on disagreement which raises the question of emancipation and power. Nowhere does this show up more than when considering boundary definition. How do we agree on where a boundary, whether that be a physical or intellectual boundary, should be? It is not the intention at this point to open a discussion on power – a future text perhaps – or enter into the Foucault and Habermas debate but merely to raise this issue. In other sections of this text you will have noted that some authors have attempted to address such problems, e.g. Stowell and Ulrich and you have hopefully by now grasped the different underlying philosophy embedded in these ideas.

Third Generation Frankfurt School

We are conscious that we have excluded many influential critical theorists but deliberately limited our review to the Frankfurt School and its most influential theorists. The current director of this prestigious seat of critical theory is Axel Honneth (1949 to date), whose work focuses on power and recognition. As we indicated above, despite the discussion of emancipation which, de facto, is about the exercise and effect of power, we have chosen not to discuss the philosophical arguments surrounding power at this juncture. Our reason for this is that we feel that it would divert the readers' attention from the purpose of this chapter. That is not to minimize the importance of power; on the contrary, we feel that by not entering into a discussion within this text it serves to highlight its importance.

Critical theory and its relevance to Systems has divided opinion but its contribution cannot be disregarded because at a minimum it highlights the difficulties for the practitioner when attempting to understand 'what is' and 'what ought' to be the situation. The summary of critical theory summarized by Bullock and Trombley has some resonance with the thrust of this text when they point out that '. . . Despite its popularity critical theory resists some central features of post modernist thought retaining "modernist" commitments to logical analysis and the need to provide liberationist struggles with an objective grounding. It thereby retains both its Marxist legacy and (especially in Habermas) the traditional ambitions of the "modernist" Western enlightenment project' (Bullock and Trombley, 2000, p. 185).

Concluding Remarks

As in the case of phenomenology and hermeneutics there is a considerable literature surrounding critical theory but we can find no satisfactory definition of 'critical Systems' as such. Presumably because it is still being formulated or one does not yet exist. For example, Bammer (2003) defines it as aiming '. . . to combine Systems thinking and participatory methods to address the challenges of problems characterised by large scale, complexity, uncertainty, impermanence, and imperfection' (Wikipedia, accessed 2011): a definition which could apply equally to all Systems thinking and practice. A further search on the web reveals 'life critical' and references to computer-based 'safety critical' systems. Critical theory, like phenomenology, is an importation of some aspects of a philosophical treatise into Systems thinking. It is debatable whether it should be called critical Systems just as it is debatable whether we should use the title phenomenological Systems.

As discussed earlier in this chapter, although there have been some attempts to define critical Systems as the latest in a wave of Systems ideas, we do not find this a helpful categorization. We prefer to consider each of the ideas as part of the whole. Systems thinking and practice has benefited from many strands of ideas and contributions from different schools of thought over the past decades. Indeed the early founders of modern Systems were concerned with Systems as a meta-discipline where other ideas are embraced in the spirit of what the founders refer to as an isomorphy of concepts. We prefer to think of Systems as an idea which subscribes to the notion of wholeness and as Systemists we encourage the use of tools appropriate to the concept of wholeness to help gain insights into complex issues and situations.

You will have noted that there are some important (perhaps crucial) areas of shared interest in the work of Gadamer and Habermas. This is particularly so in the case of language, both written and spoken. There is however, a serious disagreement between the two and it is one reason for including both these influential philosophers in this text. Habermas considers the impact of historical and capitalist beliefs upon society. He sees the manipulative aspects of capitalism, technology and religion as impediments to a harmonious society and the basis of conflict and the crises that are part of modern life; his ideal is '. . . to dissolve obsolete prejudices and overcome social privileges through thought and reflection' (Gadamer, 2004, p. 570). You can be excused for imagining critical systems to be a means of fulfilling the political agenda of critical theory in particular. Habermas' aim is to challenge fallacious argument and expose what he considers to be truth with the objective of emancipation and social change in keeping with the traditional, albeit evolved, Marxist heritage.

In some areas Habermas and Gadamer have similar expectations of emancipation but it is in the underlying belief of what makes up 'the world' that they differ. Gadamer in his riposte of Habermas' criticisms draws attention to the danger of '. . . glib manipulation and incapacitation of reason . . .' and his belief in the ability of gaining understanding through persuasion (Gadamer, 2004, pp. 570–571). Gadamer's notion of hermeneutics is based upon a belief in the ability of human beings to understand which in turn helps to develop understanding, '. . . In truth hermeneutic experience extends as far as does reasonable beings' openness to dialogue' (2004, p. 570). Emancipation relies not upon the destruction of the cultural beliefs prevalent in society but upon the natural evolution of traditions and ideas and above all the ability to exchange and accept other views. The notion of a fusion of horizons is to accept that the interlocutors should recognize and attempt to divorce themselves from their opinions. To deny this possibility is to deny the importance of tradition in developing society, as it depends on being made conscious and openly debated. Gadamer challenges such an assertion as being *tantamount* to a defence of the status quo. He points out that dialogue is '. . . the structure of verbal understanding and characterised it as a dialectic of question and answer' (2004, p. 578). In this exchange the participants recognize their own opinions (*Weltanschauung* if you will) and attempt to lay them to one side in pursuit of understanding.

In this chapter we have excluded many significant contributors such as Kierkegaard, Foucault, Derrida and Popper as well as more recent contributors such as Giddens and many current authors. We have also limited our brief discussion to core texts of the key figures in hermeneutics and critical theory. This is because our intention in this chapter is to provide a brief account of ideas which we consider to be key to modern Systems practice rather than an introduction to sociological and philosophical theory. If this chapter opens a debate about Systems thinking and practice within the Systems community then we feel that it will have served its purpose.

CHAPTER 7

Systems Research

Research: The act of searching for or after a specified thing or person: Inquiry into things

(Bullock and Trombley, 2000)

Before embarking upon empirical research it is important for the researcher to be clear about their intellectual position. They should be clear about their position in the intellectual universe, so to speak. For many researchers the dominant paradigm of reductionism inhibits thinking outside the toolbox that accompanies the scientific method. As Winograd and Flores (1986) acutely observe 'Science, is the very paradigm of what it means to think and be intelligent' making alternatives difficult to contemplate. But as we have pointed out in this text the methods of natural science are not always suited to the kinds of complexity that characterize human social interaction and so in this chapter we consider a method more suited to Systems research, namely Action Research.

We start the journey by reminding ourselves of the origins of the methods favoured by natural science. Most of us will have been taught that the way that we approach problems is to break things down into smaller components. The English Franciscan friar William of Ockham, c. 1288 – c. 1348, advocated this idea which was based upon the argument that the explanation of any phenomenon should make as few assumptions as is possible and eliminate those that make no difference in the observable predictions of explanatory hypothesis or theory. This notion, popularly referred to as Ockham's razor, has had a significant impact upon the way that we attempt to unravel difficult problems.

But it was Descartes' highly influential treatise 'Discours de la Méthode' (1637) that laid the foundation stone of the method of modern science that still predominates today. Simply stated, Descartes method consists of four stages:

(i) Only accept as true what you know is the case – i.e. there are no doubts;
(ii) Break the problem down into the smallest parts necessary;
(iii) Address the easiest problems first; and finally
(iv) Make comprehensive lists to be sure that you have forgotten nothing.

Descartes' work was to provide a degree of certainty to understanding. His ideas suggested that the foundations of knowledge hitherto had been based upon opinions, speculations and unverifiable observations and as such offered little contribution to understanding. The key to Descartes' thinking was his belief in the power of reason and that his method was true.

The impact of these ideas upon what we might think of as the modern scientific method was enhanced with the establishment of the Lucasian 'Chair of Mathematic' in 1663. Notable incumbents include Isaac Newton and latterly Stephen Hawking. But it was the advent of state education (Education Act, or Forster Act, of 1870) in the UK that provided the infrastructure for the dissemination of what we can call a reductionist or scientific approach to problem solving. Methods of reductionist practice began to yield important discoveries, which have, and are making, a significant impact on our lives (it has to be said not always for the better!). However, the success of this approach has become so persuasive that other approaches to understanding complexity have declined and attempts to revisit the way that we approach the understanding of problems have had difficulty in gaining respectability.

Nevertheless, in recent times there has been a growing awareness that certain aspects of scientific rationalism are deficient when addressing some areas of our concerns, particularly those involving human interaction. Moreover, there is a realization that wider, rather than narrower, perspectives might be helpful in gaining understanding of some of the current problems we face. For example, we are increasingly aware of the damaging effects that our actions are having upon the planet; the recent global economic crisis has also served to heighten our awareness of the interconnectedness of all things. For example, the continuous development of technological artefacts combined with market forces are acting to accelerate our consumption of raw materials and are creating major problems for the disposal of waste. An example of the latter problem is the mobile telephone, which is now a telephone, a camera and a fashion accessory; it is a *must have* item for most people on this planet. The changes in fashion and the attractive developments in technology provide an easy way to encourage people to discard the old in exchange for something new. Yet how many consider the impact of this enormous consumption of materials and minerals, some of which are rare, or the problem of waste disposal on a scale never experienced before?

Whilst the importance of reductionism in addressing problems and problem solving cannot be denied we should recognize that techniques found to be useful in the laboratory are often found to be deficient when used to address problems of a social nature. Objective inquiry and analysis, which is at the heart of reductionism, is not beyond dispute and a counter argument for Descartes' reasoning can be found in the writings of Heidegger (1889–1976), in particular his notion of *Dasein*.

Dasein means 'being' in the ontological sense. He argued that *Dasein* is always being engaged with the world which is in contrast with the reasoning of Descartes, who made thinking an introspective act; turning in on ourselves. Heidegger argued that we are 'there' as part of the world and being influenced by and also influencing it. In other words we cannot be dispassionate observers. Gadamer (1900–2002) took these ideas further and argued that in hermeneutics, which is essentially interpretation, we should remember that we are a part of that which we seek to explain. The thrust of the argument is that to view our world as if it can be observed objectively is not possible and to explain existence in an abstract form is to ignore the past and its part in the evolution of ideas and practices. Gadamer argued that human society functions through the tacit acknowledgement and acceptance of a common practice and purpose, and through evolving and continual development of social practices and not with reference to abstract theory. These ideas cast doubts on a major tenet of scientific rationalism, which assumes objectivity as its major plank in methods of gaining understanding for areas involving human society. If what we observe is influenced by tradition, culture, physical characteristics and the like there can be no single explanation and no universally acceptable account. As a consequence we cannot ignore the influence of subjectivity and historicity. If we accept this argument then we need to consider methods of inquiry that embrace this view: non-reductionist methods.

By non-reductionist methods we mean those that recognize the importance and effect of subjectivity in any situation. We accept that such methods are open to the criticisms of lack of rigour and validation, but we argue that it is possible to have checks and balances appropriate to this paradigm. For example, in Chapter 3 we expressed a view of organization based upon the notion of maintaining relationships and learning. To view an organization like this implies a different mind-set to that related to the traditional view and to organizational problem solving. In order to gain understanding of complex situations we need an approach capable of embracing a view such as that expressed in Chapter 3 and of the wider dimensions of social problems. In this chapter we describe the notion of 'action research' and its relevance to carrying out a subjective inquiry and analysis. Whilst this chapter offers an 'academic' argument for the use of action research it will also show how the theory and practice of this kind of inquiry can be brought together and provide a practitioner, be they academic or manager, with a means of 'learning and finding out'.

Research and Reductionism

The central notion of positivist empiricism is that situations are 'set up' and an attempt is made to observe objectively the manipulation of variables by value-neutral techniques. This idea of course relates to the Cartesian idea of method and realism. A challenge to the positivist, reductionist, empiricist perspective is to accept its deficiencies and recognize that there are other ways of addressing complex issues. There have been many researchers who have questioned the positivist philosophy because such an approach does not easily translate across to all aspects of inquiry within the social sciences.[1]

Stowell and West (1994, p. 121) in their text *Client-Led Design*, provide a useful summary of what they refer to as the positivist empiricist perspective. They cite Maturana (1978, p. 28) who offers a summary of positivist empiricism, which he argues is concerned with the following:

(i) Observation of a phenomenon that, henceforth, is taken as a problem to be explained;

(ii) Proposition of an explanatory hypothesis in the form of a deterministic system that can generate a phenomenon isomorphic with the one observed;

(iii) Proposition of a computed state or process in the system specified by the hypothesis as a predicted phenomenon to be observed; and

(iv) Observation of the predicted phenomenon.

We can consider these key points when we think about inquiring into problems of a social nature since we recognize that:

[1]NB There are numerous examples of similar discussions including: Lewin, 1948; Weber, 1949, 1964; Emery and Trist, 1965; Berger and Luckmann, 1966; Gadamer, 1975; Checkland, 1981; Reason and Rowan, 1981; Lincoln and Guba, 1984; Winograd and Flores, 1986; Checkland and Scholes, 1990; Jackson, 1991; Stowell and West, 1994; Champion and Stowell, 2003.

(i) Human situations are complex;

(ii) They cannot be treated as rational since

(iii) Judgements by humans are affected by human experience;

(iv) Humans can appreciate the value of a situation as well as a factual description;

(v) The situation is ever re-forming (Vickers' flux of events) and there are no universal laws of behaviour;

(vi) An analysis of situation by participants will be different (validity of interpretation) and the concerns of those involved are highly personal.

In the afterword to Gadamer's excellent, although dense, text *Truth and Method* (2004) he takes up the point about methodological purity. He points out that fore-understanding impacts itself on all research and the researcher's position can be found in the results of the research. He says 'In a time when science penetrates further and further into social practice, science can fulfil its social function only when it acknowledges its own limits and conditions placed on its freedom to manoeuvre' (Gadamer, 2004, p. 556).

In the following discussion we review those areas of the practice within positivist science which have been identified by researchers such as those listed above as being inappropriate when transferred to particular aspects of social science and in particular inquiry into social situations.

Objectivity and the Notion of 'Reality'

If we think about Heidegger's notion of *Dasein* we can think of it, for the sake of simplicity, in terms of ourselves as a part of the world that we seek to understand. Being a part of that 'reality' means that we bring with us knowledge of what went before and that we possess the ability to presume what might result from what we see. But experiments based upon reductionist methods are in contrast with this idea; they are designed to test a given hypothesis, which is the basis of positivist empiricism incorporating the notion that the 'observer' is outside the influence of the experiment. It is the observer who can control and manipulate variables in the situation being tested so as to be able to define general laws that explain it. This presupposes that the 'observer' is neutral and can objectively analyse and manipulate the experiment without influencing its behaviour. The view that the world consists of 'things to be discovered' is one favoured by researchers in the natural sciences but it is inappropriate when transferred to some areas involving social interaction. To suppose a universal consistency of human behaviour as individuals or in groups is fraught with difficulty. As we indicated in previous chapters the view of social reality adopted in this text can be described as nominalist; universals do not exist. By that we mean that we view 'reality' as a product of an individual's consciousness; so-called universals are considered to be abstract entities and each person's 'real world' is a function of their take on their existence. Research into human situations based on objective observation is one that is difficult to support. By adopting an approach in which the situation is observed from outside, so to speak, we are making an assumption that the entity or 'thing' observed can be expected to behave in a 'knowable' or predictable way, and our research will yield results that can be repeated anywhere; much as adding sodium to water in Milton Keynes will have the same effect if repeated in Boston. But to apply reductionist methods to the study of human beings is deficient, '. . . unlike objects in nature, humans are self-aware beings who confer sense and purpose on what they do' (Giddens, 2001, p. 640). In other words the outcomes of human social systems are difficult to predict and the actors cannot be relied upon to behave in the same way even when confronted with the same situation; there are no universal laws of human behaviour. Moreover as Mayo observed, in the well-documented Hawthorn experiments (1949), the presence of the researcher will influence the behaviour of the actors in the situation. You will also realize that you, the researcher, will (i) interpret the situation (ii) be aware of the potential for the method itself influencing the outcome and interpretation.

By now you will be aware that the researcher/practitioner should possess the knowledge and skills of an organizational analyst and be capable of taking on the role of guiding and directing the inquiry. But as we have warned this should not be done by the imposition of models and technological constraints, but through the practice of an appropriate mode of inquiry with a policy of full client involvement. Intervention into the social setting cannot be ignored since it is where most Systems research takes place and it is most likely to affect the behaviour of those being observed. It is for this reason that emphasis is placed upon the need for the researcher/practitioner to recognize themselves as a participant in the situation rather than an outside observer. '. . . [A]ll human understanding is ultimately interpretation. A perspective of the world is always just that; it is never an unmediated picture of the way things really are, it is necessarily provisional and limited and can never be a view of the way things really are because the way things are is as illusory as the philosopher's stone. What we must never forget is that we are always a part of what we seek to understand . . .' (Lawn, 2006, p. 39). Moreover, our involvement in the system of interest will disturb the 'system' being investigated and act to influence its behaviour.

In questioning the applicability/appropriateness of scientific principles when undertaking research involving human actors we begin to see the significance of discussions and concepts put forward in previous chapters. We have argued that an approach based upon the reductionist methods where there is an assumption that social systems conform to a uniform set of behaviours is unlikely to yield as rich an understanding as one which recognizes complexity. In Chapter 6 we reflected upon Gadamer's argument that we cannot ignore the influence of the past upon everything we undertake and he makes a point germane to research where he says '. . . when naïve faith in scientific method denies the existence of effective history, there can be a deformation of knowledge' (Gadamer, 2004, p. 300). In their text *Client-Led Design* (1994) Stowell and West discuss a similar point about the relevance of history and research that is key to the ideas of Sir Geoffrey Vickers. Stowell and West say that '. . . the concept of "history" (in terms of both events and ideas), is central to the notion of "Appreciation"'. Vickers argues that it is through interaction with the continuous interacting flux of events and ideas that actors develop their judgements of reality and value, which in turn enable the individual or group to make decisions about appropriate action (Vickers, 1965, pp. 100–101) (Stowell and West, 1994, p. 123). The point being made here is that for inquiry such as those found in a business enterprise, it is important that '. . . the researcher . . . views each business organisation as a product of its own particular history and as a consequence thinks of each business as being unique' (1994, p. 123). As such the method of inquiry, and subsequent design and development, should also be capable of embracing this view rather than take it as given.

Scientific Rationalism and Objectivity

As we have discussed earlier, the methods of research used in the natural sciences have been widely adopted in research involving human actors. For example, research undertaken within the fields of psychology, cognitive science, management science and computing science. But there is a body of research that has developed based upon finding the means of gaining a subjective appreciation of human behaviour. These researchers follow the direction of early social thinkers such as Weber and Durkheim. Influenced by the Kantian notion of freedom and autonomy and the revolt against positivism and the support for subjectivity Weber created the basis of modern methodology in which he attempted to question objective positivism and the role of subjective value judgements. Although accepting that observation of human behaviour could be described numerically he recognized that understanding what this might be rested upon a subjective interpretation of meaning and values. Following on from this perception there has developed a body of research that can loosely be described as being interpretivist: for example, ethnography, Soft Systems and participatory approaches to problem definition. This tradition of understanding through engagement includes a long line of researchers stretching back over several decades.[2]

---

[2]Researchers such as Berger and Luckmann, 1966; Garfinkel, 1967; Schutz, 1970; Giddens, 1976; Checkland, 1981; Lincoln and Guba, 1984; Silverman, 1985; Heron, 1990; Stowell and West, 1994; Ulrich, 1994; Schwandt, T. 2000; Reason and Bradbury, 2008.

Reductionist method embraces the notion of objective observation, designed experiment and the value-neutrality of methods used to conduct the research (e.g. questionnaires, structured interviews, surveys, personality tests). But as we have pointed out earlier the choice of methods will have a direct influence upon the outcome of the investigation. You will recall in Chapter 5 (p. 112) we drew attention to Churchman's comment about the value neutrality of the method that the method chosen should not '. . . function according to the basic principles of its own design' (Churchman 1971, p. 249), in other words it should not require the situation to fit the requirements of the method used.

We have offered criticism of positivist empiricism not because it has failed but to draw attention to the fact that it does not lend itself to understanding the complexity that human social problems generate. The way in which functionalist models are sometimes used as a means of generating information about a problem situation does, as Susman and Evered pointed out, tend to leave much unknown about the problem situation that can often be explained through what the actors involved describe as 'intuition, hunch, interpretation' (1978, p. 586). Checkland makes the point about the deficiencies of reductionism in gaining insight into the complexities of human society when he says that '. . . the method of science, so powerful in the natural sciences, has not yet, and will not easily be applied to the investigation of social phenomena' (Checkland, 1999, p. 71). If we agree that methods based upon objectivity are deficient for examining social phenomena then the approach that we chose to intervene in such situations must be capable of addressing such difficulties. The potential value of knowledge gained from 'within' is offered by the method of action research, which offers the opportunity to develop 'a deeper understanding of the organisational values, encourage consideration of new organisational forms, and facilitate recognition of clues to the new forms the organisation might take' (Susman and Evered, p. 586). Such an aim can be seen as an attempt to maintain the focus of attention upon the total problem situation and its environment (Clark, 1980, p. 153).

A researcher who adopts the method of action research focuses upon understanding the everyday action of those involved by being a part of it – *Verstehen* – rather than observe behaviour dispassionately from the 'outside'. One difficulty for the researcher is how to record their experiences. This difficulty can be addressed to a large degree through the method of inquiry which is used. For example, in Soft Systems Methodology the research can be recovered though the Rich Pictures and ensuing models. In the Appreciative Inquiry Method the researcher's pathway might be recovered through the systems maps and resultant models. Some action researchers attempt to address this problem by note keeping and even recording the situation in some way. However, we can argue that by doing so they are incorporating a degree of positivism in their research. Attempts to formalize the conduct of the research tend to move it towards positivism; for example, Eden and Huxham propose 15 characteristics of action research and despite this '. . . they fail to provide any means of establishing the validity of the learning outcomes . . .' (Champion, 2001, p. 65).

The criticism is often made that non-reductionist research lacks integrity and rigour. One reason for this criticism is that we do not offer a means of validation and verification of our results because we consider them inappropriate, preferring instead the notion of 'authentication' (Champion and Stowell, 2003, p. 27). Authentication places the credibility and acceptance of outcomes upon those most affected or concerned. Checkland also proposes that by declaring a framework of ideas in advance of the work undertaken A/R will have academic rigour (Checkland, 1985; Checkland and Scholes, 1990). This proposal was extended by Checkland and Holwell (1998) who suggest that a way of achieving this is by 'recoverability'. That is to say an interested person ought to be able to 'recover' the research process after the event. In addition to this Champion and Stowell propose the use of the mnemonic PEArL to support '. . . reflection upon the enquiry process' (Champion and Stowell, 2001, p. 3; 2003, pp. 28–33).

Compare the approach of subjective appreciation of human society to that of scientific empiricism. Here we find the formulation and refutation of hypotheses to be a fundamental part of inquiry accompanied by what seems to be a nihilistic view of any other approach to the study of human behaviour (e.g. Popper, 1959; Plutchik, 1974, pp. 180–181; Schwartz and Jacobs, 1979, pp. 3–4; Checkland, 1981, pp. 50–58, Giddens, 2001, pp. 697–698). We see that accompanying the idea of testing hypotheses is the notion of repeatability as it is seen that only by the repetition of an experiment and the observation of identical results can 'scientific knowledge', or 'truth', be established (Checkland, 1981, p. 53). Closely associated with the notion of repeatability is that of measurement since measurement allows values from experiments to be recorded and repeated. The more specific and definable the measurement then the more successfully we can compare results. A result of this situation is described by Checkland when he explains: 'Hence the potentially most powerful scientific facts are those expressed as the quantitative results of experiment' (1981, pp. 54–55).

If we consider the above within social systems intervention, it presupposes that first of all, human actors behave in identical fashion in the same circumstances and second, that all aspects of human action can be accurately and sufficiently measured in quantitative terms. Qualitative measurements are far more difficult to deal with and, consequently, recognition of the need to use them is often countered by an attempt to quantify them by further breaking down the elements into definable and measurable chunks (e.g. goals). It is worth noting that as levels of quantification increase, so too may margins for error. Undertaking research in social situations in a similar way to that undertaken in a laboratory is fraught with difficulty. As Checkland (1989b) points out human consciousness and the ability to act on impulse make it difficult to replicate any situation (pp. 38–39). Because it is difficult, some say impossible, to quantify human action in all its possible combinations it suggests that inquiry into human activity should include qualitative as well as quantitative measurements.[3]

Scientifically proven knowledge generally develops from within its own framework of knowledge, reinforcing its own theoretical foundations and methods: positivist science 'is itself a product of the human mind' (Susman and Evered, 1978, p. 586). Gadamer (2004) points out that 'they (the representatives of critical rationality) are so caught up in the methodologism of theory of science that all they can think about is the rules and their application' (p. 559 – our parenthesis). He points to the importance of what he calls productive prejudice as a contribution to understanding and by implication objectivity denies the researcher the opportunity to gain a full understanding. There is no single answer to be discovered from objective inquiry; things are changing continuously. A similar point is made by Popper who says that all knowledge and learning and the method of science 'consists of the modification (possibly the rejection) of some form of knowledge or disposition, which was there previously' (1983, p. 71). Kuhn (1962), makes the point in describing the way in which formulation of hypotheses to be refuted in scientific research are consistent with current accepted knowledge which makes particular investigations meaningful. He describes the body of acceptable knowledge that influences scientific research as a 'paradigm' which from time to time undergoes shifts that influence the choice of hypotheses and the direction of useful research. In a practical sense, positivist empiricism seems to have become the de facto standard for research into our world, whether natural or man-made. Winograd and Flores (1986, p. 16) argue that this is a direct result of what they refer to as the 'prestige and success of modern science' and the 'deep-seated pre-understanding' of what science is.

The lesson we must learn from the previous arguments is that the way in which we select and use the methods and techniques can never be neutral since through our involvement we bring our own understanding and interpretations, fore-understanding, to bear upon their application. If we reflect upon these arguments we then begin to question the neutrality of the methods we chose and the notion of objectivity. As Gadamer points out 'The very idea of a situation means that we are not standing outside it and hence are unable to have any objective knowledge of it' (Gadamer, 2004, p. 301).

---

[3]e.g. Lewin, 1948; Weber, 1964; Garfinkel, 1967; Schutz, 1970; Blumer, 1975; Schwartz and Jacobs, 1979; Reason and Rowan, 1981; Lincoln and Guba, 1984; Gill, 1986; Cooperrider and Srivastva, 1987; Stevens, 1990; Checkland and Holwell, 1998; Champion and Stowell, 2003.

Positivist researchers rely on models that are then used to structure an inquiry which results in the acquisition of knowledge relevant to the model and not necessarily to the problem situation (remember Churchman's warning about the value neutrality of the method?). In many instances such models are inappropriate to social inquiry because they force the situation into the framework of the method and concentrate upon the identification of activities that relate directly to it. Even where the use of a 'soft' approach has been attempted it is not uncommon to find it has used it as a recipe rather than a framework to help to gain insight and appreciation of the situation. Functionalist models concentrate upon the identification of activities that relate directly to the model used and to the 'reality' that they are supposed to represent rather than to the reality perceived by those involved. In questioning the appropriateness of 'reductionist method' for all areas of social inquiry some researchers have sought an alternative framework for research which is more suited to the 'interpretive' character assigned by such researchers to areas of social science. A framework for research resulting from this concern has become known as 'action research'.

Action Research as a Framework for Systems Research

It should be clear that we favour an interpretive approach to Systems thinking and practice and it follows that we support a method of inquiry and research that could relate to this point of view. As you will have learnt, Systems thinking is about taking a holistic view of things. It is not just that Systems thinkers attempt to take into account the wide perspective of what interests, but they use ideas which allow them to concentrate upon the system of interest without losing sight of the wider implications of their inquiry. In many respects Systems research has much in common with Gadamer's idea of philosophical hermeneutics. You will remember in Chapter 6 that we discussed this idea and the cycle of learning (which is similar to that of action research in that the research recognizes that understanding) is a never-ending process. As with Systems thinking the whole is understood in relationship to its parts and the parts in relationship with the whole.

The notion of action research can be traced to two sources. The first to Kurt Lewin (1948), of the University of Michigan, USA, and the second the Tavistock Institute of Human Relations in Britain. We first became aware of the term when Lewin, with his roots in Gestalt theory, described the process as 'rational social management'. Lewin describes research needed for social practice as a type of action research, a comparative research on the conditions and effects of various forms of social action, and research leading to social action. For Lewin, research that produces nothing but books will not suffice (Lewin, 1948, 202–203). Action research 'proceeds in a spiral of steps each of which is composed of a circle of planning, action, and fact-finding about the result of the action' (1948, p. 206). The idea of a circle shares much in common with the hermeneutic circle (e.g. Schleiermacher, 1766–1834, Dilthey, 1833–1911, Gadamer, 1900–2002; see Chapter 6) and was offered by Lewin as a practical means of carrying out the two main concerns of the action researcher. First, the practical concerns of people in an immediate problematic situation; and second, the goals of social science by joint collaboration within a mutually acceptable framework. Rapoport and later McTaggart (1996, p. 248) make an important observation. Rapoport says that '. . . it is a mistake to think that following the action research spiral constitutes "doing action research" . . . action research is not a "method" or a "procedure" for research but a series of commitments to observe and problematise through practice a series of principles for conducting social enquiry' (Rapoport, 1970, p. 499). In other words they are emphasizing the importance of involvement. However we might take issue with the verb 'observe' preferring instead 'be a part of'. We share Champion's view that:

> . . . research within social situation ought to be characterised by those involved in the situation participating in the inquiry process and collaborating with researchers . . . These characteristics have become accepted in the literature, as standard elements of inquiry within an Action Research framework' (Champion, 2001, p. 63).

Lewin's ideas influenced the work of researchers at the Tavistock Institute, where it is acknowledged on the Institute's web page which states 'An important and ongoing early influence was Kurt Lewin and his pioneering action research approach which is used at the Institute, both in the research-based approach to consultancy and in the often engaged and learning-focused evaluation studies' (Tavistock Institute of Human Relations, 2011). However, the two approaches were different in practice – as Stowell and West point out (1994, p. 127), the main difference between Tavistock and Lewin was that the latter's work was more academic in orientation, with close links to experimental psychology, while the work of the Tavistock Institute was more orientated to the practical need 'to get collaboration from members of an organisation while attempting to help them solve their own problems' (Rapoport, pp. 500–501).

The tasks of client participation and problem ownership are at the heart of action research – an idea which is based upon a cycle of learning in which all concerned are enabled to gain understanding of the depth and scale of the problems and opportunities that exist within the situation of interest. Researcher involvement is an essential part of this process in which the researcher engages and interacts with the clients. For Gadamer understanding is always part of a dialogue through which understanding emerges. Lawn sums up Gadamer's argument thus, '. . . meaning conforms not to the logic of the proposition but to the logic of question and answer' (Lawn, 2006, p. 98). In other words the proposition contains the viewpoint of the proposer and it is through the resultant questions and answers that understanding is achieved through the interchange of ideas and knowledge. Checkland (1983, 1985) suggests that thinking about the world and experiencing the world are equal in importance and together they create a cycle of learning that helps to make sense of new experiences. We can liken this to Husserl's 'life world – *Lebenswelt*' that emphasizes the importance of living in the world. As Hermberg (2006) puts it *Lebenswelt* underlies every intentional act (p. 74). If we accept this it means that the action researcher becomes actively involved in the situation of interest and engages in conversation with other participants in order to gain that understanding. The engagement with the participants is important as Champion points out: 'For the research to be judged as being *useful* . . . the research was tackled in a manner that is perceived *by others* to have been a credible effort undertaken with due care and attention' (Champion, 2001, p. 65).

An important point to remind the reader about action research is that unlike other methods of inquiry, e.g. Actor Network Theory, it does not view human actors as 'objects' of inquiry but as 'purposeful systems' that can initiate changes of ideas and action and can choose to behave 'capriciously' (Checkland, 1989b, pp. 38–39). This is a move away from reductionist methods that place importance upon objective observation, emphasizing instead, '. . . the individuality of human actors, and of groups of actors, and highlights the need to view each new problem situation as a result of its own context and history' (Stowell and West, 1994, p. 131). That is to say adopting the notion of *Lebenswelt*, which is the world of lived experience that emphasizes the importance of sharing human experience, in which the 'artistic, historical and lingual is construed as designating the reservoir of meaning . . .' (Ricoeur, 2004, p. 592). It follows then that each inquiry should be treated as a unique experience and the researcher should avoid imposing preconceived ideas about similar situations upon it. As we have already commented action research is 'hermeneutics in action' and as such its prime purpose is to create an environment in which participants can learn and exchange ideas and experiences about the situation of interest as a means of addressing its opportunities and threats.

The Framework of Thinking

The action research cycle offers a means of reflecting upon the development of theory from the experience of doing, and the development of practice from a sound theoretical base. The influential paper by Susman and Evered (1978) in which they describe the stages of action research suggests five basic elements, namely: (i) diagnosing, (ii) action planning, (iii) action taking, (iv) evaluating and (v) specifying learning (see Figure 7.1).

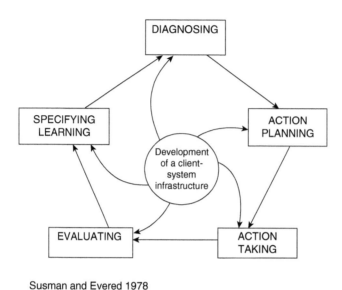

Susman and Evered 1978

Figure 7.1:   Action Research as a Cyclic Process (Susman and Evered, 1978, p. 588)

It is important to recognize that the steps are iterative and the framework should not be used as if it were a step-by-step technique. The outcomes of research into social situations cannot be predicted and so the method of research used within the A/R cycle should be one which is not predicated on a particular kind of outcome, or desired end. This is an additional 'burden' for the action researcher in that it is necessary to ensure that the planning stage and outcomes are undertaken such that they will bear scrutiny from a wider audience. The researcher is faced with the twin dilemmas of demonstrating rigour and at the same time avoiding restricting the cycle of learning that is at the core of action research.

Central to action research is that the theory/practice cycle is a means of learning about a situation and acting collaboratively upon this learning in order to address the problems and opportunities that the system of interest offers. The iterative process, that is an important feature of action research, represents an important difference to the research practices of positivist empiricism and '. . . a move away from the methods of scientific enquiry that value "objective observation" and "measurable results . . ."' (Champion, 2001, p. 66). We can describe the process of action research as a method by which knowledge about a particular situation is acquired by an individual or group through the process of interacting with that situation. It is important to note that A/R is about learning and we should be mindful of the importance of discussion and dialogue in this process. Here we take Gadamer's view:

> To conduct a conversation means to allow oneself to be conducted by the subject matter to which the partners in the dialogue are orientated. It requires that one does not try to argue the other person down. But one really considers the weight of the other's opinion. Hence it is the art of testing. But the art of testing is the art of questioning. (Gadamer, 2004, p. 361)

We must remember that in conversation there is as much unsaid as said, which underlines the importance of dialogue as a means of achieving a fusion of horizons as we engage with others' views about the topic of interest. This knowledge is then used to develop strategies for addressing issues relevant to that particular problem situation. But participation is not without criticism as the influence of power and authority within any social grouping can surface difficulties that require '. . . great sensitivity and tact . . .' (Checkland, 1999, p. A20).

Of equal importance to the process of learning are the practical outcomes that the participants consider to be important. For the research to be deemed a 'success' the ideas should be surfaced that are deemed appropriate to the expressed concerns. Action research is where '. . . knowledge is produced and reality modified simultaneously; each occurring due to the other' (Oquist, 1978, p. 145). It will be clear to you now that action research involves the continued development of an individual's understanding of 'reality' created by reflecting upon the cycle of previous action and, in turn, reflecting upon this action. In their book *Client-Led Design* (1994), Stowell and West draw attention to Oquist's explanation of the relationship between practice and theory in which he says:

> Action by itself is not of value without the consciousness which allows humans to purposely interact with their physical and social environment. Action without thought is meaningless . . . theory and practice are dialectically related in that they conform a unity of opposites. One necessarily implies the other. (1975, p. 158)

A prime purpose of action research then is to promote meaningful and appropriate action (or practice of that theory), the results of which add to the theoretical knowledge about social theory and to the knowledge about the given situation that will help indicate the action to be taken (Stowell and West, 1994, p. 130).

The approach to A/R described here has synergy with Systems ideas that we believe is suited to undertaking empirical research. It provides a method of learning about the situation within a 'cycle of learning' that helps to raise the awareness of the clients' appreciation of the situation of interest and involve them in a partnership (see

Figure 7.1). Participation in the inquiry process provides a platform for all participants to bring their own areas of expertise to the debate.

As you think about the learning cycle that takes place in the process of inquiry the question 'How then do we know when to stop?' springs to mind. It has been argued that the 'completion' of a study is when its outcome is accepted or authenticated by those involved. Champion and Stowell (2003, p. 7) argue that

> . . . as Action Researchers it is important that we pay due regard to establishing that an inquiry was a credible, responsible and *authentic* attempt at exploring and learning about a complex social situation not just amongst fellow collaborators, but amongst a wider audience of interested individuals. The manner in which an inquiry process was conducted must be capable of being scrutinized, so that a *public* perception of authenticity (or otherwise) can gradually emerge.

They suggest that thinking in terms of *authenticity* is helpful and that such a notion can promote public acknowledgement of the credibility of the actual process of inquiry. In other words the clients judge the outcome of the inquiry and resulting recommendations. If the clients feel that the outcome is satisfactory then that is the stage at which this line of inquiry/activity stops. In the case of a research project it is the point at which the researcher begins to see what their contribution to the body of knowledge is. It is when the researcher, the supervisors and those involved in field research feel that the subject of interest has been fully investigated. Authentication is done in a variety of ways but can be summed up as a word, that is used to describe the process of judging that an experience or a complex series of events 'is convincing; one that can be believed' (Burchfield, 1998, p. 79).

Putting A/R into Practice

There are many papers that discuss the advantages and suitability of action research but few examples showing how to do it. For some, action research means going out into the 'real world' and talking to people, for others it is the way that it is carried out: the method used. It is important to remember that the cycle of learning is a key feature of action research and the method chosen should be capable of achieving this. As a starting point we believe that the researcher is better equipped to undertake A/R if they are aware of their own position in the intellectual universe. By this we mean the researcher should be aware of the epistemology they have adopted, whether it is a functionalist or an interpretivist approach. Do they subscribe to the notion of objectivity or subscribe to subjectivity? A similar point is made by Reason (1993) who argues that the validity of any knowledge gained is credible only if the epistemology is declared;

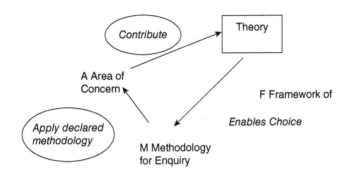

Figure 7.2:   FMA model after Checkland and Scholes 1990 (p. 283) (Checkland and Holwell, 1998, p. 23)

a similar point is made by Checkland (Checkland 1985, Checkland and Scholes, 1999). By reflecting upon where you are coming from – so to speak – the philosophical thread of the research will be maintained which should help to guard against inconsistencies within the study.

Checkland (1985) has suggested the mnemonic FMA, which he proposed as a practical check on the way that research is undertaken. This check is useful to the practitioner too as it helps to frame the approach and avoid inconsistency (see Figure 7.2). By thinking in these terms the inquirer is able to fulfil Susman and Evered's (1978) suggestions of planning and action taking. In the FMA model the F stands for the framework of ideas of the research, highlighting the epistemology adopted by the researcher (see Chapter 6). The M stands for the methodology to be used in the inquiry (see Chapters 2 and 3) and A is the area of interest or concern. The latter will involve the notion of boundary and environment of course (see Chapters 1 and 4).

The second consideration is to think about the area of interest and the method of approach. The selection of a method or methodology requires that the researcher, or Systems practitioner, understand the framework of ideas upon which their approach resides and what methods are suited to these ideas and how can they be used. The choice of method for action research is important. Here we must sound a note of warning as in adopting an approach which attempts to understand from within, one opens it to criticisms of being little more than anecdotal and general opinion. (Although given the subjective nature of social inquiry, a similar criticism can also be made against case study and ethnographic research too.) But as Champion reminds us 'no matter how detailed the documentary evidence . . . such evidence can still fail to explain the outcome' (Champion, 2001, p. 119). As we discussed earlier in this text, to overcome this criticism Checkland and Holwell (1998) suggest the idea of 'recoverability'. By this they mean that a third party ought to be able to 'recover' the research process after the event. They argue that an open declaration of the aims of the inquiry and also of the intended research method, prior to involvement in the situation of interest, is essential and 'without that declaration, it is difficult to see how the outcome of [Action Research] can be more than anecdotal' (Checkland and Holwell, 1998, p. 14).

As we have discussed earlier (Chapter 1 and Chapter 4 – in the sections on boundary) as the inquiry progresses things will change. The boundary of the study might alter, the participants might change and, as they learn more about the situation, the problems/ opportunities they perceived earlier might change too. This is a special difficulty for the Systems researcher. Checkland and Holwell's (1998) suggestion that by declaring in advance the method and approach to be used, one provides a safeguard for the researcher and defence against criticisms of what they refer to as 'creative outcomes', or outcomes which are hoped for rather than discovered. By declaring in advance the inquirer provides a route for the work to be authenticated (Champion and Stowell, 2003) by a third party.

By suggesting that the researcher establishes the authenticity, or otherwise, of an inquiry Champion and Stowell (2003) argue that it adds to the rigour of Systems research whilst maintaining the underpinning philosophy of interpretivism. They argue that if an inquiry process is acknowledged as being 'authentic', it is more likely that concerned individuals will accept the 'validity', or relevance, of any design proposals resulting from the learning. Their work led them to devise a means of gaining under-standing about the context and culture of the situation which they were investigating. This idea is contained within the elements of the mnemonic PEArL which helps to support reflection on the inquiry process (Champion and Stowell, 2001; Champion, 2007; Stowell and Cooray, 2006; Stowell, 2009a). They argue that PEArL enables the character of an inquiry to be appreciated by anyone interested, whether or not those individuals physically participated in the inquiry. PEArL is summarized as follows:

P – Participants
   Who are involved?
   Why are they involved?
   What is their role in the study?
   Who has been excluded and why?
   Are there transitory participants, if so why?

E – Engagement
   How will 'P' engage?
   Can you identify the boundary between 'P' and 'non P'?
   Describe the environmental influences in which the engagement takes place.

A – Authority

Formal authority associated with role – assess strength (e.g. control of resources).

Influences from the environment (e.g. policies).

What embedded authority do the tools for engagement have? Describe why were they chosen and how might they influence the outcome.

r – relationships

Insights into the commodity of power and the control strategies that are used and managed within the participant group(s).

L – Learning

Theoretical and practical outcomes.

Judgement about how this was achieved and assessment about the ownership of outcome.

They propose that the elements within the PEArL mnemonic support interested individuals in scrutinizing the manner in which their inquiry was undertaken. They argue that PEArL allows the practitioner to facilitate the making by interested individuals of a judgement on the character of the inquiry process and that involvement will be reflected through the level of participation, manner of engagement, authority for action and the relationships that develop between the researcher(s) and collaborators.

It is important to emphasize that 'more' involvement is not inherently 'better'. What is fundamental to others scrutinizing the research is the ability to gain some appreciation of the quality of interactions and of how interactions were achieved and maintained.

A successful conclusion of an organizational intervention is when the clients 'take ownership' of the outcome and address them, with the practitioner's role now reduced to that of benign participant. There are examples of consultancy and research where this approach has been adopted successfully and the study has been practitioner led. The extensive report of the study into 'Waverly Randall' (a fictitious name but an accurate report of a real study) example in *Client-Led Design* (Stowell and West 1994, pp. 137–200), Champion's report of her research in a multinational company (Champion, 2001, pp. 121–162) and Cooray's research into a city library (2010, pp. 100–136) all make significant contributions and provide examples of participative design.

Concluding Remarks

It is difficult to give an unequivocal definition of action research since different commentators place different emphasis upon various concepts and merits of the approach.

What we have attempted to do in this chapter is to advocate the value of action research for complex social problems using interpretivist Systems thinking. We have argued that methods of research based on those used in natural science are not always best suited to the complexities of areas of human interaction. We discuss a method of action research we have found useful in exploring difficult areas involving human actors, the culture and historicity that surround it. In this approach we underline the importance of the cycle of learning which we see as a means of gaining an appreciation of the whole situation. We have highlighted difficulties of undertaking A/R and suggested how such research might be carried out. We have raised the importance of the choice of method and suggest that Soft Systems Methodology and the Appreciative Inquiry Method (AIM) provide an approach which fulfils the criteria for action research, but not exclusively. The key point is that whatever approach is selected it should not get in the way of the process of learning.

PART IV

CASE STUDIES

Chapters 8 and 9

Chapter 8 provides worked examples of the way in which selected methods from the earlier chapters have been used to address specific problems/opportunities. These examples show how Systems thinking can be used to address a variety of problems. One example also shows how a method used to address a 'known' problem may reveal the problem to be something unexpected.

In Chapter 9 case studies are provided for the serious learner to hone their skills by using one or more of the methods or methodologies that they have learnt from the earlier chapters. The case studies are intended for the benefit of all those who use this text and not as a set of 'end of text' exercises. For example, there is no reason why those learners who have completed the first section should not use the case studies in this chapter to help improve their understanding and practice of what they have learnt from the early stages of the text. Indeed, in addressing the situations depicted in the case studies using the simple ideas expressed in Chapters 1–3 might act as an incentive to study further the ideas described in the later chapters.

Pulling it All Together

I n this chapter, we have set out two expanded case studies as illustrations of the usefulness of Systems approaches in practice. The first case is about a group of people who restore a disused railway line to operation and the decisions they need to make in order to keep it running. We have discussed how some of the methodologies outlined in this book could be applied to assist the actors described in the case study to analyse and structure their perceived problems.

The second case relates to a university department responsible for the management and operation of overseas programmes of study, which is going through a period of change. Here we discuss how the Appreciative Inquiry Method can be applied to help the engaged actors to explore their ideas in the context of developing a new information system.

Please read these cases in conjunction with the ideas presented in Chapter 5 of the text, and use them to reflect on ways in which you might use these thinking techniques in your own work context.

Case 1: The Dengie Peninsular Railway

The history of the railway goes back to 1854 when the Dengie Peninsular Railway Company was formed and a parliamentary bill was passed for construction of a line

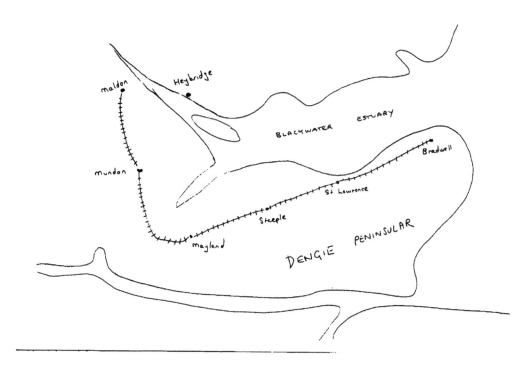

Figure 8.1:   The Dengie Peninsular Railway

from Bradwell in the East, along the north side of the peninsular to Maldon in the West[1] (see Figure 8.1). Construction was completed in 1863 with the opening of Maldon South station. Here, passengers could transfer on foot to the Maldon-Witham branch line and thence to the Great Eastern Railway. Both passenger and freight services originally operated on the line, due to a thriving fishing port at St Lawrence but the decline in fisheries led to the closure of freight services shortly after World War I. The freight terminal at St Lawrence was taken over by a local coal merchant. Passenger services continued until World War II, but the line gradually became less and less profitable. St Lawrence and Mundon stations became request-only halts in 1944. Following the Beeching Report in 1963, closure of the line was recommended. In 1967, the line closed and the track was lifted. Maldon South station was purchased by a local firm as a storage depot. Steeple and Mayland stations became private houses and the buildings of Bradwell station were closed and boarded up. Parts of the old permanent way were adopted by the local authority as footpaths for local people and tourists wishing to enjoy views across the Blackwater Estuary.

---

[1]This scenario is entirely fictitious. Although a thriving branch line exists to the south of the Dengie peninsular along the Crouch Vale, there is not (and to the best of my knowledge never has been) a railway line along the northern boundary.

However, the old line and the days of steam locomotives were not forgotten and several groups of enthusiasts got together with a view to preserving and celebrating the heritage of the Dengie Peninsular Railway. In 1978, a number of groups merged to form the DPR Society and obtained permission to renovate the old Bradwell station buildings as a museum and visitor centre. Over the next five years, fund raising efforts resulted in a sum of money sufficient to enable DPRS to purchase the freehold and re-lay a small amount of track on which a steam locomotive could be driven. A licence was obtained to offer tourist rides over this half mile stretch of track. Subsequently, the DPR Trust was established as a charity with the aim of preserving the heritage of the local railway. The Trust formed a trading subsidiary company to manage the museum and operate trains on the relaid track, while Trustees themselves concentrated on fund raising appeals, educating the public about the DPR and attracting new volunteers and members. The founders of the DPRS comprised three main groups. The South West Essex branch of the Society for Sustainable Transport campaigns continually for extension of more ecologically friendly forms of transport. The closure of the branch line on purely financial grounds appeared to this group to be a mistake, leading to congested roads and consequent wasteful and polluting use of fossil fuels. This group was supported by many local people, not least parents of children who had no means to travel to the High School in Maldon other than a long and convoluted bus route or private cars of parents. The second founder member of DPRS was the Maldon and District Steam Railway Society. This group of enthusiasts came together to organize trips to operating steam railways and the Chappel Railway Museum. They endeavoured to preserve knowledge from the age of steam and to promote opportunities for hobbyists to enjoy participating in such ventures as becoming amateur engine drivers, stokers, signalmen, etc. The third group, the Dengie Historians, were interested in promoting public understanding of the heritage of Dengie, including the bygone fisheries, agriculture, civic development and religious foundations. The DPR was a key area of interest to the Historians as it had played a major role in the life of the Peninsular.

During the 1970s and 1980s, the Trust was able to accumulate funds from appeals and tourist operations to enable further sections of track to be relaid. The local authority was supportive in making over sections of the old permanent way to the Trust and some parcels of private land were also purchased. Two locomotives were purchased and renovated and some other suitable rolling stock was acquired. In 1987, a new track was in place between Bradwell and Steeple, with a passing loop at St Lawrence, controlled by a ground frame in place of signals. Thus, in the summer season it was possible to operate a tourist service offering four return rides per day from the DPR museum to the newly reconstructed Steeple station. This provided impetus for the continuing redevelopment of the line and finally, in 2002, the link through to Maldon was re-established. Unfortunately, the vision of a fully working public transport facility remained elusive since Maldon was no longer connected with main line services, the

Witham–Maldon line having closed in 1966. By now, diesel locomotives had been added to the rolling stock, being cheaper to run and to maintain. DPR Trading still relied on volunteers in all areas: management, operation of trains, maintenance and customer service.

In 2010, a new strategic plan was produced. The key challenge was summarized as 'To rectify, within five years, inadequacies in operating facilities, including maintenance and accommodation of rolling stock, workshops and equipment, volunteer and staff facilities, exhibition space, and commercial outlets.' A new Vision Statement expresses a view that DPRT should become 'A public transport service for the people of North Dengie and visitors to the area, catering both for real service needs and a heritage railway environment that all may enjoy.' The aims of the Trust were reaffirmed as preservation of and education about the heritage of the DPR, and fundraising in order to achieve these ends; the subsidiary Company being responsible for operation of trains and other services, and all other matters not permitted to the Trust by reason of its charitable status. The Plan also set out details of core responsibilities and targets for the coming period:

DPRT's core responsibilities:

1. Directing Railway policy in accordance with its charitable status and the wishes of the membership;
2. Managing the finances of the Trust with prudence and caution such that the Railway always lives within its means and requiring the DPR Company to do likewise;
3. Raising funds to support the work of the Trust, both generally and for specific projects;
4. Directing DPRC to return a net surplus each year as required by the Charity Commission (to be retained with the SRC for operating purposes or covenanted to the DPRT for improvement and development projects);
5. Encouraging members and volunteers, directly and indirectly, to contribute to the work of the Trust;
6. Developing the DPR's Museums, and its heritage and educational goals;
7. Raising public awareness of the DPR and making it accessible to all in the community;
8. Securing such additional assets as may be required for the long-term benefit of the DPR;
9. Leading the DPR's overall communications strategy;

10. Enhancing the standing of the DPR in the community and in the heritage and railway industries;
11. Media liaison on all strategic matters.

DPRC's core responsibilities:

1. To operate a safe railway;
2. To operate within the policies set by the DPRT;
3. To exercise financial prudence in all respects;
4. To manage a rolling programme of maintenance and investment in the DPR's assets;
5. To recruit, manage and motivate staff and volunteers;
6. To deliver an annual surplus as directed by the Trust and as required by the Charity Commissioners;
7. To manage projects and associated risks;
8. Media liaison on all operational matters.

The Trust, as the senior body, governs the activities of the trading company and all members belong primarily to the DPR Trust, which is run as a cooperative – all members having a right to participate in managing the DPR. Consensus decision making (as promoted by the Seeds for Change Network of co-operatives) has always been practised. As the size of the membership has grown, some members have grumbled that this approach tends to favour maintenance of the status quo and stifle debate.

Unfortunately, there has been disagreement among Trustees over the past two years regarding the priorities that should be pursued and the current Strategic Plan represents a compromise approach. Although a congenial atmosphere has been maintained, lengthy and sometimes heated discussions have taken place. In particular, some members have been pushing for faster progress in developing capacity to provide a public service. The picturesque area around St Lawrence attracts many summer visitors and the volume of traffic through the old village has become a problem. (No by-pass is planned and the local terrain would make this difficult to engineer in any case.) A smaller group, but one supplying a large number of volunteers, wishes to concentrate on acquiring and renovating a steam locomotive which ran on the DPR in its heyday. This they consider vital to the educational mission of the Trust and they believe it will also help to attract more visitors to the museum. A third group is concerned about achieving financial stability and believes that capital investment should focus on acquiring the old, disused station buildings of Maldon South. This could be turned into a shop, restaurant and community facility and they believe it could be developed into a commercial venture yielding useful revenue.

Perspectives for Analysis

The Viable Systems Model

As we have seen (Chapter 5, pp. 121–128) Stafford Beer (1981) considered the necessary conditions in which an organizational system could be viable by using the analogy of the human body. The body has muscles and organs which enable the human being to carry out actions and a nervous system that carries back signals to the brain. Elements in the brain are concerned with coordinating and controlling actions and seek to optimize the internal environment. Other aspects of the brain's functioning relate to interactions with the world outside, through interpretation of sensory signals from the nervous system and through cognitive processes of forecasting and planning. By analogy, the Viable Systems Model considers three aspects: environment, operation and a meta-system which monitors and controls both internal and external interactions so that operational units work in harmony.

VSM helps us to consider a system in terms of what is needed to enable it to come together as an integrated whole. Thus, we might begin by asking what *operational activities* the system in focus needs to perform and what needs to be managed in order to facilitate this. Each operating unit needs to be autonomous but must cooperate with other units so that they can come together as a coherent, viable system. We can examine the DPR's plans for clues as to the operational units needed, e.g. fund raising (financial management); recruiting volunteers and staff (human resource management); communicating, both internally and externally (management of communication channels); operating railway services (risk management); acquisition and maintenance of track, rolling stock, signalling equipment, etc. (financial, human resource and risk management).

Thus, System 1 in VSM (Primary Activities) is established and we have ideas as to what must be dealt with in the meta-system.

System 2 is concerned with maintaining the *stability* of the whole. It therefore deals with conflict resolution. In any set of coordinated activities with an overall common aim, there are likely to be conflicts of interest and differences of opinion. For example, when limited funds become available, should they be used to upgrade rolling stock, renovate buildings or generate publicity about the railway? All of these fall within the Society's vision statement and aspects of its strategic plan. DPRT have adopted principles of consensus decision-making. This approach is easy to implement when small numbers of people are involved. A small community of enthusiasts working in the same environment on different aspects of operational activities can down their tools at any convenient time and discuss the next phase of activities without much trouble. However, when all members are entitled to participate in decision making but their activities are diverse and spread out over many locations and times, the process becomes more complex. System 2 may be in need of re-design, perhaps by making use of the 'spoke model' suggested by the Seeds for Change Network[2] for achieving larger group consensus. Possibly, further modifications need to be considered if there are particular blockages to achievement of consensus that must be addressed, e.g. undue conservatism resulting from current processes. Possibly, the Trust may need to consider whether its needs are best served by a cooperative model or whether its size and the scale/complexity of its operations require a different constitutional basis.

Once stability has been achieved, the job of System 3 must be addressed: how to *optimize* interactions in order to achieve the aims of the whole. System 3 must be designed to take a continuing overview of the complexities of the system in focus, in order to bring about synergy. This aspect of the meta-system is dependent upon effective feedback from operational units and its essential task is to regulate System 1. The various management tasks we identified above must be taken into account. Aspects of System 3 must therefore be designed to ensure that resources are available to the operational units, sufficient to their individual needs but managed in order to gain maximum utility from funds raised. We can immediately see here that there is an interaction (feedback loop) between System 3 and System 2, since members will wish to negotiate over optimal use of scarce funds. There is also an interaction with System 4 here (see below) since the Society is also obliged to remain in surplus and needs to make prudent provision for the future. Human 'resources' need to be motivated, protected and deployed effectively. System 3 must be designed to cater for this. When volunteers are recruited, they bring certain skills with them to the Society and will need to be trained in others so that their contributions can bring optimum advantage to the Society in pursuing its various aims. Thus, a volunteer who is by day a professional accountant may come forward because s/he has always wanted to drive a train, but someone may need to persuade them to offer their financial skills from time to time too. It will be necessary to consider the risks involved in operating a railway, and, for instance, design appropriate safety routines (here System 3 interacts with System 4) and take out appropriate insurance policies to cover activities by volunteers and public use of the railway; failure to do so could jeopardize future activities, if, say, a large compensation payment had to be made following an accident (impacting upon Systems 1 and 2).

---

[2] http://www.seedsforchange.org.uk/free/shortconsensus.pdf.

Clearly, DPRS has taken steps to set up System 4, which is concerned with the future of the system in focus. System 4 monitors the whole, in conjunction with Systems 2 and 3, and considers adaptations that are necessary to future stability and achievement of common aims. Forward planning, based on interpretations of feedback from System 3, and strategic management are the business of System 4. Currently, all members of the trust are entitled to participate in System 4's sphere of responsibility and have currently interacted using consensus decision making in order to generate the 2010 strategic plan. In doing so, they have enabled some areas of conflict to surface, e.g. whether educational or sustainability goals should take precedence. This highlights an interaction (loop) between System 4 and System 2, in order to maintain the ongoing stability of the whole system.

System 5 is responsible for pulling the whole system towards achievement of its overall purpose. System 5 provides ground rules for all activities of participating units, together with means for enforcing them. This is what we often refer to as policy and it is closely related to the constitutions of organizations. DPRS is constituted as a trust and operates as a cooperative. Its responsibilities are partly governed by law, e.g. the general duties of trustees in a context of charitable status. The underlying principles of members who own and control the Society are of course influential upon policy-making, e.g. a view that the environment should be respected and that sustainability is important; or another view that heritage should be preserved and transmitted. At times, such underlying principles may come into conflict, generating interaction between Systems 2 and 5. At times, the desires of members may conflict with the duties imposed on them by the social environment, e.g. activities may be curbed because as Trustees they have a duty to deliver a surplus not a deficit.

We can see from this example how an organization operates through working units carrying out primary and secondary tasks. In order to do so, the organization needs to maintain stability in its relationships with internal and external environments, and seek ways to optimize its performance and make progress towards its aims. The meta-system (Systems 2–5) thus provides a service to operational units (in one sense) and to the system as a synergistic whole (in another).

System Dynamics

As discussed in Chapter 5 (see pp. 101–106), techniques known as System Dynamics may be used to model the ways in which feedback influences the ongoing behaviour of systems. There are a number of powerful dedicated software tools designed to help with the complex mathematical modelling underlying System Dynamic analyses. However, a more familiar software tool for many people is the humble spreadsheet. This can also be used to model the dynamics of ongoing complex systems such as those underpinning the Dengie Peninsular Railway Society's activities.

If you are not already familiar with spreadsheet software, e.g. Microsoft Excel, then it can best be described as an active, electronic grid of cells each of which can hold a numeric value, a formula or a text-based label. Data can be entered into cells upon which formulae entered in other cells will operate, e.g. a column of figures can be entered in cells A1–A5 and cell A6 can contain a formula asking the software to calculate the sum of these figures (or perhaps the arithmetic mean, standard deviation or any of a range of other functions). Cells can also contain references to the values in other cells in the same worksheet, or another worksheet in the same spreadsheet file. Thus, in the example above, if cell A6 contains a formula to sum the values of cells A1–A5, then the resultant value can become an input to another calculation by a formula in a cell located in another part of the worksheet, which refers to A6. Thus, a book-keeper might list administrative expenses incurred in cells A1–A5 and calculate the total in cell A6 by formula. A cell in a separate worksheet headed Profit and Loss Account can then reference cell A6 in the original sheet for that total, which will in turn be an input value to calculation of net profit. Furthermore, it is possible to conduct 'What if?' analysis.

Figure 8.2 shows the Indirect Expenses for the Railway Company for 2008 and 2009. Compare this with Figure 8.3. This contains the formulae by which the expenses posted in each category in the spreadsheet were totalled. These expenses form part of the accounting system which works out whether the company is making a profit. Figure 8.4 shows the Profit & Loss Account in which the totalled figure for Indirect Expenses appears. This figure is taken away from the Gross Profit earned by running the company's activities in order to calculate the Net Profit earned. Figure 8.5 shows the formulae entered into cells in order to make these calculations. Note that the total for Indirect Expenses has been obtained by entering the cell reference in the expenses sheet of the same workbook (=Expenses!H43). This is the calculation we saw in Figure 8.2.

So far, the spreadsheet calculations have been quite simple. However, it is possible to turn this into a potentially powerful tool to support decision making.

Suppose that the Directors of the company are concerned about changing economic conditions which they fear will lead to increased expenditure or loss of business. It is possible to manipulate the figures in the spreadsheet to model the impact of various changes in the environment. Figure 8.6 shows how the spreadsheet can be used to model various contingencies. We call this 'What if?' analysis.

This enables the impact of changes to be considered so that appropriate strategies can be worked out for the future. Spreadsheet software incorporates more sophisticated modelling features so that statistical functions, for instance, can be embedded into a

DENGIE PENINSULAR RAILWAY COMPANY LIMITED				
INDIRECT EXPENSES YEAR ENDING DECEMBER 2009				
	2009		2008	
	£	£	£	£
ADMINISTRATIVE EXPENSES				
Personnel costs				
Wages	548,554		509,264	
Less: wages recharged to DPRT	−4,800		−3,192	
National Insurance	42,945		40,844	
		586,699		546,916
Establishment expenses				
Rent	22,921		26,315	
Contribution for use of museum buildings	27,498		25,454	
Rates	23,532		22,063	
Heat, light and water	23,021		16,083	
Insurance	40,228		46,238	
Cleaning and laundry	7,518		11,697	
Repairs and maintenance	147,656		89,817	
Marketing and publicity	47,609		26,668	
		339,983		264,335
General expenses				
Motor and travelling expenses	11,210		4,533	
Telephone	10,470		12,854	
Printing, stationery and postage	24,813		28,224	
General expenses	14,214		13,725	
Legal and professional fees	7,900		6,888	
Auditors remuneration	4,900		4,750	
Depreciation	90,575		106,742	
Repayment of loans	−22,970		−5,507	
Profit on disposal of fixed assets	−378		nil	
		140,734		172,209
Financial costs				
Bad debt write off	7,600		−300	
Bank charges	11,254		4,128	
Credit card charges	8,186		7,676	
		27,040		11,504
		1,094,456		994,964

Figure 8.2:   Indirect Expenses for the Railway Company

spreadsheet. There is also a scenario building tool so that 'What if?' analysis can be carried out to compare the outcomes of a variety of different conditions without rebuilding the entire spreadsheet or changing the values of live cells in the main workbook. Figure 8.7 shows how this tool has been used to model the impact of three possible management strategies.

	DENGIE PENINSULAR RAILWAY COMPANY LIMITED			
	INDIRECT EXPENSES YEAR ENDING DECEMBER 2009			
	2009		2008	
	£	£	£	£
ADMINISTRATIVE EXPENSES				
Personnel costs				
Wages	548,554		509,264	
Less: wages recharged to DPRT	–4,800		–3,192	
National Insurance	42,945		40,844	
		=SUM(H9:H11)		=SUM(J9:J11)
Establishment expenses				
Rent	22921		26315	
Contribution for use of museum buildings	27498		25454	
Rates	23532		22063	
Heat, light and water	23021		16083	
Insurance	40228		46238	
Cleaning and laundry	7518		11697	
Repairs and maintenance	147656		89817	
Marketing and publicity	47609		26668	
		=SUM(H15:H22)		=SUM(J15:J22)
General expenses				
Motor and travelling expenses	11210		4533	
Telephone	10470		12854	
Printing, stationery and postage	24813		28224	
General expenses	14214		13725	
Legal and professional fees	7900		6888	
Auditors remuneration	4900		4750	
Depreciation	90575		106742	
Repayment of loans	–22970		–5507	
Profit on disposal of fixed assets	–378		nil	
		=SUM(H25:H33)		=SUM(J25:J33)
Financial costs				
Bad debt write off	7600		–300	
Bank charges	11254		4128	
Credit card charges	8186		7676	
		=SUM(H37:H39)		=SUM(J37:J39)
		=SUM(I19:I41)		=SUM(K9:K41)

Figure 8.3: Indirect Expenses sheet, showing formulae

Soft Systems Analysis

We have seen in the case study that there is some disagreement among the Trustees about the future direction for the development of the railway. We can see that SSM might be used here to generate a more positive decision-making environment, enabling participants to express the unstructured problem situation in which they find themselves; identify and model systems perceived to be relevant to future development;

DENGIE PENINSULAR RAILWAY COMPANY LIMITED							
INDIRECT EXPENSES YEAR ENDING DECEMBER 2009							
ADMINISTRATIVE EXPENSES				2009		2008	
Personnel costs			£	£	£	£	
Wages				548,554		509,264	
Less: wages recharged to DPRT				−4,800		−3,192	
National Insurance				42,945		40,844	
					586,699		546,916
Establishment expenses							
Rent				22,921		26,315	
Contribution for use of museum buildings				27,498		25,454	
Rates				23,532		22,063	
Heat, light and water				23,021		16,083	
Insurance				40,228		46,238	
Cleaning and laundry				7,518		11,697	
Repairs and maintenance				147,656		89,817	
Marketing and publicity				47,609		26,668	
					339,983		264,335
General expenses							
Motor and travelling expenses				11,210		4,533	
Telephone				10,470		12,854	
Printing, stationery and postage				24,813		28,224	
General expenses				14,214		13,725	
Legal and professional fees				7,900		6,888	
Auditors remuneration				4,900		4,750	
Depreciation				90,575		106,742	
Repayment of loans				−22,970		−5,507	
Profit on disposal of fixed assets				−378		nil	
					140,734		172,209
Financial costs							
Bad debt write off				7,600		−300	
Bank charges				11,254		4,218	
Credit card charges				8,186		7,676	
					27,040		11,504
					1,094,456		994,964

Figure 8.4: Profit & Loss Account

		DENGIE PENINSULAR RAILWAY COMPANY LIMITED			
		PROFIT & LOSS ACCOUNT AS AT DECEMBER 2009			
		2009		2008	
		£	£	£	£
TURNOVER					
Passenger takings			1620820		1314897
Shop income			175427		151837
Catering income			289131		232468
Car park income			111963		101369
Driver experience takings			12317		24596
Grants and loans			Nil		Nil
Allocation from DPRT			69793		20107
Sundry income			35142		16254
			=SUM(I7:I14)		=SUM(K7:K14)
COST OF SALES					
Locomotive running costs		−245058		−181851	
Special event costs		−96189		−93389	
Shop purchases		−116354		−99055	
Catering purchases		−122287		−113217	
Infrastructure costs		−15900		−17827	
Locomotive hire		−183075		−178465	
Repairs to rolling stock		−120238		−100442	
Car park running costs		−45657		−42173	
			=SUM(H20:H27)		=SUM(J20:J27)
GROSS PROFIT			=SUM(I17:I29)		=SUM(K17:K29)
OVERHEADS					
Indirect expenses			=Expenses!H43		=Expenses!J43
OPERATING PROFIT			=I32−I35		=K32−K35
Interest received			61		422
			=SUM(I37:I38)		=SUM(K37:K38)
Interest payable			−4828		−15978
NET PROFIT			=SUM(I41:I43)		=SUM(K41:K43)

Figure 8.5: Profit & Loss Account showing formulae

		Current State		What if? (a)		What if? (b)	
What if? (a)	Takings fall by 25% but expenses remain level						
What if? (b)	Takings fall by 25% but locomotive running costs rise by 15%						
			£		£		£
		£		£		£	
Takings			1,620,820		1,215,615		1,215,615
			175,427		175,427		175,427
			289,131		289,131		289,131
			111,963		111,963		111,963
			12,317		12,317		12,317
			Nil		Nil		Nil
			69,793		69,793		69,793
			35,142		35,142		35,142
			2,314,593		1,909.388		1,909.388
Locomotive running costs		−245,058		−245,058		−281,817	
		−96,189		−96,189		−96,189	
		−116,354		−116,354		−116,354	
		−122,287		−122,287		−122,287	
		−15,900		−15,900		−15,900	
		−183,075		−183,075		−183,075	
		−120,238		−120,238		−120,238	
		−45,657		−45,657		−45,657	
			−944,758		−944,758		−981,517
Gross profit			1,369,835		964,630		927,871
			0		0		0
			1,369,835		964,630		927,871
			61		61		61
			1,369,896		964,691		927,932
			−4,828		−4,828		−4,828
			1,365,068		959,863		923,104

Figure 8.6: What if? Analysis

Scenario Summary	Current Values	Scenario 1: Reduce wage costs	Scenario 2: Reduce travel costs	Scenario 3: Reduce running costs
Changing Cells:				
Wages	548,554	500,000	548,554	548,554
G25	6,000	6,000	6,000	6,000
Heating	23,021	23,021	23,021	20,000
Maintenance	147,656	147,656	147,656	100,000
G20	7,518	7,518	7,518	5,000
Result Cells:				
H43	1,089,246	1,040,692	1,089,246	1,036,051

Notes: Current Values column represents values of changing cells at time Scenario Summary Report was created. Changing cells for each scenario are highlighted in gray.

Figure 8.7:   Scenario building with MS – Excel

consider the differing worldviews underpinning the apparently conflicting suggestions, and so create a more measured and reflective decision-making environment.

Case Two: Information System Development and CLICS

The following example illustrates the information systems development cycle following the CLICS cycle. This example is taken from a 'real' study undertaken by Cooray in 2009 as part of a research project. The authors wish to express their thanks to Shavindrie Cooray (2010) and Stowell and Cooray (2006) for the inclusion of the example.

In Chapter 3 we introduced AIM as a means of gaining appreciation of a system of interest. In the same chapter we introduced the notion of CLICS (an evolved CLD – see Stowell and West (1994)) as a means of developing, with the clients, an information system. In this chapter we provide an example of CLICS that was used in practice.

As part of her empirical research Cooray (2010) explored the use of interpretive ideas in the development of an information system. She started from the premise that technical developers require a technical specification and in most cases this amounted to something like a class diagram. Her objective was to build upon the work of previous researchers in this field (e.g. Stowell and West, 1994; Guo et al., 1999a and 1999b; Stowell and Champion 2002; Champion et al., 2005) and attempt to establish ways in which the client, or non technical end-users, can navigate their way to an initial technical specification but which is advanced enough for technical developers to use to guide them. Cooray's research takes this idea a stage further, developing some of the processes within the CLICS cycle developed by Stowell (2000) Champion and Stowell (2000).

In keeping with the idea behind CLICS (see Chapter 3 for discussion of CLICS) it is important that the entire development can be traced back to each preceding stage. In this way the clients can see that their ideas are driving the whole design and that they are in control of the development process rather than the technical developers thereby increasing the sense of ownership.

We suggest that the development and design process can be ably assisted through the use of AIM or if the situation is unclear SSM; the outcome of either of these approaches is then linked via the activity diagram to produce a relationship diagram, which is then used to produce a class diagram as the basis for the technical specification. An earlier example of this process was published in Champion et al. (2005). The evolved CLICS cycle is shown in Figure 8.8:

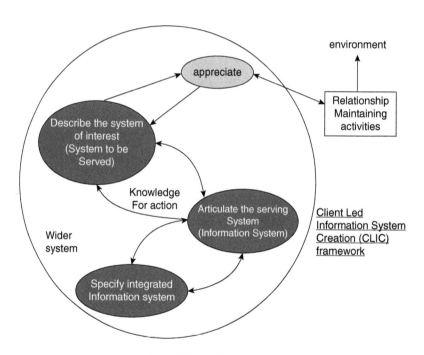

Figure 8.8: CLICS framework

Cooray's Study (2010): The Situation of Interest

This small study was a precursor to a much larger study undertaken in the public sector but provides a useful example of the use of Systems ideas and how they were linked to a technical specification. The study was carried out in a University department responsible for the management and operation of overseas programmes of study – let us call it Distance Programmes (DP). The department was undergoing change following the appointment of a new senior manager. In this case Cooray wanted to use

Systems ideas for all involved to express their understanding of the situation and develop a model of how they thought it 'ought' to operate. Inspired by Champion et al.'s 2005 paper Cooray wanted to see if she could take the resultant model to another level, namely produce a technical representation of some aspects of its operation. Cooray then reflected upon the CLICS framework and decided that her approach would be as depicted in Figure 8.9:

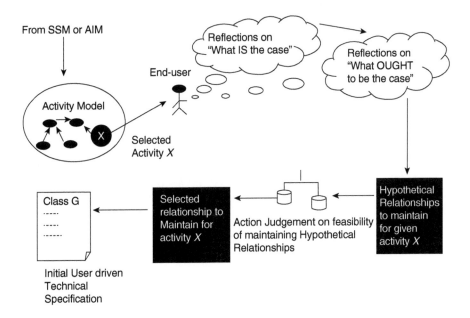

Figure 8.9:   Important elements of CLICS (after Cooray, 2010, p. 86)

The field study was carried out in three stages. The first stage was to produce a Rich Picture (RP) of the situation. This was developed from discussions with the Department Manager, the Administrative Manager, Academics and the Administrative Staff. Each participant was asked to talk about their involvement with and perceptions of the programme. The information generated was recorded in the form of a Rich Picture (see Figure 8.10). After each meeting with individual participants the RP was further enhanced to reflect the views expressed. At least two meetings were conducted with each individual participant and the iterative process of RP building resulted in a deeper appreciation and learning by the researcher and participants of the operation of the module in the real world.

Once the RP had been developed to the satisfaction of all involved problem themes were identified and from this, relevant systems. The most important problem theme and relevant system was identified and a Root Definition (RD) produced. The RD was discussed with each participant as part of the process of learning. This resulted in the

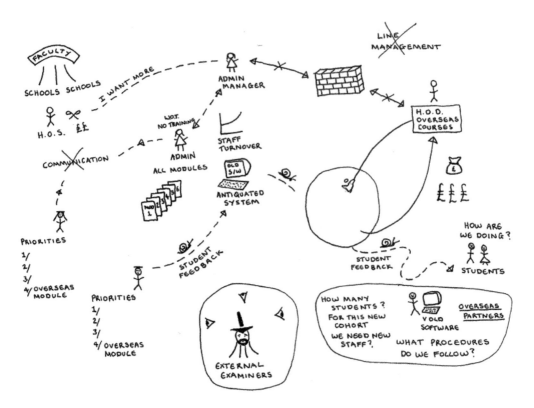

Figure 8.10:   Rich Picture of situation

production of an activity model that was also discussed with the participants as a sense-making device (see Figure 8.11). Once the model was agreed the activities in the model were grouped into sub-groups based on what had been learnt and agreed by the participants. Once each individual had become familiar with the activities in the model the researcher and participants grouped these activities into sub-groups based on their understanding of the situation. Next the participants selected what they considered the most important activity from each sub-group.

The activity models are 'ideas for action' (Champion et al., 2005) and the next stage is to think how we might turn these into action. Champion (2001) argued that the client should be provided with the means to *navigate* from ideas for action to ways of converting them into practice using tools that can be understood by both non-technical and technical participants. The significance of the term navigate is to emphasize that the participants are monitoring and controlling the process of moving from one state, in this case a model of actions described in natural language and which fulfil a particular need into a form which can be shared by all concerned. It is the '. . . end-users that

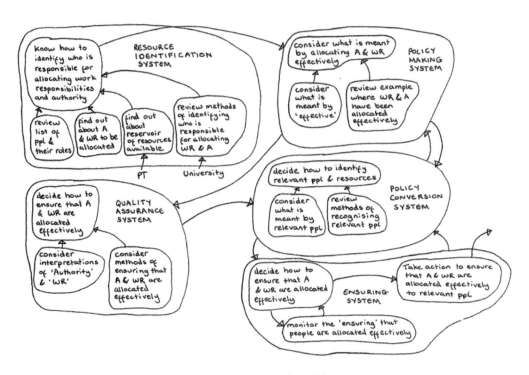

Figure 8.11: Activity model

possess ideas for action, but it is the technical developer who holds the expertise needed to operationalise those *ideas for action*' (Cooray, 2010, p. 93).

In the project Cooray discussed with the participants which of the activities in the sub-grouping were the most important. By taking each activity in the activity diagram and using PEArL (see Chapter 7) as a sense-making device clients were assisted in gaining a richer appreciation of each activity as well as promoting group discussion. The questions generated by PEArL helped the participants to express 'what IS the case' for the time for each activity, which corresponds to what Vickers called reality judgements, leading on to the value judgements of 'what OUGHT to be the case' (see Chapter 4).

In this case participants were asked to elaborate upon their thinking using PEArL once again (see Figure 8.12), but remember that this time it was to explore 'what ought to be the case'. The participants are asked to think in terms of the ideal functioning of the activities being considered. It is the interaction between the two results in a set of hypothetical relationships considered to be significant enough to change the selected activities in some way.

Elements	Issues to Reflect upon "What is the case" for each activity (Reality Judgements)	Issues to Reflect upon "What ought to be the case" for each activity (Value Judgements)
P- Participants	Who is involved in the activity, who is excluded and why? Why are they involved? What is their role in the activity?	Who ought to be involved/excluded in the activity and why? What should be their role in the activity?
E- Engagement	How are the participants involved? What methods are used to engage participants? What are the environmental influences in which an activity takes place?	How should participants be involved? What methods should be used to engage participants?
A- Authority	Formal authority associated with activity. What are the environmental influences? What embedded authority do the tools for engagement have? Why were they chosen and what influences the outcomes?	What should be the formal authority associated with activity?
r- relationships	What kind of informal power or commodities (Stowell, 2000) do people use to influence others (Examples include the use of gender, sociability, and verbal skills)	What kind of informal power or commodities (Stowell, 2000) do people use to influence others (Examples include the use of gender, sociability, and verbal skills)
L-Learning	The theoretical and practical outcomes from the activity, judgements about how these were achieved and assessment about the ownership of outcomes	What should be the theoretical and practical outcomes from the activity? Who should have the ownership of outcomes?

Figure 8.12:   Elements of PEArL corresponding to 'What is' the case and 'What ought' to be the case (after Cooray, 2010, p. 89)

The outcome from this set of discussions provides information which could be used to inform a relationship model. In the development of a new 'system' we advocate the involvement of the clients throughout which enables them to reinvest what they have learnt as they developed their respective maps and activity diagrams. In this example Cooray was able to develop a simple relationship diagram from the answers that the participants gave when questioned through the PEArL mnemonic about 'what ought to be the case'. Cooray used answers given against P and A as roles and the answers to E, r and L she used as the relationships between these roles. This decision meant that there was logical coherence and traceability, which is one aim of CLICS.

The relationship model was presented to the participants for their comment. This was followed by an influence analysis for each of the important relationships in the rela-

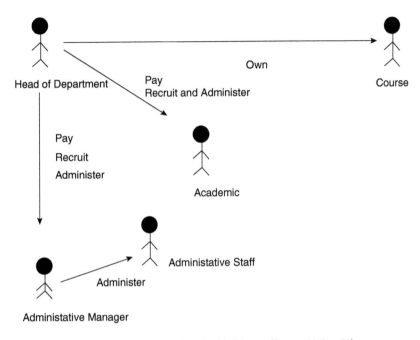

Figure 8.13: Example of Relationship Diagram (Cooray, 2010, p. 94)

tionship model in order to investigate the relationship processes and attitudes that might arise from mismatches between 'what is and what ought' to be the case. The clients will consider relationship processes and attitudes that might be influenced if the relationships were to be implemented. This part of the process is undertaken by all the participants with the aim of producing an 'agreed' relationship diagram following a discussion about which of the relationships are important. Cooray (2010, p. 95) argues that by enabling the end-users to reflect, dwell, learn and expand on the judgements that they have made they are then able to select the relationships most likely to be implemented. In a sense this was to enable the clients to consider the feasibility of what was being proposed. The outcome of this was action judgements, actions which need to take place if the selected activity was to be implemented. The outcome of this resulted in a modified relationship model (see Figure 8.13). The outcome of this activity is what Vickers refers to as an action judgement.

Once the relationship diagram has been agreed then a one-to-one mapping takes place between the relationship diagram and the class diagram. It is this class diagram which provides the technical specification. In this example we use the circles in the relationship diagram to depict the roles and these in turn become classes in the class diagram. The relationships shown in that diagram become the classes in the class diagram. The relationships in the relationship diagram become the methods of those classes in the class diagram. Provided that the class diagram has included all the information in

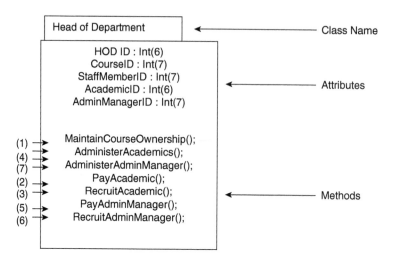

Figure 8.14:   User-driven Class Diagram (after Cooray, 2010, p. 96)

the relationship diagram the clients and technical experts can trace back the source and hence provide the required transparency and logical coherence required of CLICS.

The result of the mapping of the relationship diagram shown above and the class diagram is shown in Figure 8.14. In this diagram the role 'head of department' (hod) becomes a class and the relationships to hod become methods in the hod class. We repeat Cooray's example here in which she has numbered the relationships in the relationship diagram and the corresponding methods in the class diagram. It is worth reminding ourselves that this diagram is one that has been produced by the clients and can be traced back by them to the previous models which they created. The class diagram (and this is a simple example to illustrate the point) is not the final technical specification but sufficiently developed that it can be used by the technical engineers. (An additional example of the way in which this approach is used can be found in Champion, Stowell and O'Callahan, 2005).

CLICS as a Means of Developing a Technical Specification?

The participants commented that whilst the proposals in the models including the class diagram were timely and necessary they also felt that due to the limitations of bureaucracy and politics the implementation of these decisions in the real world might be difficult. However, they did state that the class diagram produced accurately sum- marized 'what they wanted' or 'what they had specified' throughout the inquiry. As such the exercise could be considered successful in the sense that the participants themselves drove the inquiry process, which culminated in an initial class diagram, which summarized their needs. The initial class diagram was then presented to a set of software engineers at another university (for an objective assessment) to establish whether it could be used to produce an initial technical output. Their response was that the initial client-driven class diagram produced from the process could indeed be used as a frame for implementing a technical program. Their opinion was that once the clients had encapsulated their needs as an initial technical specification they would only need to add in technical elements such as arrays and variables to implement the program. The basic structure of the client-driven initial class diagram would remain intact.

Lessons Learnt and Outcome

The study provides an example of the way in which CLICS is used to define an information system. However, the approach also yields a greater understanding of the situation as a whole. For example, although Cooray's intention was to research how to enable clients to lead in an information systems design it was apparent during the study that there was a significant problem with the distance programmes (DP).

The responsibilities and management of the administrators was outside the control of the head of DP. The academics employed on the programmes were also part of the University Faculty of Technology and any work that they undertook for DP was considered to be in addition to their normal timetable commitments. In practice this meant that the duties of the administrative manager were determined by the demands of the Faculty who administered DP staff, but who were located within DP.

The workload of the department was considerable with a number of programmes operating in two countries in Asia. The responsibilities of the head of DP meant that he and at least one of the administrative staff and one member of the faculty had to travel out to the counties involved every four months for 10 days at a time. The administrative staff also had to liaise with the external examiners and arrange for travel for the whole team each quarter. The head of the newly formed school (which was a merger of three departments) within the Faculty of Technology was reluctant to allow staff to participate in DP unless it was entirely under his control. This was bound to create friction as the income from DP was significant and the newly appointed head felt it should come to his school.

One of the problem themes that was acknowledged by the DP staff was that of 'conflicting responsibility for the allocation of human resources'. However, although it was agreed by the participants that this was outside the remit of the study, the head of DP and the administrative staff were made aware that this was their main problem theme and was likely to become a major difficulty in the future.

Note: Shortly after the study took place the DP was merged into the newly formed school resulting in the head of DP resigning and the administrative team being broken up. It is not known how many of the programmes formerly managed by DP are still running. Within a year of these changes taking place the newly appointed Head of School also resigned.

CHAPTER 9

Cases

This chapter contains further case studies which can be used as self-learning tools or material for discussion in formal classroom settings. Two substantial cases are provided that can be used as a basis for exploring Systems ideas and the methods discussed throughout the text. Four short cases are provided, all of which relate to common management problem situations from contemporary settings. These are accompanied by links to further relevant material you can explore for yourself. You may be able to find other links by searching your own library or on the Web.

The purpose of the cases in Chapter 9 is to act as a springboard for discussion using Systems concepts, for instance at management development sessions or in a classroom setting.

Part 1 – Substantial Cases

The first extended case relates to a fictitious hospital whose managers have difficult choices to make and need to structure their problems effectively in order to find the right solutions.

The second case in Part 1 relates to an airline company needing to develop a new information system to support its business.

Part 2 – Outline Cases

The Forgotten Heroes of the Falklands War
Action on 'Garden Grabbing'
Sustainable Ports
Airport Security

Part 1

Case 1 – Princess Monica Hospital

The first case study is about a fictitious hospital whose management has difficult decisions to make in order to meet government cost savings targets. This case study is
intended for a group of at least 15 participants where each person has a particular role
assigned to them.

The case study should be read and absorbed by all the participants before any action
is taken or roles are assigned. The idea is to divide the participants into sub-groups of
five to six. First, the whole group reads and absorbs the case study. Once this has been
done one participant per group is then assigned the role of management consultant.
Using a suitable method of enquiry such as Soft Systems Methodology (SSM) or the
Appreciative Inquiry Method (AIM) the small team set about making sense of the situation. The outcome of the exercise is a set of recommendations to the client.

Before embarking upon the consultancy you, the management consultants, should
decide the boundary of the study, i.e. what is and who are, inside and outside the
boundary and what is in the environment. You should represent this diagrammatically
with an explanation of how you arrived at this decision. You are then in a position to
find out the views of those who work at the hospital. Your first action now is to assign
roles to those within your boundary, not forgetting the influence of those outside. To
help you in this task you could use AIM or SSM (see Chapter 3).

Roles

Management Consultant (one per sub-group)
Medical Consultant (cottage hospitals)
Medical Consultant Pediatrician
Medical Consultant Cardiology
Patient Representative, Princess Monica Hospital
Social Services
Senior Hospital Administrator

Union Representative for cleaning staff
Trainee Nurse
Senior Staff Nurse
Junior Doctor

The Exercise

You are part of a small team of analysts tasked with researching the way in which Princess Monica Hospital management can make recommendations for efficiency savings to the hospital's senior administrator. Other members of the group are part of the hospital staff and should work with the analysts to arrive at a set of recommendations.

Participants in the Study Include

Team leader (the facilitator), management consultants and representatives from each of the client groups. The management consultants, in conjunction with the team leader, will decide the time allowed for each activity.

There are six main groups of staff representing the hospital: (i) Medical consultants, (ii) Hospital administration, (iii) Medical staff, e.g. nurses, junior doctors, trainees, (iv) Non-medical staff, e.g. auxiliary, catering and maintenance staff, (v) Patient Representative Committee and (vi) Social Services. Your team should decide how you plan to learn what the requirements of these staff are. Your team leader has decided that the best way to achieve this is to form into sub-groups of five to six per group and through them identify the parts of the problem and then discuss what has been learnt followed by recommendations at Plenary sessions organized by the team leader.

The District and the Hospital

Princess Monica (PMH) is one of three large general hospitals in the Sunshine county, which, together with nine 'cottage' hospitals serve the region. The population of the Sunshine Region is presently around 1,250,000, of which 10.5% are over 75, 17% between 60–74, 30% between 6 and 18 and 20.5% 5 years of age and under, the remaining 22% being between the age of 19 and 60 years. The male to female ratio is 54% female to 46% male with 5.5% of the over 75 age group being female.

At the last census 42% of the population of the county live in Portcity. The population across the Sunshine region has been increasing over the past decade at an average rate of 5.1% per annum. Between PMH and the associated cottage hospitals there are 5285 patients awaiting general surgery and of these 10% have been waiting for more than one year, which is the highest figure recorded for 15 years. The total number for the region as a whole is 15,875. The number of alcohol and obesity-related illnesses has increased dramatically over the past five years (25% nationally) accounting for 1 in 6 admissions and an increase in expenditure for specialist equipment. (There has been a 5.7% increase in alcohol-related crimes in the area.) Each PMH consultant offers specialist cosmetic treatment ranging from tattoo removal through to liposuction; these procedures are undertaken in the 10% time available for private consultancy.

The Haywood Ward is typical of all surgical wards in the hospital (there are 15 other similar wards in PMH) and each one has 12 beds. Each surgical procedure has been given a bed occupancy figure and cost of treatment. For example, a cataract operation: £786 to £1164; heart valve surgery: £9788 to £10,199; heart bypass: £6911 to £8080; hip replacement: £5319 to £5568; hernia surgery: £956 to £1219; knee replacement: £5788 to £6182; major breast surgery: £2386 to £2497; varicose vein removal: £752 to £1376; any treatment or occupancy which falls outside the hospitals standards (compiled by the hospital administrative team) is subject to an inquiry.

On arrival each patient undergoes a series of tests including blood and urine samples, x-rays and ultrasound tests if necessary and then recording of personal details including name, date of birth etc. Most doctors admitting patients prefer to carry out their own checks rather than rely on computer-based records. Efficiency statistics are published each year under government policies on standards in public services.

Princess Monica has 74 active wards including maternity, emergency and geriatric. The occupancy rate of the wards has been an average of 87% over the past five years but increases to 100% during inclement weather. 10% of the beds are occupied by patients transferred from the cottage hospitals and 1% of the beds are occupied for 75% of the time by patients who have no accommodation with adequate care available to them. Arranging suitable accommodation is the responsibility of the small team of resident Social Service officers. Some wards still have mixed occupancy, which is against government policy. The average stay per patient is nine days and the average cost per patient is £675 per day.

Three qualified nurses and one enrolled nurse staff each ward: the staff are supervised by a senior nurse or sister. Each ward is assigned to a consultant who has one senior registrar and two junior doctors per three wards. During the night there is one senior nurse, two nurses and one enrolled nurse and one doctor for every five wards with two more on call. Each ward has a central administrative point for medical staff. The cottage hospitals have a pool of consultants who are specialists in one of the main health priorities. These consultants are assigned to the cottage hospitals and rarely come into PMH.

Within PMH each ward is visited three times per week by any of the 25 consultants or 21 senior registrars accompanied by three junior doctors. Approximately 30% of the visits are for training purposes providing the junior doctors with experience of diagnosis and recommending treatment. A similar system exists in each of the cottage hospitals.

Outpatients

On discharge in-patients are given an appointment for subsequent visit to the outpatient department, which on average takes about eight weeks. Until three years ago the first appointment was five to six weeks. Typically patients are discharged after one visit but the average overall patient discharge rate is 1.75 visits.

Upon arrival each patient reports to reception, which has a record of each patient and the name of the medical practitioner who will see them, although recently there have been several occasions when the reception desk had no record of patient or consultant. The average waiting time from the time of registration until being seen by a medical practitioner is 25 minutes and the total time spent per patient from arrival to departure is 45 minutes.

General Points

Although part of the government ring-fenced funding PMH must demonstrate efficiency savings. This has meant staff reductions and greater reliance on cost-cutting actions such as outsourcing cleaning and ward catering. The latter action is unpopular with the medical staff and patient representatives. There are claims that because of inadequate cleaning this has led to an increase in patient infection. There are also claims that patients are not getting proper meals; this is especially the case for the elderly who are sometimes unable to feed themselves. Outsourcing is also unpopular with patients and relatives who say that the overalls worn by these staff are confusing as they find difficulty differentiating between someone who serves tea and the medical staff. The patient representatives want overalls standardized to help with identification.

The patient representatives are also pushing for more 'creature comforts' in the wards such as bedside TV monitors similar to those found on airplanes, bedside telephone access and better menus.

The record system still has a significant part processed by hand and held as paper records. There is a general mistrust of the computer-based systems throughout the hospital as there have been errors in the recent past. Moreover many consultants are aggrieved that so much NHS funding has been spent and they were not consulted about the need for such patient record systems. This problem is exacerbated by the fact that many of the specialist computer budgets were cut in order to pay for the patient record system.

The cost of administration has increased in recent times by 7% over what it was five years ago and there has been an increase in administrative staff of 3% compared to a 1% increase in medical staff. The increase in administrative staff is said to be because of the new patient records and booking systems.

There are plans to extend the hospital at a cost of £250 m but these have to be submitted to the Ministry of Health. If approved this submission will provide 15 new wards which will be assigned for specialist treatment but discussions about the submission have proved controversial. For example, each hospital in the county must put forward a case for one of three specialist areas and one minor area of specialism; the applications will then be considered and then specialisms nominated by the regional health authority. This process, over which each hospital has no control, has caused rifts between the hospital consultants, the local community and the other three major hospitals in the county. For example Princess Monica Hospital has a specialist unit for children which, should the plans be approved, may be moved to a major city in the south of the region, Southsea. If approved at least three of the cottage hospitals will close and those patients will have to attend PMH or one of the hospitals in a neighbouring county or go to Southsea. Southsea is likely to lose its specialist renal centre to Westsea.

PMH senior management has learnt that those bids which can demonstrate efficiency savings are the most likely to succeed. There is no guarantee that all three of the county's major hospitals will be awarded funding. The current economic downturn may result in the Ministry's budget being cut which has encouraged PMH management to be prepared to take radical steps to cut expenditure. A meeting between the senior management of the three hospitals has been scheduled much to the angst of the hospital staff resulting in the possibility of trade union action. The unions have been excluded from all discussions thus far.

The following role summaries should not be generally available but allocated to the individual role players following the boundary drawing exercise.

Roles – (To be Allocated Following Boundary Definition)

Consultant (Cottage Hospitals)

You are a highly regarded cardiologist with responsibility for all cardiovascular patients attending two of the cottage hospitals under your care. You have three years to retirement at age 60 with the prospect of a few years' lucrative private consultancy which, added to your generous pension, should allow you to have a very comfortable retirement. Whilst you can see advantages if PMH were to win the grant and open a specialist cardiology department it would almost certainly mean that you will have to work within PMH. This will add a total of 1hr 30 minutes to your journey each day. Whereas you are more or less in charge of your own domain at the moment you would join the staff at PMH as a senior consultant but be under the line management of a much younger person (who is the driving force behind the funding bid). You also feel that your patients, many of them elderly, would find the journey to PMH exhausting. You would much rather have £65,000 which will allow you to purchase software that you believe will directly benefit your patients rather than large sums of money being spent on an expensive wing of what is already a very large and expensive medical centre. You will take some persuading to support any move in that direction. However, you have always and will always put the best interests of your patients first no matter what the personal costs might be.

Patient Representative, Princess Monica Hospital

You have become increasingly concerned about the rise in the number of postoperative infections found in patients. You are convinced that the problem lies in the outsourcing of ward cleaning. You have been pressurizing the hospital management to return to the policy of hospital employed and managed cleaners. You have also received a number of complaints from relatives of patients in the geriatric wards who are concerned that their loved ones are not getting proper attention at meal times. Too often you hear of elderly patients being asked if they would like a dinner and when told 'No' the plate is taken away without any attempt to persuade. This is the fault of the overall time-tabling of the ward caterers who do not have the time to have even a brief conversation with the patients. You regret the passing of hospital employed ancillary and catering staff and think the interests of the patients would be better served if PMH were to return to this structure. You are generally supportive of the proposed changes but not at the cost of patient care.

Social Services

Your task is to ensure that when patients are discharged they have a secure place to return to. Too often elderly patients live alone and cannot look after themselves. Your job is to make all the necessary contact with relevant welfare and voluntary organizations to arrange for care before discharge. The problem is that the number of patients has risen dramatically but the number of staff to undertake this work has not and is too small. This has led to either a patient being discharged with no after-hospital care being arranged or they have to continue to occupy a bed long after they should have been discharged. As a non-medical member of staff you do not have access to the record system and so have the task of creating your own. You have made representations to the hospital administrators for limited access but as yet this has not happened. In your view the need to create your own records is an unnecessary burden.

Senior Hospital Administrator

You have been given the task of putting together the submission for an expansion of PMH. The hospital governors are emphatic that this bid be successful and are prepared to support you in the face of resistance. Although you have experience of the newspaper industry, where you made your name for being ruthless, you have little experience of the NHS. Despite your reputation you are charming and able to get your way without resorting to threats. You have never been known to raise your voice. Your initial thoughts are that there can be considerable savings made by closing several of the cottage hospitals as most of the serious cases end up in PMH so it makes sense to rationalize the service. Moreover, two of the consultants are within three years of retirement and may well be persuaded to accept voluntary redundancy which will allow for new – and possibly cheaper – appointments.

Trainee Nurse

You are 19 years of age and have been a trainee for nine months. You love the work and are following a family tradition. Your mother was a nurse and your father a doctor. However, the stress of the job is having its effect. There do not seem to be enough nursing staff on duty especially at night and weekends. At certain times of the year such as Christmas and New Year you do not feel that patients are getting proper care as you are rushed off your feet. You are suspicious of the quality of cleaning but are afraid to voice your views, as you are so new in the post. Like most of the nursing staff you are unhappy about the increase in the numbers of administrative staff when the hospital desperately needs more medical staff. Although you have heard about the proposed submission you, as well as the other nursing staff, have little knowledge of what this means. No one has spoken to the nursing staff and as far as you are aware the doctors are in the dark too, at least the junior doctors that you have spoken to know little about the proposal. You do not want to get into any debate about changes as you are too busy with getting to grips with your role as a nurse.

Consultant Cardiologist (In Favour)

The proposal is a very good idea. You are a senior consultant and in charge of cardiology at the hospital. You are ambitious and very keen to get a specialist cardiology department at PMH. You have given every support to the senior administrator and tried to do as much lobbying as you can. You have heard about some consultants wanting money for specialist software but you think this is not as important as getting support for the changes to the hospital. You have spent some time researching the equipment and materials that a specialist unit will need. It will be a difficult argument to win as Southsea already have a fine specialist unit but you are banking on the population figures to support the need for a second specialist unit in the area.

Consultant Pediatrician (Against)

You have built a significant reputation for Pediatrics but PMH stands to lose the specialist children's unit to Southsea. You would be forced to transfer to Southsea if what is rumoured happens. Aside from the additional travelling you do not think that you would get the senior post. You have considerable support from parents in the area and are not averse to leaking what is happening should the loss of your 'empire' be on the cards. However, you are good at concealing your hostility to the proposal preferring to work behind the scenes.

Union Representative for Cleaning Staff

The Union officer is unaware of any changes or of the proposal. You object to the criticisms made about your staff as you feel the problem, if there is one, lies with the management. The hospital staff were laid off and all offered the same job at lower pay and restricted hours two years ago. Aside from the anger that many felt the time allowed for the activities is too short to do a proper job. This resulted in many of the old hospital staff leaving and staff new to this kind of cleaning, recruited. You have been mounting a campaign to get the cleaning staff and catering staff reinstated as hospital staff. You have the support of the patient representative in this matter. You are presently holding talks with hospital management, which seem to be going well. You think that you get on well with the senior administrator.

Senior Staff Nurse

You have been a senior staff nurse for five years and a staff nurse for 10. Your area of specialism is urology and renal services, so it is your wards that have been affected most by the increased number of alcohol-related cases in recent times. Your department is short of specialist equipment and there have been occasions when you have had to transfer patients to London because your department was unable to provide the specialist care. PMH has been a good place to work up until the efficiency drive. In practice this has meant changes to shift hours and shift cycle times. The result, in your view, is a lowering of patient care. You and your staff work tirelessly but the strain at night and weekends has had a deleterious effect on your nurses, particularly the young ones. Five staff have left over the past year because of the stress of the job. You find it very difficult to defend the increase of administrative staff to your colleagues when you clearly could do with more medical staff. You too think that returning to the good old days when nurses wore uniforms, which marked them out as nurses, would be a good idea. You have met the senior administrator several times at staff meetings and like him. You are unaware of the detail of the proposal although you had heard that something is taking place but assume that it will not affect you.

Junior Doctor

You are at the end of the first year on the wards. Like your colleagues your biggest concern is getting enough rest. What is going on in the hospital management passes you by. You are unaware of the proposal that is being developed but in any case have no view about what it might contain. You hope to specialize in pediatric care and get on well with the consultant. You have recently purchased a house in the area and are struggling a bit financially. You do not get on with the Union representative who you think has no real grasp of the problems that patients report. You have made your views known to the senior consultant who is in agreement and have promised to take it up with the hospital management. You are concerned about the number of nursing staff on at the weekends and have raised this matter several times with hospital management. Although you make full use of the computer-based record system you are aware of one case in another hospital where the records were incorrect and the patient concerned almost died because of an error in medication. For these reasons you always check the data with a test of your own before you prescribe treatment.

Case 2 – Major Air

This case study can be used either to develop investigative skills, or those of an Information System Development consultant, or both! Client-led design will make a suitable framework of approach that can be 'front-ended' with either SSM or AIM (see Chapter 3).

The object is to produce a model of the information system required for the company. The way that the company has developed reflects the way that the markets dictated but it is becoming increasingly apparent that the basis upon which decisions are made is deficient. Each sector of the company seems to be working in isolation united only by a fixation on the bottom-line.

You are a senior manager in the company in charge of information systems provision but feel that you do not have the power or influence to implement what the company needs. Attempts to get you promoted to the Board of Directors have hitherto failed. An opportunity has recently presented itself as the owner of the company has become increasingly concerned that the root cause of the company's problems is related to the lack of information provision and availability. He is unable to obtain a comprehensive overview of the company's operations and has to reply on what he suspects are 'massaged' reports from each of his directors. He intends to raise this matter at the next Board meeting. He has tasked you and your team to produce an outline design for an information system for Major Air. The information system should include provision for marketing data, financial data, passenger numbers, airfreight and human resources. We are looking for the way in which the information system will operate, some of it supported by technology and some resulting from human actions. The exercise will enable you to identify the system of interest, the serving system and identify those parts that can be supported by some form of technology (see Chapter 3). The activity models produced provide the basis for Object Oriented models which lead to a technical specification for those areas that will be served by technology (see example in Chapter 8).

Major Air is a large multinational airline based in Great Britain. The company functions by regular meetings of the small Board of Directors who enjoy complete autonomy within their region. Each region compiles the feedback of all data, financial and personnel, and a summary is sent to HQ one week in advance of the Board meeting. Marketing is undertaken by each region and although company policy is decided by the Board its implementation is at the discretion of the regional director. There is fierce resistance by the current members of the Board to the suggestion by the chair to increase the Board by the addition of a technical director.

The Problem Situation

Major Air

The company was set up in 1985, initially with the aim of providing a cheaper cost alternative Atlantic carrier to other British airlines flying to the United States. Despite attempts to put the company out of business Major Air survived the 1990s well and generated enough wealth to increase the number of aircraft and develop routes flown. The company now has daily flights to New York, Boston, Houston and San Francisco and more recently Tokyo, Singapore and Hong Kong. Plans are in hand to start flights to Australia in the New Year.

Despite the initial 'cut price' philosophy the company has, for the past five years, turned the company into a 'great value for money' airline and claims to provide a better standard of service at a lower price than any other airline in all classes of seating, namely: 1st Class, Business Class, Premium Economy and Tourist Class. The company has steadily replaced its aircraft and is a keen participant in the Boeing customer-led design approach to aircraft design, where alongside the engineers are assembly workers, mechanics, tooling experts and customers.

The competition in the passenger air transportation market is fierce and Major Air have been accused of saving money by cutting back on safety and hiding the real cost of travel. For example, the lowest Tourist Class ticket costs 15% less than its nearest rival but the passengers have to pay for any meals or alcohol consumed. Snacks and refreshments are provided within the ticket price but the main meals are not. In overall terms the passenger might end up paying 10% more than on other airlines depending upon the choice of food and drink. Online seat reservations, which is a free service on other airlines, costs 0.2% of ticket price and there is a charge for baggage too large for the overhead lockers.

Major Air deny any cut back on safety and claim savings are made through the use of computer-based fault diagnostic equipment and a sophisticated in-flight monitoring system of all aircraft equipment. Despite Major Air's excellent safety record it has lost 5% of its total Atlantic passenger population over the past year. The criticisms of lack of safety by other airlines seem to have found credibility probably because of two incidents on its cargo service. In each case, involving a serious fire on board, the investigation showed the company was not at fault, but the general population seemed to have gained the impression (encouraged by other carriers) that the fires had occurred because of inadequate maintenance. A recent 'near miss' incident at Heathrow Airport involving Major Air and another airline has added to passenger anxiety. In this case the fault was found to lie with the other aircraft, which was found to have a minor technical defect in its navigation system. Nevertheless the perception of the public, fuelled by competitors, is damaging the company.

The Company

Major Air is managed by a Board of Directors operating through a management hierarchy located in each geographical division. The Board of Directors of the company comprises the Company Chairman, Philip Major, the Director of Finance, Brian Feltham, and a Director from each of the various operations as part of the company. The Board meets once every three months at the company headquarters at Heathrow. The standard topics on the monthly agenda are:

1. Profit/Loss account
2. Passenger numbers
3. Total freight
4. Review of annual plan.

Additional items to the agenda are included when considered necessary. The latter rarely happens as each Director jealously guards their part of the company and does not wish to provide an opportunity for criticism of their area at the main Board meeting.

The company is divided into five divisions – these are USA, Japan, Hong Kong, newly created Singapore and Australia and global freight. The USA division has three directors: North, East and West Coast, which deal with passenger carriage only. All freight, of which 80% is between the USA and UK, is operated by one director and represents 51% of the total profit for the company – the target is to build this to 60% within the next five years which will allow freight to subsidize the passenger side of the company and allow Major Air to continue to undercut competitors' fares.

Philip Major has many other business interests including a communications company and a software house specializing in computer games. His latest project includes the development of virtual reality systems which can be marketed in the leisure industry but which will have spin-offs of business applications (e.g. to aid in training for aircraft maintenance, pilot training). He is very keen on the use of technology to provide his directors with up-to-date information to aid them in their decision making and enable the company to operate as a single entity. There is a highly regarded information systems manager who is based at the GB HQ that Major believes would make an excellent addition to the Board but so far his attempted appointment of an Information Systems Director has been rejected, although only by a slim majority. The Information Systems Manager is concerned that Major Air are being left behind by other airlines as they have to rely on data from other sources and do not take advantage of the Information that they could collect from their global company, nor do the various Directors share data they do have – except when it is politically expedient.

Philip Major is very much a 'hands on' type of individual which sometimes results in his neglect of certain parts of the company whilst he pursues an interest. But recently he has become alarmed by both the sudden drop in passenger numbers and the predicted fall in freight carrying that were revealed at the last Board meeting. The two questions he intends to ask at the next Board meeting are 'Where do we get our information from?' and 'How reliable is it?' as the beginning of his determination to appoint a Director of IS. He sees information as an essential commodity for any business and no more so than with a global business like his. He has become more and more convinced that information is the 'glue' that binds a company together. Equally if it is not available to all the decision makers then the company is in danger of failing.

USA

The USA link is highly competitive within the company and each of the North, East and West Coast branches of the operation work as independent companies. The Director of the West Coast operation feels that the USA operations as a whole would benefit if they operated as one unit instead of three but this suggestion is greeted with scorn by the East and North divisions who claim that the suggestion has only been made because the West Coast operations are small (22% of the total USA passengers, with East 33% and North 45%). The Director of the North division has worked for Major Air for 15 years and has secured many agreements with tour operators, car hire companies, hotels and food suppliers which enable this division to take 10% of the total UK/New York market. He believes quite firmly that if he maintains the link with the fundamental factors of passenger transportation everything else will follow. His policies are devoted to the maintenance of these factors. He is totally unconcerned by the fall in passenger numbers or the reputation for cutting corners on safety that the company seems to be getting.

The Director of the East Coast division has only recently joined the company and is determined to make a success of the operation. In her last company, one of Major Air's main competitors, she had the reputation for being a good tactician, and a shrewd politician but a poor staff administrator. She had, in her last post, been blamed for several staff disputes which subsequently were shown not to be of her making but senior colleagues, anxious not to create any difficulties for themselves, were willing to let her take the blame and to 'assist' her to make a decision to leave the company. This she has refused to do and is determined to overturn what she sees as a male dominated cabal. It was for these reasons that she was reluctant to support the Director of the West Coast division and his suggestion to work as one unit. Her hidden agenda was to improve the standing of the Eastern domain and, from a position of strength, embrace the suggestion to make a single operation of which she would become the head. Her major concern was to exploit the weaknesses of her two colleagues and maintain the overall percentage of the market but shift the balance of trade from North to East.

The Director of the West Coast division felt that if the company operated as one unit they could increase Major Air's total market share. For example, he noted that many passengers wanting to travel to Minneapolis or St Louis would fly to Houston or New York then change airlines for the last leg of their journey. Some passengers travelled to San Francisco from New York with one of Major Air's competitors. He was also concerned by the rumour about safety, particularly as he knew what importance Philip Major placed upon safety and the amount the company invested in safety. As the accidents had happened in the USA he felt there was a need to communicate to the public the many safety innovations the company had introduced before competitors could do more damage to trade. He also felt that the virtues of the company (e.g. customer-led design of aircraft) were not being communicated to the public and, equally as important, the views of the customers about aircraft departure, availability and disembarkation problems were not being communicated to the company. He was also quite confident that mutually beneficial arrangements could be made with rivals of Major Air (e.g. aircraft availability, transfer of passengers, internal flights).

Major Air acts like most other air carriers as far as check-in and baggage collection are concerned. The First Class passengers are collected from and delivered to their hotels (providing the hotel is located in the city nearest to the airport), Business Class passengers have the use of a special lounge where they can purchase drinks and order a meal, which they can take in the sectioned-off portion of the airport dining area. The bulk of the passengers, Tourist Class (85%), use the general facilities of the airport. There is a suggestion that Economy Class passengers could purchase a pass to use the Business Class lounge at major airport hubs but a recent poll of business travelling passengers found this to be unpopular and has been shelved for the moment although the newly appointed Director for Singapore and Australia intends to make this happen as he feels that this will be welcome for passengers travelling on the long haul flights and will give Major Air the edge over competitors on these routes. The Director for Hong Kong and Japan is openly hostile to this suggestion. He is also suspicious that he will lose the Hong Kong route to the ambitious Director for Singapore and Australia.

The air-crew, stewards and stewardesses are specially trained to Major Air standards although the final decision about the training courses attended rests with each divisional director. The prime task of the cabin crew is to look after passenger comfort which includes flight entertainments and frequent refreshments (at an extra cost for standard/tourist class passengers). The pilots are also expected to avoid unnecessary passenger discomfort (e.g. avoid turbulence). One major area of concern is the distress felt by passengers when the aircraft becomes part of a stacking system over airports (note: ways of reducing passenger anxiety need to be considered by your consultancy). At present the responsibilities of the cabin crew begin the moment the passengers step on to the aircraft and end when the last passenger leaves. The North Division (USA) Director feels that one way of reducing costs is to cut down on the number of stewards/stewardesses per passenger and bring the company in line with other airlines. The Director of the Eastern division (USA) feels that the cost of the meals should be included in an increased basic fare. The fare should be set at a level which, initially, represents a saving in the cost of food purchased by each passenger but over a 12-month period reduce the quantity of food to allow a profit to be made. The Director of the Western region was in favour of surveying passengers' opinions but the other two Directors did not support his suggestion on the grounds that if the company did not do what the customers proposed then the company stood a greater chance of losing their custom.

Far East

The Directors for the Far East were unanimous in their support for existing levels of stewards and stewardesses to be maintained and emphasize the need for passenger comfort, which is a major selling point of Major Air's competitors. They were united in opposing a charge for advance seat booking and additional charges for luggage of any kind. They feel that the more attention that is paid to customers the better it is for business.

The Directors in this part of the company feel that their sector is rapidly expanding but Major Air is not expanding at the same rate as they believe it should. This assertion is dismissed by the Directors from the USA as an attempt at empire building. However, at a recent meeting in Singapore they decided to start an information gathering exercise to find out what is happening in their market. On hearing this, the other Directors have tried to stop it as being too costly. This item is likely to be added to the next agenda and provides Major with the opportunity to suggest the inclusion of an Information Systems Director to the Board.

The Environment

The company's prime competitors had learnt from Major Air innovations and had installed many of them themselves. In financial terms they know that Major Air cannot sustain the Atlantic passenger price difference much longer and that they will be forced to make radical changes either to the operations of the company or to their pricing strategy. Public accusations by Major Air about a 'dirty tricks' campaign carried out by their competitors are considered to be normal tactics in a highly competitive industry. The use of such tactics, however, is unsustainable as a long-term policy and will be seen by the general public as a smokescreen to hide difficulties.

A recent survey of the travelling public shows that the competitive edge in the airline business lies in the quality of service rather than in a low-cost operation. This is bad news for Major Air and one that should be discussed sooner rather than later. The survey showed that long-haul flight passengers were less concerned with saving £20 than they were with comfort and good quality service. The Board of Directors has dismissed this as yet another tactic from the other airlines. However, they do not have any evidence to the contrary and since they meet so infrequently, if it is true, they could find the company losing even more revenue and with empty aircraft.

Part 2

Short Cases

Four short cases appear below:

The Forgotten Heroes of the Falklands War
Action on 'Garden Grabbing'

Sustainable Ports
Airport Security

Each of these cases consists of a summary plus links to further relevant sources on the Web or in the Press. Searching using a Web browser will easily uncover more of these. They are intended to replicate unstructured problem situations which could be of interest to individuals and groups in their working or private lives.

The cases are intended to provide an opportunity for you to think about the application of some of the ideas we have covered in this text. You might, for instance:

- Draw a rich picture reflecting your understanding of this problem situation.
- Create a systems map reflecting your view of the situation.
- Identify some systems of interest. Choose one of these, set a boundary and draw up a Root Definition and conceptual model.
- Consider which of the approaches and/or methodologies that we have discussed in this volume could be most useful in exploring such a problem situation.
- Apply some of the tools and techniques of your chosen approach to explore the situation further.
- Discuss your analysis with colleagues or classmates.

The Forgotten Heroes of the Falklands War

Of the 30,000 British personnel who served in the Falklands War (1982), it is estimated that 9% (2700) are suffering or have suffered post traumatic stress disorder (PTSD). The actual number is unclear, but what is known is that some 300 of these war veterans have since committed suicide. There is also evidence to show that many have succumbed to alcoholism and depression, sometimes leading to homelessness, violence and crime. A relatively high proportion of the prison population has previously served in the armed forces. Many veterans were unaware that they suffered from PTSD, or simply felt that they should rise above their negative feelings in the spirit of the 'stiff upper lip'. In some cases, the full impact of their experiences did not surface until 20–25 years after the war was over. What is clear is that the social cost of ignoring the invisible harm done to veterans has been considerable – not just for the veterans themselves but for the whole of British society. Yet we have known about PTSD (or shell shock as we once called it) for very many years. Elsewhere, the social impact of emotional damage to Vietnam War veterans in the USA has been very well documented. Many of those who served in the Falklands campaign are now receiving the help that they need. However, four times as many people have taken part in the conflicts in Afghanistan and Iraq in recent years. It is important that we reflect upon the needs of these people as they are reintegrated into civil society, and the impact that their experiences will have on their lives and those of their families and our wider society.

Below, you will find links to a variety of sources in which these issues are discussed. Consider these sources, and any others you can find:

http://news.bbc.co.uk/1/hi/uk/1758301.stm
http://www.portsmouth.co.uk/news/local/east-hampshire/forgotten_heroes_of_
  falklands_conflict_1_1272119
http://www.independent.co.uk/news/world/americas/the-fallen-amp-the-forgotten-the-
  falklands-war-25-years-on-441691.html
http://www.pension4army.co.uk/supportadvice/menu-options
http://www.guardian.co.uk/world/2007/jan/21/falklands.uk1
http://ptsd.about.com/u/ua/causesanddevelopment/overcomingptsdua.htm

Action on 'Garden Grabbing'

For many years, British governments have encouraged developers to look for brown field sites on which to build much needed extra housing, in order to protect rural areas from encroachment. However, developers prefer sites which are not previously built upon, since the building process is then simpler and less costly. One result of this has been a rise in the numbers of gardens associated with existing buildings being acquired for development. Figures suggest the proportion of houses built on such sites increased from one in ten in 1997 to one in four in 2008. Many people have begun to express concern over this practice, since it tends to increase population density in urban areas without a proportionate increase in services. Pressure on schools, hospitals and transport systems has grown in consequence. The former Labour government defended the practice, emphasizing the benefits of development within existing urban areas. However, the coalition government's Department for Communities and Local Government has taken a view that communities deserve more protection from so-called 'Garden Grabbing'. Greg Clark, Minister for Decentralisation, has introduced legislation to remove gardens from the category of land designated as 'brown field' and claims to be taking steps to ensure that decisions on development are taken at a more local level.

A further area of concern in relation to urban and suburban development has been the impact of paved areas around residential housing. In past decades, residential plots tended to consist of a dwelling house with a back and/or front garden area containing flower beds, lawns, etc. However, as we became increasingly addicted to private transport during the latter half of the 20th century, more garden space was paved in order to create parking space. At the same time, with increased leisure time available, many people created paved patio areas in order to enjoy barbeques, hot tubs and other outdoor facilities. Not only did these paved areas change the character of neighbourhoods, with less visible green spaces, but they led to concern about the impact on water tables. Where rainwater was no longer absorbed into the soil, existing drains were unable to cope with the volume of water running off suburban properties. In some cases, local flooding resulted. Legislation to deal with this issue was enacted in 2008, since when planning permission has been needed to lay down an impermeable surface around residential property. However, this does nothing to reduce the impact of hard surfaces already in place.

Below, you will find links to a variety of sources in which these issues are discussed. Consider these sources, and any others you can find:

http://news.bbc.co.uk/1/hi/8728633.stm
http://www.communities.gov.uk/multimedia/newsroom/1638697
http://www.rhs.org.uk/Gardens/News/New-powers-to-prevent-garden-grabbing
http://www.legislation.gov.uk/uksi/2008/2362/pdfs/uksi_20082362_en.pdf
http://www.drivewayexpert.co.uk/ecological-environmental-driveway.html

Sustainable Ports

Britain is a maritime nation with an economy dependent upon trade and transport. Over the past few decades, the world has seen growth in the volume of trade and increasing containerization and automation of the ports upon which it relies. Seaports developed during the 19th century have ceased to be fit for purpose, both in terms of the berths available to ships and the mechanisms for loading, unloading and processing cargoes. This affects not only the ports themselves but the infrastructure of the surrounding areas, especially road transport networks. Our seaports have undergone periods of rapid expansion and more modernization is still needed, including creation of new ports. However, at the same time it is recognized that development of the ports cannot be considered in isolation. It is necessary to look at the impact on zones and communities local to those ports, in terms of both benefits and challenges for the economy and infrastructure. It is also necessary to look into environmental impact on the hinterlands surrounding the ports themselves and beyond. The sea is, of course, not biddable. We cannot readily engineer the wind and tide or their impact on our dynamic coastline. It is important therefore that design and development of new and existing ports take into account changes that can be predicted by geographers, geologists, meteorologists and others.

It is vital that policy makers devise ways in which we can develop the economic potential of our trading ports without sacrificing precious resources in the process. There are a number of principles which must be adhered to:

- Development must take into account real pricing, not simply project-based accounting. The impact on all stakeholders, both direct and indirect, must be taken into account.
- Future proofing is needed. It is not acceptable to develop resources for the benefit of current generations when the negative impacts may be felt far into the future.
- Holistic thinking is required which does not privilege the well-being of maritime regions over the well-being of the whole country, or indeed other parts of the world.

Below, you will find links to a variety of sources in which these issues are discussed. Consider these sources, and any others you can find:

http://environment.abports.co.uk/env_sustainable.htm
http://www.sustainableports.com/
http://www.trb.org/Main/Home.aspx
http://www.portoftruro.co.uk/files/downloads/2011/07/sustainablestrategy.pdf

Airport Security

In 2000 it was estimated that the world's commercial jet airlines carried approximately 1.09 billion people on 18 million flights, while suffering only 20 fatal accidents, suggesting that air travel is technically a relatively safe activity. However, since 9/11 we have all been concerned about our safety in the air for reasons of a non-technical nature. Civil aviation authorities around the world have imposed restrictions on the types of luggage we may carry and the items we may take with us into the cabin of the airliner. At the same time, screening of baggage and other items, as well as techniques of body searching, have been introduced at airports. Travellers are now accustomed to queuing to go through electronic surveillance barriers and to carrying identification documents to obtain access even to internal flights.

However, the incidence of terrorist attacks on planes remains low when compared to the huge volume of air travel undertaken every day. Terrorists succeed by planting fear of what might happen, without necessarily needing to take more than minimal action against target populations. What we sometimes lose sight of is the cost to us of maintaining our vigilance, because the catastrophic costs of failing to do so are so evident.

Airport security systems can fail in two ways: they can fail to detect a genuine risk, or they can fail by generating false alarms which bring about costly and inconvenient delays causing harm to both private lives and the economy. An example occurred in March 2006 at LaGuardia Airport in New York. A man successfully walked through a metal detector but was called aside for a random check of his shoes. Whether or not he was a terrorist is not known because he declined to be checked and fled back into the crowded airport. There was no choice but to evacuate the whole terminal and subsequently rescreen 2000–3000 passengers. The delays to flights backed up the system for several days, causing problems for air traffic controllers, airport services and, of course, customers. The knock-on effects of this problem cannot be known but will have impacted on many aspects of the lives of those customers, the companies for whom they worked, other companies with whom their employers did business, and of course social events which were missed. Connecting flights were missed, pick-up arrangements disrupted, and so on. A very high cost of this failure was borne by many stakeholders around the world. Can we design better security systems that fail more gracefully when they do fail? Are we making the best use of technology to speed up screening and improve confidence in our travel systems?

Below, you will find links to a variety of sources in which these issues are discussed. Consider these sources, and any others you can find:

http://www.schneier.com/blog/archives/2010/11/me_on_airport_s_1.html
http://www.youtube.com/watch?v=Y4ycfgXxwoo
http://www.direct.gov.uk/en/TravelAndTransport/Foreigntravel/AirTravel/index.htm
http://www.bbc.co.uk/news/business-11632944
http://eur-lex.europa.eu/LexUriServ/LexUriServ.do?uri=CELEX:32006R1546:EN:NOT://
    science.howstuffworks.com/transport/flight/modern/airport-security.htm

Glossary

Algedonic alerts: warnings of deviation from target output, used in VSM.

Algedonic loop: a heuristic, which cannot be precisely specified although we know what we want.

Anastomotic reticulum: a complex network with many branches which intermingle such that it is no longer possible to sort out how the messages traverse the reticulum.

Appreciation: gaining an understanding about the whole situation and the context within which it resides.

Appreciative settings: conditions our perceptions of new experiences, but are also modified by them.

Appreciative System: Vickers' description of the way in which we gain a holistic understanding of a situation. Appreciation manifests itself in the exercise through time of mutually related judgements of reality and value. Appreciative judgments are a set of readinesses which distinguish some aspects of a situation rather than others – to classify in this way rather than that. These readinesses are what Vickers describes as the Appreciative System (Vickers, 1983, p. 67).

Autopoiesis: this literally means 'self-creation' and expresses something which is self-sustaining or productive of reproduction.

Black Box: a means of modelling the changes that the input to a System has upon its output.

Bremermann's Limit: the maximum computational speed of a self-contained system in the material universe, i.e. 2.56×10^{47} bits, which number is known as Bremermann's Limit.

Causal Loop: a diagram to depict the dynamic relationship between a set of variables.

Cloud: these are the symbols used in SSM to represent activities within a conceptual model. A cloud is used rather than a circle as a means of emphasizing its contents to be ideas and the result of thinking about the situation rather than concrete 'things' that exist.

Commodity: a metaphor used in this text as a means of describing attributes and exercise of individual uses of 'informal' power.

Constructivism: theory that knowledge is not something we acquire but something we produce.

Critical Systems: depends upon the school of thought. For some this relates to Foucault and emancipation, for others Habermas and the universality of morality amongst the participants.

Entropy: states of increasing probability and decreasing order (Bertanlaffy).

Epistemology: theory of knowledge which differentiates the diversity of ideas which lie within.

Functionalist: an approach in which a description is made of the parts of a system of interest and how these support the system to survive. The observations are made from an objective view of the situation.

Goal: an end which individuals or groups seek to achieve.

Heuristics: find out, discover; trial and error kind of procedure.

Hierarchical systems: entities treated as wholes built upon smaller entities.

Hierarchy: an arrangement whereby its contents are organized in such a fashion as to show their dependencies upon each other.

Holism: looking at the world as a series of inter-connected systems rather than taking things in isolation.

Homeostat: ultrastable system.

Interpretivism: concerned with interaction and meaning. This stems from the German ideas of hermeneutics: an attempt to understand an actor's description of the situation. Interpretivism rejects the notion of neutral observation.

Interpretivism: concerned with trying to understand the world as it is e.g. Schütz (1899–1959).

Languaging: flows of meaning including sounds and gestures.

Level of resolution: level of detail of the constituent parts of a 'model of something'.

Logical dependencies: the reliance of one activity upon the other expressed by its logical relationship.

Metaphors: a phrase or word applied to something which is not literally true. A comparison made between two unlike things that have something in common (e.g. commodity of power).

Neurocybernetics: in cybernetics the study of communication and automatic control systems.

Neurophysiological: branch of physiology that deals with the functions of the nervous system.

Notional boundary: an imaginary (sometimes concrete) line to encapsulate a situation of interest.

Notional system: a system identified by an individual but recognized to be a personal view which may alter over time, accepting that someone else might describe it in another way.

Organization: for the purposes of this book we will assume an organization to be something created by human beings for a purpose.

PEArL: a mnemonic developed to assist in understanding participant contribution and interaction.

Perturbations: factors that influence system behaviour.

Phenomenology: the study of structures of consciousness as experienced from the first-person point of view: An attempt to describe our existence directly as it is.

Power: in a social setting a sense of what is done to influence people, to cause things to happen.

Readinesses: to distinguish some sets of a situation rather than others and to classify and value these in this way rather than in that. Our (often unconscious) willingness to make a judgement about something.

Reductionist: someone who reduces the situation into its smallest manageable component. Typically decomposing a higher level system into its parts (Sarkar, 1992).

Relationship maintenance: the ongoing maintenance of our relationship in an ever-changing environment.

Reticulum: a netlike formation or structure; a network.

Serving system: a system which provides essential support for another system in order for it to function.

Singerian: never-ending process of learning – it has no terminating point. It has the purpose of creating knowledge.

Socio-Technical Approach: an approach to complex organizational work design that recognizes the interaction between people and technology in workplaces.

Symbolic Interactionism: sociological perspective that places emphasis on micro-scale social interaction, which is particularly important in subfields such as urban sociology and social psychology.

System: a set of interconnected parts that, for us, seem to form a meaningful whole which we can name and draw a boundary around – it is something which, taken together, has meaning for us.

System to be served: the primary system of interest.

Systems: a general term, an epistemology we adopt to encapsulate a particular way of thinking about the world.

Teleology: developments happen as a result of the ends served by them – rather than the result of prior causes.

Weltanschauung(en):   a word taken from German that means roughly (but not entirely accurately) world view. In the earlier chapter we refer to this being a world view. We extend that simple definition to mean as Churchman (1971, p. 33) wrote 'stories of the world' or as the *Penguin Dictionary of Philosophy* (Mautner, 2000, p. 599) defines, a comprehensive philosophical view of the world and man's place in it.

References

Ackoff, R.L. (1962). *Scientific Method: Optimising Applied Research Decisions*. John Wiley & Sons Inc., New York.

Ackoff, R.L. (1999). *Re-Creating the Corporation: A Design of Organizations for the 21st Century*. Oxford University Press, New York.

Ackoff, R.L., Emery, F.E. and Ruben, B.D. (2006). *On Purposeful Systems: An interdisciplinary analysis of individual and social behaviour as a system of purposeful events*. Edition with new material, New Brunswick: Transaction Publishers, New Brunswick; originally published 1972 Tavistock Publications, London.

Ackoff, R.L. and Emery, F.E. (1972). *On Purposeful Systems*. Chicago: Aldine-Atherton.

Ackoff, R.L., Magidson, J. and Addison, H. (2006). *Idealized Design – Creating an Organization's Future*. Wharton Business School Publishing. 217–232.

Adorno, T.W., with Horkheimer, M. (1944). *Philosophische Fragmente* by Social Studies Association, Inc., New York revised (1947) as *Dialectic of Enlightenment* Querido Verlag in Amsterdam.

AIIE Committee Report (1951). Proposed Symbols and Terms for Feedback Control Systems, *Electrical Engineering*, 70, 909.

Ashby, R. (1961). *Introduction to Cybernetics*. Chapman & Hall, London.

Ashby, R. (1978). *Design for a Brain*. Chapman and Hall, London.

Ashby, W.R. (1956). *An Introduction to Cybernetics*. Chapman Hall, London.

Ashby, W.R. (1963). *An Introduction to Cybernetics*. Science Editions, John Wiley & Sons Inc., New York.

Atkinson, C.J. (1984). Metaphor and Systemic Praxis, PhD thesis, University of Lancaster, unpublished.

Austin, J.L. (1962). *How To Do Things With Words*. Oxford University Press, Oxford.

Avison, D. and Wood-Harper, T. (1990). *Multiview: An Exploration in Information Systems Development*. McGraw-Hill, Maidenhead, UK.

Avison, D., Baskerville, R. and Myers, M. (2001). Controlling Action Research Projects, *Information, Technology and People*, 14(1), 28–45.

Bammer, G. (2003). Embedding Critical Systems Thinking in the Academy. Proceedings of CMS Conference, http://www.mngt.waikato.ac.nz/ejrot/cmsconference/2003/abstracts/orsystems/Bammer.pdf, accessed 19 December 2011.

Bateson, G. (1972). *Steps to an Ecology of Mind: Collected Essays in Anthropology, Psychiatry, Evolution and Epistemology*. University of Chicago Press, Chicago.

Batty, D. (2003). 'Catalogue of Cruelty'. *The Guardian*, Monday 27 January 2003, retrieved from http://www.guardian.co.uk/society/2003/jan/27/childrensservices.childprotection, 8 December 2009.

Beckford, M. (2007). 'Road with 100 cameras is plagued by crime'. *The Daily Telegraph*, 14 November 2011, accessed at http://www.telegraph.co.uk/news/main.jhtml?xml=/news/2007/07/11/ncctv111.xml.

Bednar, P.M. (2007). Individual Emergence in Contextual Analysis. Special Issue on Individual Emergence, *Systemica: Journal of the Dutch Systems Group*, 14(1–6), 23–38.

Bednar, P. and Welch, C. (2007). A Double Helix Metaphor for Use and Usefulness in Informing Systems, *Informing Science*, 10, 273–295.

Beer, A.S. (1959). *Cybernetics and Management*. Science Editions, John Wiley & Sons Inc., New York.

Beer, A.S. (1972). *Brain of the Firm*. Allen Lane, The Penguin Press, London.

Beer, A.S. (1979). *The Heart of Enterprise*. John Wiley & Sons, London and New York.

Beer, A.S. (1981). *Brain of the Firm*. 2nd edition, John Wiley & Sons Ltd, Chichester.

Beer, A.S. (1994), *Brain of the Firm*. 2nd edition, Classic Beer Series, John Wiley & Sons Ltd, Chichester.

Berger, P.L. and Luckmann, T. (1966). *The Social Construction of Reality: A Treatise in the Sociology of Knowledge*. Anchor Books, Garden City, NY.

von Bertalanffy, L. (1940). Der Organismus als physikalisches System betrachtet, *Die Naturwissenschaften* (The organism is considered as a physical system, the natural sciences), 2(28), 521–531.

von Bertalanffy, L. (1950). An outline of General Systems Theory, *British Journal for the Philosophy of Science*, 1, 139–164.

von Bertalanffy, L. (1956). 'General System Theory'. In *General System, Yearbook of the Society for the Advancement of General System Theory*. Emery, F.E. (ed).

von Bertalanffy, L. (1968). *General Systems Theory – Foundations, Development, Applications*. Brazille, New York.

Bignell, V. and Fortune, J. (1984). *Understanding Systems Failures*. Manchester University Press, Manchester and New York.

Blumer, H. (1969). *Symbolic Interactionism: Perspective and Method*. University of California Press.

Blumer H. (1975). 'Sociological Implications of the Thought of George Mead'. In *Social Theory Revisited*, C.J. Jesser (ed). Dryden Press, Hinsdale Ill.

Bohman, J. and Rehg, W. (2009). 'Jürgen Habermas', *The Stanford Encyclopedia of Philosophy* (Summer 2009 edition), Edward N. Zalta (ed). Metaphysics Research Lab, CSLI, Stanford, CA.

Brittanica, accessed 2011 (http://www.britannica.com/EBchecked/topic/180957/eidetic-reduction).

Bullock, A. and Trombley, S. (1999). *The New Fontana Dictionary of Modern Thought*. Harper Collins.

Bullock, A. and Trombley, S. (2000), *The New Fontana Dictionary of Modern Thought*. Harpers Collins, London.

Burchfield, R.W. (1998). *The New Fowler's Modern English Usage*. Clarendon Press, Oxford.

Burrell, G. and Morgan, G. (1979). *Sociological Paradigms and Organisational Analysis: Elements of the sociology of corporate life*. Heinemann, London.

Burrell, G. and Morgan, G. (2005). *Sociological Paradigms and Organisational Analysis*. Ashgate Publishing Company, Aldershot.

Capra, F. (1996). *The Web of Life: A New Scientific Understanding of Living Systems*. Anchor Books, NY.

Capra, F. (2003). *The Hidden Connections*. Flamingo, London.

Cerbone, D.R. (2008). *Heidegger: A Guide for the Perplexed*. Continuum, London.

Champion D. (2001). Navigating the Gap between Purposeful Action and a Serving Information System. PhD thesis, De Montfort University.

Champion, D. (2007). Managing Action Research: The PEArL Framework, *Systemic Practice and Action Research*, 20, 455–465.

Champion, D. and Stowell, F.A. (2000). 'An Interpretivist Approach to Modelling Clients Requirements for Information Systems'. In *Systems Modelling for Business Process*

Improvement, D.W. Bustard, P. Kawalek and M.T. Norris (eds). Artech, London, 187–198.

Champion, D. and Stowell, F.A. (2001). PEArL: A Systems Approach to Demonstrating Authenticity in Information System Design, *Journal of Information Technology*, 16, 3–12.

Champion, D. and Stowell, F.A. (2002). Navigating the Gap between Action and a Serving Information System, *Information Systems Frontiers*, 4(3), 273–284.

Champion, D. and Stowell, F.A. (2003). Validating Action Research Field Studies: PEArL, *Systemic Practice and Action Research*, 16(1), 21–36.

Champion, D., Stowell, F.A. and O'Callaghan, A. (2005). Client-Led Information Systems Creation (CLIC): Navigating the Gap, *Information Systems Journal*, 15(3), 213–231.

Checkland, P. and Holwell, S. (1998). *Information, Systems and Information Systems: Making sense of the field*. John Wiley & Sons Ltd, Chichester.

Checkland, P. and Poulter, J. (2006). *Learning for Action: A Short Definitive Account of Soft Systems Methodology, and its use for Practitioners, Teachers and Students*. John Wiley & Sons Ltd, Chichester.

Checkland, P.B. (1981). *Systems Thinking Systems Practice*. John Wiley & Sons Ltd, Chichester.

Checkland, P.B. (1983). O.R. and the Systems Movement: Mappings and Conflicts, *Journal of Operational Research*, 34(8), 661–675.

Checkland, P.B. (1985). From Optimising to Learning: A Development of Systems Thinking for the 1990s, *Journal Of The Operational Research Society*, 36(9), 757–767.

Checkland, P.B. (1989a). 'Soft Systems Methodology'. In J. Rosenhead (ed), *Rational Analysis for a Problematic World*. John Wiley & Sons Ltd, Chichester, 71–100.

Checkland, P.B. (1989b). 'O.R. and Social Science Fundamental Thoughts'. In *Operational Research and the Social Sciences*, M.C. Jackson, P. Keys and S.A. Cropper (eds). Plenum Press, New York, 35–41.

Checkland, P.B. (1989c). SSM Present and Future, Keynote Address at the 2nd UK Systems Society Workshop. City University 18–19 December 1989.

Checkland P.B. (1989d). 'Researching Systems Methodology Some Future Prospects'. In *Systems Prospects The Next Ten Years of Systems Research*, R.L. Flood, M.C. Jackson and P. Keys (eds). Plenum Press, New York, 915.

Checkland, P.B. (1999). *Systems Thinking, Systems Practice: A Thirty Year Retrospective*. John Wiley & Sons Ltd, Chichester.

Checkland, P.B. and Casar, A. (1986). Vickers' Concept of an Appreciative System: A Systemic Account, *J. Applied Systems Analysis*, 13, 3–17.

Checkland P.B. and Scholes J. (1990 and 1999). *Soft Systems Methodology in Action*. John Wiley & Sons Ltd, Chichester.

Cherns, A. (1976). Principles of Socio-technical Design. *Human Relations*, 2, 783–792.

Churchman, C.W. (1971). *The Design of Inquiring Systems: Basic Concepts of Systems and Organisation*. Basic Books. Concise Oxford, New York.

Clark, A.W. (1980). Action Research Theory Practice and Values, *Journal of Occupational Behaviour*, 1(2), 151–157.

Cooperrider D.L. and Srivastva, S. (1987). 'Appreciative Inquiry' in *Organisational Life Research in Organisational Change and Development* Vol. 1, 129–169.

Cooray, S.F. (2010). End-user Driven Development of Information Systems – Revisiting Vickers' Notion of 'Appreciation', thesis, University of Portsmouth, unpublished.

Crowe, M, (1996). Heraclitus and Information Systems, *Systemist*, 18(3), Aug 1996, 157–176.

Denzin, N.K. and Lincoln Y.S. (eds) (2011). *The SAGE Handbook of Qualitative Research* 4th edition, Sage, California, USA.

Descartes,R. (1637). *Discours de la Méthode*, Ian Maire.

Dilthey, W. (1961). *The Essence of Philosophy*, AMS Press, New York.

Emery, F. (1978). *The Emergence of a New Paradigm of Work*. Australian National University.

Emery, F.E and Trist, E.L. (1965). The Causal Texture of Organisational Environments, *Human Relations* 18(1), 2132.

Espejo, R. and Harnden, R. (1989). *The Viable Systems Model: Interpretation and application*. John Wiley & Sons Ltd, Chichester.

Finlayson, J.G. (2005). *Habermas, A Very Short Introduction*. Oxford University Press, Oxford.

Flood, R.L. and Jackson, M.C. (1991). *Creative Problem Solving: Total Systems Intervention*. John Wiley & Sons Ltd, Chichester.

Flood, R.L., Jackson, M.C. and Keys, P. (eds) (2006). *Systems Prospects*. Plenum Press, New York, 329–334.

Forrester, J.W. (1961). *Industrial Dynamics*. Pegasus Communications.

Forrester, Jay W. (1968). *Principles of Systems*. MIT Press, Cambridge, MA.

Forrester, Jay W. (1973). *World Dynamic*. MIT Press Cambridge, MA.

Foucault, M. (1980). *Power/Knowledge: Selected Interviews and Other Writings 1972–1977*, C. Gordon (ed), Harvester Press, Brighton.

Friedrichsen, G.W.S. (1980). *Shorter Oxford Dictionary*. Clarendon Press, Oxford.

Gadamer, H. (1975). *Truth and Method*. The Seabury Press, New York.

Gadamer, H. (2002). 'Elements of a Theory of Hermeneutic Experience'. In *The Phenomenology Reader*, (D. Moran, and T. Mooney, eds). Routledge, London. 314–338.

Gadamer, H. (2004). *Truth and Method*, 2nd revised edition (trans. J. Weinsheimer and D. Marshall), Continuum, London.

Garfinkel, H. (1967). *Studies in Ethnomethodology (Social and Political Theory)*. Prentice Hall.

Garfinkel H. (1968). *Studies in Ethnomethodology*. Prentice Hall, Englewood Cliffs NJ.

Giddens A. (1976). *New Rules of Sociological Method*. Hutchinson and Co., London.

Giddens A. (2001). *Sociology*, 4th edition, Polity, Oxford.

Gill, K.S. (1986). The Knowledge Based Machine: Issues of Knowledge Transfer in *Artificial Intelligence for Society*, K.S. Gill (ed). John Wiley and Sons Ltd, Chichester. 717.

Gilmore, T., Krantz, J. and Ramirez, R. (1986). Action Based Modes of Inquiry and The Host–Researcher Relationship, *Consultation* 5(3), 160–176.

Glanville, R. (2009). *The Black Box*, Vol. III, 39 Steps, Rema edition echoraum, Wein.

Guo, M., Wu, Z. and Stowell, F. (1999a). *Developing Object-Oriented Models within the Framework of Client-Led Design*. UKAIS'99, York.

Guo, M., Wu, Z., and Stowell, F.A. (1999b). 'Information Systems Specifications Within The Framework Of Client Led Design', In *Systems Modelling for Business Process Improvement*. D.W. Bustard, P. Kawalek, and M.T. Norris (eds). Artech, London, 199–211.

Guo, M., Wu, Z., Stowell, F.A. and Cowell, J. (2000). 'AM/OO Modelling': Research, Teaching and Practice. 5th UKAIS Conference, 25–28 April, 'Achievements and Problems' In *Information Systems – Cardiff*, P. Beynon-Davis (ed), 312–321.

Gutting, G., (ed) (1996). *The Cambridge Companion to Foucault*. Cambridge University Press, Cambridge.

Habermas J. (1971). *Knowledge and Human Interests*. Beacon, Boston.

Habermas, J. (1984). *The Theory of Communicative Action; Reason and the Rationalisation of Society*, Vol.1 (trans. T. McCarthy). Polity Press, Cambridge.

Habermas, J. (2003). *The Structural Transformation of the Public Sphere*. Polity Press Cambridge.

Habermas, J. (2003a). *Truth and Justification*, (trans. B. Fultner). MIT Press, Cambridge, MA.

Habermas, J. (2004). *The Theory of Communicative Action; The Critique of Functionalist Reason*, Vol. II (trans. T. McCarthy). Polity Press in association with Blackwell Publishers Ltd, Cambridge.

Harris, S. (2006). Internet Devices Threaten NSA's Ability to Gather Intelligence Legally. (National Journal, April, http://www.govexec.com/dailyfed/0406/041006nj2.htm).

Heidegger, M. (1967). *Being and Time* (trans. J. Macquarrie and E. Robinson). Basil Blackwell, Oxford.

Heidegger, M. (2002). 'The Worldhood of the World'. In *The Phenomenology Reader* (D. Moran, and T. Mooney, eds). Routledge, London, 288–307.

Helmholz, H. (1862). 'The Relation of the Natural Sciences to Science in General'. In *Selected Writings of Herman von Helmholtz* (Russell Kahl, ed). Wesleyan University Press, Middletown, Connecticut.

Hermberg, K. (2006). *Husserl's Phenomenology*. Continuum, London.

Heron, J. (1977). *Catharsis in Human Development*. British Postgraduate Medical Foundation, London.

Heron, J. (1990). *Helping the Client: A Creative Practical Approach*. Sage, London.

Highsmith, J.A. (2000). *A Collaborative Approach to Managing Complex Systems*. Dorset House Publishing.

Holland, J.H. (2006). Studying Complex Adaptive Systems, *Journal of Systems Science and Complexity*, 19(1), 1–8.

Holwell, S.E. (1997). Soft Systems Methodology and its Role in Information Systems. PhD Thesis. Lancaster University, unpublished.

Horkheimer, M. and Adorno, T.W. (2002). *Dialect of Enlightenment: Philosophical fragments*, G.S. Noerr (ed). English translation by the Leland Stanford Junior University.

Hoverstadt, P. and Bowling, D. (2002). Modelling Organizations using VSM. Fractal http://www.systemdynamics.org/ – Website maintained by the System Dynamics Society.

Husserl, E, (2002). 'Pure Phenomenology, its Method and its Field of Investigation'. In *The Phenomenology Reader* (D. Moran, and T. Mooney, eds). Routledge, London, 124–133.

Ison, R. (2005). Guest Editorial: Geoffrey Vickers 2004: Contemporary applications and changing appreciative settings, *Systems Research and Behavioral Science*, 22(4), 277–284.

IT Governance Institute (2008). Enterprise Value Governance of IT Investments: Getting Started with Value Management.

Jackson, M.C. (1991). *Systems Methodology for the Management Science*, Plenum Publishing.

Jary, D. and Jary, J. (1995). 'Sociology', *Collins Dictionary*, Harper Collins, London.

Klein, H.K. and Myers, M.D. (1999). A Set of Principles for Conducting and Evaluating Interpretive Field Studies in Information Systems, *MIS Quarterly*, 23(1), 67–94.

Kotter, D. (1995). Leading Change: Why Transformation Efforts Fail, *Harvard Business Review*, Mar/Apr, 59.

Kuhn, T.S. (1962). *The Structure of Scientific Revolutions*. Chicago University Press, Chicago.

Laertius, Diogenes http://en.wikipedia.org/wiki/Diogenes_Laertius (1925). *Lives and Opinions of Eminent Philosophers in Ten Books*. Book IX, Chapter 1, Heraclitus http://classicpersuasion.org/pw/diogenes/dlheraclitus.htm, (trans. R.D. Hicks). Harvard University Press.

Langefors, B (1966). *Theoretical Analysis of Information Systems*. Studentlitteratur.

Lawn, C., (2006). *Gadamer, A Guide for the Perplexed*. Continuum, London.

Leleur, S.,(2005). *Systemic Planning*. Polyteknisk Forlag, Copenhagen.

Lewes, G.H. http://en.wikipedia.org/wiki/George_Henry_Lewes (1875). *Problems of Life and Mind* (First Series), 2. Trübner, London.

Lewin, K. (1948). *Resolving Social Conflicts; Selected papers on group dynamics*. Gertrude W. Lewin (ed). Harper and Row, New York.

Lewin, K. (1948). 'Action Research and Minority Problems.In *Resolving Social Conflicts*, G.W. Lewin (ed). Harper, New York, pp 201–220.

Lincoln Y.S. and Guba E.G. (1984). Naturalistic Inquiry. California Sage.

Lindblom, C.E. (1959). The Science of 'Muddling Through', *Public Administration Review*, 19(2), (Spring, 1959), 79–88.

Little, W., Fowler, H.W. and Coulson, J. (edited and revised C.J. Onions) (1980). *The Shorter Oxford English Dictionary*, on 'Historical Principles'. Clarendon Press, Oxford.

Littlejohn, S.W. and Foss, K.A. (2008). *Theories of Human Communication*, 9th edition. Thomson Wadsworth, Belmont, CA.

Luhmann, N. (1990). *Essays on Self-reference*. Columbia University Press, New York.

Luhmann, N. (2006). What is Communication? *Communication Theory*, 2(3), 251–259.

Lyytinen K.J. and Klien H.K. (1985). *The Critical Theory of Jurgen Habermas as a Basis for a Theory of Information Systems in Research Methods in Information Systems* (E. Mumford, R.A. Hirschheim, G. Fitzgerald and A.T. Wood-Harper, eds). Elsevier Science Publisher B.V., Amsterdam, 219–231.

Macintyre, D. (1996). 'Why my son will go to grammar school, by Harriet Harman', *The Independent*, Saturday, 20 January 1996, retrieved online 7 December 2009.

Maturana, H. (2004). Biology, Love and Social Responsibility, address to Systems Practice for Managing Complexity network event, 6 September 2004, St Anne's College, Oxford, unpublished.

Maturana, H.R. (1978). *Biology of Language The Epistemology of Reality in Psychology and Biology of Language and Thought Essays in Honor of Eric Lenneberg* (G.A. Miller and E. Lenneberg, eds). Academic Press, New York, 27–64.

Maturana, H.R. and Varela, F.J. (1980). *Autopoiesis and Cognition: The realization of the living*. D. Reidel Publishing Company, Dordrecht.

Mautner,T. (2000). *Penguin Dictionary of Philosophy*. Penguin Books, London.

Mayo, E. (1949). *Hawthorne and the Western Electric Company, The Social Problems of an Industrial Civilisation*. Routledge, London.

Mayr, O. (1970). *The Origins of Feedback Control*. MIT Press, Cambridge, MA.

McCarthy, T. (1988). *The Critical Theory of Jürgen Habermas*. MIT Press, Cambridge MA.

McKeon, R. (ed) (1941). *The Basic Works of Aristotle* (trans. W.D. Ross). Random House, New York.

McTaggart, R. (1996). 'Issues for Participatory Action Researchers'. In O. Zuber-Skerritt (ed) *New Directions in Action Research*. Falmer Press, London.

Meadows, D., Randers, J. and Meadows, D. (1972). *The Limits to Growth*. Universe Books, New York.

Midgley, G. (2000). *Systemic Intervention: Philosophy, Methodology and Practice*. Kluwer Academic/Plenum Publishers, New York.

Midgley, G. (2003). *Systems Thinking*, Vol I: *Systems Science, Cybernetics and Complexity*. Sage, London.

Miles, R.K. (1985). Computer Systems Analysis: The constraint of the 'hard' systems paradigm, *Journal of Applied Systems Analysis*, 12, 107–112.

Mill, J.S. (1843). *System of Logic*. 8th edn, 1872. Longmans, Green, Reader, and Dyer, London.

Miller G.A. (1956). The Magic Number Seven, Plus or Minus Two: Some Limits of Our Capacity for Processing Information, *Psychological Review*, 63(2), 343–355.

Mingers, J. (1990). The What/How Distinction and Conceptual Models: A Reappraisal, *Journal of Applied Systems Analysis*, 17, 21–28.

Mingers, J. and Stowell, F. (eds) (1997) *Information Systems: An Emerging Discipline?* McGraw-Hill, London.

Moran, D., and Mooney, T. (eds) (2004). *The Phenomenology Reader*. Routledge, London.

Morecroft, J. (2007). *Strategic Modelling and Business Dynamics: A Feedback Systems Approach*. John Wiley & Sons.

Mumford, E. (1995). *Effective Systems Design and Requirements Analysis: The ETHICS approach*. Macmillan Press, Basingstoke.

Mumford, E. (2006). The Story of Socio-technical Design: Reflections on its successes, failures and potential, *Information Systems Journal*, 16, 317–342.

Mumford, E., and Weir, M. (1979). *Computer Systems in Work Design – The ETHICS Method: Effective Technical and Human Implementation of Computer Systems: A Work Design Exercise Book for Individuals and Groups*. Associated Business Press, London.

Onions, C.T. (ed) (1980). *The Shorter English Dictionary*, Volume II, Clarendon Press, Oxford.

Oquist, P. (1978). The Epistemology of Action Research, *Acta Sociologica*, 21(2), 143–163.

Palmer, R.E. (1969). *Hermenuetics*, North West University Press, USA. web ref http://books.google.co.uk/books?id=9EzNdD4LmT0C&pg=PA12&lpg=PA12&dq=hermeneuein&source=bl&ots=Xhft4iYwZb&sig=hmCfjQ3rB_lDze5RbrmP3Kk2XA8&hl=en&ei=3tX0TPXwCobRhAfu7J3JBQ&sa=X&oi=book_result&ct=result&resnum=2&ved=0CCEQ6AEwAQ#v=onepage&q=hermeneuein&f=false.

Pasmore, W.A (1988). *Designing Effective Organizations: The Socio-technical Systems Perspective*. John Wiley & Sons Inc., New York.

Peppard, J. (2001). Bridging the Gap between IS Organisation and the Rest of the Business-Plotting a Route, *Information Systems Journal*, 11, 249–270.

Peters, M. and Robinson, V. (1984). The Origins and Status of Action Research, *Journal of Applied Behavioural Science*, 20(2), 113–124.

Pidd, M. (1984). *Computer Simulation in Management Science*. John Wiley & Sons Ltd, Chichester.

Pidd, M. (2004). *Systems Modelling: Theory and Practice*. John Wiley & Sons Ltd, Chichester.

Pirsig, R.M. (1974). *Zen and the Art of Motor Cycle Maintenance*. Corgi, Aylesbury, England.

Plutchik, R. (1974). *Foundations of Experimental Research*. 2nd edition. Harper and Row, New York.

Popper, K.R. (1934). *The Logic of Scientific Discovery* http://en.wikipedia.org/wiki/The_Logic_of_Scientific_Discovery as Logik der Forschung, (English translation 1959), Routledge.

Popper, K.R. (1959). *The Logic of Scientific Discovery*. Hutchinson, London.

Popper, K.R. (1972). *Objective Knowledge: An Evolutionary Approach*. Revised edition, 1979, Oxford.

Popper K.R. (1983). *Objective Knowledge An Evolutionary Approach* (revised edition). Oxford University Press, Oxford.

Popper, K.R. and Eccles, J.C. (1977). *The Self and Its Brain*. Springer International, New York.

Porter, M.E. (1985). *Competitive Advantage: Creating and sustaining superior performance*. Free Press, New York.

Powersim. (2006). Announcement of release of Powersim 7, *Powersim Newsletter*, December 2006, http://www.powersim.co.uk/news.htm, accessed 11 April 2012.

Prigogine, I. (1967). 'Dissipative Structures in Chemical Systems'. In Stig Claesson (ed), *Fast Reactions and Primary Processes in Chemical Kinetics*. Interscience, New York.

Prigogine, I. and Lefever, R. (1968). Symmetry Breaking Instabilities in Dissipative Systems. II, *Journal of Chemical Physics*, 48, 1695–1700.

Prigogine, I. and Nicolis, G. (1977). *Self-Organization in Non-Equilibrium Systems: From Dissipative Structures to Order Through Fluctuations*. John Wiley & Sons Inc., New York.

Prior, R. (1990). Deriving data flow diagrams from 'soft systems' conceptual model. *Systemist*, 12(2), 65–75.

Rapoport, R.N. (1970). Three Dilemmas in Action Research, *Human Relations*, 23(6), 499–513.

Reason, P. (1993). Sitting between Appreciation and Disappointment: A Critique of The Special Edition of Human Relations on Action Research, *Human Relations*, 46(11), 1253–1270.

Reason, P. and Bradbury, H. (2008). *The Handbook of Action Research: Concise Paperback edition: student edition*. London: Sage Publications Ltd.

Reason, P. and Rowan, J. (eds.) (1981). *Human Inquiry: A sourcebook of new paradigm research*. John Wiley & Sons Ltd, Chichester.

Ricoeur, P. (1988). *Hermeneutics and the Human Sciences*. Cambridge University Press, Cambridge.

Ricoeur, P. (2004). 'Phenomenology and Hermeneutics'. In *The Phenomenology Reader*, D. Moran and T. Mooney (eds). Routledge, London, 579–600.

Robb, F. (1992). 'Autopoiesis and Supra-human Systems', *International Journal of General Systems*, 21, 197–220.

Roberts, N., Anderson, D,. Deal., E., Garet, M. and Shaffer, W. (1983). *An Introduction to Computer Simulation*. Addison Wesley, Reading, MA.

Roberts, N., Anderson, D., Deal, R., Garet, M. and Shaffer, W. (1997). Introduction to Computer Simulation – A System Dynamics Modeling Approach. *Journal of the Operational Research Society*, 48, 1145.

Sadovsky, V. N. (1991). 'Philosophical and Methodological Foundations of Systems Theory'. In S. Umpleby and V. N. Sadovsky (eds), *A Science of Goal Formulation: American and Soviet Discussions of Cybernetics and Systems Theory*. Hemisphere Publishing Corporation, New York, Washington, Philadelphia, London, 9–17.

Sarkar, S. (1992). Models of reduction and categories of reductionism, *Synthese*, 91, 167–194.

Sauer, C. (1993). *Why Information Systems Fail: A Case Study Approach*. Alfred Waller, Henley.

Schleiermacher, F.D.E. (1998). *Hermeneutics and Criticism and Other Writings* (Hermeneutik und Kritik mit besonderer Beziehung auf das Neue Testament, 1838). (trans. Andrew Bowie). Cambridge University Press, Cambridge.

Schoderbek, P.P., Schoderbek, C.G. and Kefalas, A.G. (1990). *Management Systems: Conceptual Considerations*. 4th edition, Richard D. Irwin, Homewood, IL.

Schutz, A. (1943). 'The problem of Rationality in the Social World'. In *Sociological Theory and Philosophical Analysis*, D. Emmett and A. MacIntyre, eds. (1970), Macmillan, London.

Schutz, A.(1964). *Collected Papers II, Studies in Social Theory*. Martinus Nijhoff, The Hague.

Schutz, A. (1966), *Collected Papers III: Studies in Phenomenological Philosophy* (I. Schutz, ed). Martinus Nijhoff, The Hague.

Schutz, A. (1970). *On Phenomenology and Social Relations: Selected Writings* (H. Wagner, ed). University of Chicago Press, Chicago.

Schwandt, T. (2000). 'Three Epistemological Stances For Qualitative Inquiry'. In N. Denzin and Y. Lincoln, (eds), *Handbook of Qualitative Research*. Sage Publications Inc., London, 189–213.

Schwartz H. and Jacobs J. (1979). *Qualitative Sociology: A Method to the Madness*. The Free Press, New York.

Seddon, J. (2008). *Systems Thinking in the Public Sector: The failure of the reform regime and a manifesto for a better way*. Triarchy Press.

Senge, P., Kleiner, A., Roberts, C., Ross, R., Roth, G. and Smith, B. (1999). *The Dance of Change: The challenges of sustaining momentum in learning organizations*. Nicholas Brealey Publishing.

Shannon, C.E. and Weaver, W. (1949). *The Mathematical Theory of Communication*. University of Illinois Press, Urbana, IL.

Silverman D. (1981). *The Theory of Organisations: A Sociological Framework*. Heinemann, London.

Silverman, D. (1985). *Qualitative Methodology and Sociology: Describing the Social World*. Gower Publishing Ltd.

Simon, H. (1991). Bounded Rationality and Organizational Learning, *Organization Science*, 2(1), 125–134.

Smith, A. (1979 [1776]), *An Inquiry Into The Nature and Causes of The Wealth of Nations*. Clarendon Press, Oxford, cited in E. Mumford (1996). *Systems Design: Ethical Tools for Ethical Change*. Macmillan.

Smith, S. (2001). *Modelling Complex Decision-making: Contribution Towards the Development of a Decision Support Aid*. University of Paisley.

Smyth, D.S. and Checkland, P.B. (1976). Using a Systems Approach: The Structure of Root Defintions, *Journal of Applied Systems Analysis*, 5(1).

Steier, F. and Jorgenson, J. (2005). 'Patterns that connect patterns that connect', foreword to special issue *Cybernetics and Human Knowing – Gregory Bateson: Essays for an ecology of ideas*, 12(1–2), 5–10.

Stevens, R. (1990). *Humanistic Psychology in Introduction to Psychology* Vol. 1 (I. Roth, ed). Hove Lawrence Erlbaum Associates in association with the Open University. 418–469.

Stowell, A. (2012). Organising eWaste. Doctoral Thesis, Lancaster University Management School, unpublished.

Stowell, F. and West, D. (1995). *Client-led Design: A Systemic Approach to Information Systems Definition*. McGraw-Hill, Maidenhead.

Stowell, F.A. (1985). Experiences with SSM and Data Analysis, *Information Technology Training*, 1, 48–50.

Stowell, F.A. (1989). Change, Organisational Power and the Metaphor 'Commodity', PhD thesis, Lancaster University, unpublished.

Stowell, F.A. (1990). Systems Analysis and the Design of Information Systems. Paper presented at the 8th International Congress of Cybernetics and Systems, City University, New York City, pp 116 and 119.

Stowell, F.A. (1991). Towards Client-Led Development of Information Systems, *Journal of Information Systems*, 1, 173–189.

Stowell, F.A. (ed). (1995). *Information Systems Requirements Analysis, The Contribution of SSM*. McGraw-Hill, London, 140–158.

Stowell, F.A. (2000). 'Modelling Information System Requirements for Complex Systems', in *Systems Modelling for Business Process Improvement*, D.W. Bustard, P. Kawalek and M.T. Norris, (eds), 171–186, London: Artech.

Stowell, F.A. (2005). Why IS Fail, An Interactive Theory of IS Development, seminar University of Paisley, January 2005.

Stowell, F.A. (2006). Revisiting IS Development, *European Journal of Information Systems (submitted)*.

Stowell, F.A. (2008), Information Systems or Systems of Information? *Journal of Information Systems and Systems Approach*, 1, Jan–June, 25–36.

Stowell, F.A. (2009a). Soft Systems and Research, Kybernetes, *The International Journal of Systems and Cybernetics*, Emerald Group, 38(6), 883–900.

Stowell, F.A. (2009b). On Systems Science: An Interview with Professor Frank Stowell, *International Journal of Information Technologies and Systems Approach*, 2(2), July–Dec, 66–76.

Stowell, F.A. (2012) The Appreciative Inquiry Method – A Suitable Candidate for Action Research? *Systems Research and Behavioural Science*, in press.

Stowell, F.A. and Champion, D. (2000). 'Interpretivist Modelling for Information Systems Definition'. In P. Henderson (ed), *Systems Engineering for Business Process Change: Collected papers from the EPSRC research programme*. Springer, Chapter 9, 106–116.

Stowell, F.A. and Champion, D. (2002). 'A Unified Mechanism for Information System Definition in Action'. In *Systems Engineering for Business Process Change: New Directions*, P. Henderson (ed), EPSRC publication. Springer, London, 138–149.

Stowell, F.A. and Cooray, S. (2006). Client Led Information System Creation (CLIC) – Reality or Fantasy? 15th International Conference on Information System Development Methods and Tools and Theory and Practice, Budapest, Hungary, 30 August–1 September 2006.

Stowell, F.A. and Cooray, S. (2010). *The Notion of Appreciation and Information Systems Development*, Submitted.

Stowell, F.A. and West, D. (1990). 'The Contribution Of Systems Ideas During The Process Of Knowledge Elicitation'. In *Systems Prospects: The Next Ten Years Of Systems Research*, R.L. Flood, M.C. Jackson and P. Keys (eds). Plenum Press, New York.

Stowell, F.A. and West, D. (1994). *Client Led Design*. McGraw Hill, Maidenhead.

Susman, G.I. (1983). 'Action Research: A Sociotechnical systems perspective'. In *Beyond Method: Strategies for Social Science Research*, G. Morgan (ed). Sage Publications, London.

Susman G.I. and Evered, R.D. (1978). An Assessment of the Scientific Merits of Action Research, *Administrative Science Quarterly*, 23, 582–602.

Tavistock Institute of Human Relations (2011). web page entry, British Library, Management and Business Studies Portal, http://www.mbsportal.bl.uk/taster/subjareas/busmanhist/tavistock/tavistock10.aspx.

Thomassen, L. (2010). *Habermas. A Guide for the Perplexed*. Continuum, London.

Thompson, J.B. (1983). *Critical Hermeneutics, A Study in the Thought of Paul Ricoeur and Jurgen Habermas*. Cambridge University Press, Cambridge.

Ulrich, W. (1988). Systems Thinking, Systems Practice and Practical Philosophy: A Programme of Research, *Systems Practice*, 1, 137–163.

Ulrich, W. (1994). *Critical Heuristics of Social Planning: A new approach to practical philosophy*, 2nd edition. John Wiley & Sons, New York and London.

Ulrich, W. (2003). A brief introduction to 'Critical systems thinking for professionals & citizens', Werner Ulrich's Home Page, http://www.geocities.com/csh_home/cst_brief.html.

Vickers G. (1965). *The Art of Judgement: A Study of Policy Making*. Chapman and Hall, London.

Vickers, G. (1970). *Value Systems and Social Process*. Penguin Books.

Vickers, G. (1972). *Freedom in a Rocking Boat*. London: Penguin.

Vickers, G. (1983a). *Human Systems are Different*. Harper and Rowe.

Vickers, G. (1983b). *The Art of Judgement: A Study in Policy Making*. Harper and Row.

Vickers, G. (1984). *Human Systems are Different*. Paul Chapman.

Vickers, J. (1991). *Rethinking the Future: The correspondence between Geoffrey Vickers and Adolph Lowe*. Transaction Publishers.

Weaver, W. and Shannon, C. (1963). *The Mathematical Theory of Communication*. University of Illinois Press.

Weber, M. (1949). *The Methodology of the Social Sciences*. Free Press, Glencoe IL.

Weber, M. (1964). *The Theory of Social and Economic Organisation*. New York Free Press.

West, D. (1991). Towards a Subjective Knowledge Elicitation Methodology for the Development of Expert Systems, Thesis, University of Portsmouth, unpublished.

West, D. (1992), Knowledge Elicitation as an Inquiring System: Toward a subjective knowledge elicitation methodology, *Journal of Information Systems*, 2, 31–44.

West, D. (1995). 'The Appreciative Inquiry Method: A Systemic Approach To Information Systems Requirements Analysis'. In *Information Systems Requirements Analysis, The Contribution of SSM*, F.A. Stowell (ed). McGraw-Hill, London, 140–158.

West, D. and Thomas, L. (2005). 'Looking for the Bigger Picture: An Application of the Appreciative Inquiry Method in RCUS' In, Conference Proceedings 'Information Systems Unplugged', D. Wainwright (ed). Northumbria University, April 2005.

Wikipedia (2011). http://en.wikipedia.org/wiki/Critical_systems_thinking.

Wilson, B. (1984). *Systems: Concepts, Methodologies and Applications*, 2nd edition, John Wiley & Sons Ltd, Chichester.

Wilson, T.D. (1981). On User Studies and Information Needs, *Journal of Documentation*, 37(1), 3–15.

Winograd, T. and Flores, F. (1986). *Understanding Computers and Cognition: A New Foundation for Design*. Ablex, Norwood, NJ.

Winter, M.C., Brown, D.H., and Checkland, P.B. (1995). A Role for Soft Systems Methodology in Information Systems Development, *European Journal of Information Systems*, 4, 130–142.

Wood, J.R. (1992). Linking Soft Systems Methodology (SSM) and Information Systems (IS). *Systemist*, 14(3), 133–135.

Index